SADDAM'S SECRETS

IRAQI GENERAL

GEORGES SADA

AN INSIDER EXPOSES
PLANS TO DESTROY
ISRAEL, HIDE WMDs,
AND CONTROL
THE ARAB WORLD

SADDAM'S
SECRETS

HOW AN IRAQI GENERAL DEFIED
AND SURVIVED SADDAM HUSSEIN

IRAQI GENERAL
GEORGES SADA
WITH JIM NELSON BLACK

TIMETABLE OF KEY EVENTS

Pre-modern history	Land of Iraq ruled by Assyrians, Babylonians, Persians, Greeks.
800-750 BC	Ministry of prophet Jonah in Nineveh, the capital of Assyria.
First century AD	Christian gospel comes to what is today Iraq.
634 AD	Arab conquest of what is today Iraq; introduction of Muslim religion.
762	Baghdad made capital of Iraq and the Islamic caliphate.
1700s–1800s	Iraq a battleground between Ottoman Turks and Persians.
World War I	Iraq taken from Ottoman control and put under British mandate.
1921	League of Nations and British name Faisal I, a Hashemite, king of Iraq.
1932	British mandate (governing oversight of Iraq) ends.
1933	King Faisal I dies, and his son Ghazi succeeds him.
1958	King Faisal II overthrown by military coup; Gen. Abdel Karim Qassem becomes the new president.
	Georges Sada enters Iraqi Air Academy after high school.
1959	Saddam leads a failed assassination attempt on Gen. Qassem.
	On February 9 Cadet Georges Sada begins pilot training in Russia.

1959–1963	Saddam remains in hiding in Syria.
1963	Gen. Qassem ousted by Col. Abdel-Salam Aref.
1964–1965	Georges Sada sent for advanced instrument training in Texas.
1966	Col. Abdel-Salam Aref is killed in a helicopter crash; he is succeeded as president by his brother, Abdel-Rahman Aref.
July 17, 1968	Revolution in Iraq; Abdel-Rahman Aref ousted; Gen. Ahmed Hassan al-Bakr made president; appoints Saddam Hussein as his chief bodyguard, and later his deputy. Soon Saddam demands officer's rank in the army and is appointed a four-star general despite his lack of military training.
July 17, 1979	Saddam forces President Al-Bakr out of power; Saddam becomes president and prime minister of Iraq.
1980	Iraq goes to war with Iran.
April 8, 1980	Grand Ayatollah Muhammad Baqir al-Sadr and his sister Amina assassinated by order of Saddam to squelch any thought of religious revolution in Iraq.
June 7, 1981	Israeli F-16s destroy Iraq's Osiraq nuclear reactor.
1983	Kurds attacked with chemical weapons by Saddam; eight thousand lives lost.
1986	Georges Sada involuntarily retired from Iraqi Air Force.
1988	Halabja attacked by Saddam's forces with chemical weapons; 5,000 killed; 182,000 Kurds killed at Anfal.
August 8, 1988	Iraq's war with Iran ends; Saddam voluntarily ceases hostilities and signs compromise agreements that were very costly to Iraq.
August 2, 1990	Saddam orders the invasion of Kuwait.
	Air Vice Marshal Georges Sada is recalled to active duty in Iraqi Air Force and put in charge of POWs.
January 17, 1991	Beginning of first Gulf War (Operation Desert Storm); General Sada escapes missile strike on headquarters by seventeen seconds.

February 28, 1991	End of first Gulf War.
March 6, 1991	Coalition prisoners freed from Iraqi prisons.
1996	U.N. Oil-for-Food program begins.
1998	Georges Sada becomes involved with the International Centre for Peace and Reconciliation and related activities in Iraq.
March 19, 2003	Start of Operation Iraqi Freedom to remove Saddam from power.
April 9, 2003	End of war; statue of Saddam torn down in Baghdad's Fardus Square.
December 13, 2003	Saddam Hussein is found hiding in a spider hole.
February 24, 2004	Signing of the "Baghdad Religious Accord" at Babylon Hotel, and formation of the Iraqi Institute for Peace (IIP) in Iraq; Georges Sada named as executive secretary of IIP.
October 15, 2005	New Iraqi constitution approved by 79 percent of voters in national referendum—hailed as the first democratic national charter in Arab history.
December 15, 2005	The first constitutional elections in Iraqi history to establish a National Assembly.

CONTENTS

FOREWORD

You are about to learn some of the previously unpublished secrets of the most tyrannical leader since Adolf Hitler, as told by a most courageous man: Georges Sada, retired Iraqi general, fighter pilot, and a man of faith who faced certain death at the hands of Saddam's mad son, Qusay.

Though we came from worlds apart, our lives crossed during the darkest days of the first Gulf War. I had waited twenty years for the opportunity to enter the battle skies in the service of my country. As a United States Air Force pilot, I grew up in the shadow of those who served in Vietnam. Squadron assignments in Europe, Asia, North America, and the Middle East exposed me to all aspects of fighter tactics, and I accumulated more than 3,400 flying hours. But like most airmen, I never thought much about the prospect of being shot down by enemy fire.

Then in early August 1990, as part of the U.S. response to Saddam's invasion of Kuwait, I was deployed to southwest Asia, and subsequently participated in the opening air strike by coalition forces. On the third night of the war, January 19, 1991, the unimaginable happened and the F-15E Strike Eagle I was flying was hit by a surface-to-air missile near the town of Al Qaim in northwest Iraq. In an instant, through a brilliant white flash, I was transformed from hunter to hunted.

I managed to evade capture for three nights and even made it to the Syrian border. But I was eventually taken prisoner at gunpoint, and after two days, I was taken to the POW compound in Baghdad. There, in an underground bunker, I was led blindfolded to the interrogation room. Suddenly I found myself in the presence of a man who, despite the power he had over me, still seemed to respect my human dignity.

As I reported in my book, *Faith Beyond Belief*, death threats were common during the days and weeks that followed, and the wrath of the guards at the intelligence headquarters and the Abu Ghraib Prison was often demoralizing. During forty-three days in Saddam's prisons, my primary mission was just staying alive, but as the ranking POW, I also had to defend the rights of the others and insist on humane treatment for them as well. Locked away, where daylight and darkness were just another part of an endless nightmare, my faith sustained me and gave me the courage to face the challenges beyond my cell door.

The book in your hands is an amazing story from the other side of the blindfold. Georges Sada, who had been recalled from retirement after the attack on Kuwait, was Saddam Hussein's special advisor and the man Saddam put in charge of prisoners of war. A fighter pilot throughout his long and distinguished career, Gen. Sada[1] had not only been tested in battle, but he had faced Saddam's wrath on more than one occasion himself.

In late 2004, thirteen years after that first formal interrogation, I spoke with Georges Sada, and discovered that he was the man on the other side of the blindfold. Only then did I understand the source of his strength and the respect that I had sensed from him that night. This man, a former air vice marshal in the Iraqi Air Force, had held my life in his hands. But it wasn't until our first telephone conversation that I understood the risks he had taken to save me and my fellow prisoners of war from a swift and certain death at the hands of Saddam's son, Qusay.

Our friendship has grown since that time, and I have learned first-hand of Georges Sada's remarkable journey. As the bombing of Baghdad intensified, Qusay had ordered him to execute all the pilots. But Georges wouldn't do it. He argued that the rights accorded to prisoners under the Geneva Convention were inviolable, and by the grace of God he was able to convince Saddam that the captured pilots must not be killed. Nevertheless, he was arrested on January 25, 1991, by the Republican Guard and held prisoner under the threat of death.

In the pages that follow, you will discover the answers to many questions about Saddam—who he was, what he was really like, and what he was doing to terrorize the world. The book explains how this brutal tyrant was able to deceive the world for so long, and how he was able to expand his power and control beyond all logical limits. It was a world of extremes, of revenge and hatred, and of incredible cunning and duplicity; yet, Saddam Hussein trusted Georges Sada because he was different from all the other advisors that surrounded him.

An Assyrian and a Christian with roots that go back to Bible times, Georges was not a member of the Baath Party and he was not interested in the politics of power. Unlike most of the officers in Saddam's inner circle, General Sada had no ax to grind and no political ambitions. Speaking the truth to Saddam was always risky, but somehow Georges managed to do it without losing his own head.

Now that I know the man who was once my jailer, I can tell you that Georges Sada is an honest and honorable man. As senior advisor to the National Security Council of the new government in Iraq, he has been recognized in his own country and by leaders in many countries as a man of remarkable character. He is a man of his word, and the Word lives in him. And perhaps most remarkable of all, he is a faithful witness to the last days of one of the most tyrannical regimes of modern times.

I am delighted that you will have the opportunity in these pages to learn secrets of the Iraqi dictator that few men could share in such a way. By coming forward now—not because he sought to tell this story, but because he was persuaded to do so by others—he has again put his own life at risk. It takes enormous courage to do something like this. But being too transparent in naming names, he could also put the lives of others at risk, and this is why he has chosen not to give the names of his family members and certain others in this account.

As a fighter pilot myself, I also recognize another characteristic in Georges that may need some explaining to an American audience. Gen. Sada is a true son of the Middle East. He doesn't mince words, and he speaks of his exploits as a pilot, a military officer, a top advisor, and now as a leader in the peace and reconciliation movement, with a directness that may at first seem brash or boastful. But I can assure you he is a gentleman in every sense of the word, and I hope you will find the candor and directness of his words refreshing.

Whenever I've been asked to speak about my experiences in the Gulf War, I often say that I harbor no ill will for the Iraqi people. We were at war and I fully appreciate the situation they were in. Today I respect the people of Iraq for what they've endured, and I understand the degree to which Saddam had corrupted everything he touched. As Georges Sada puts it, Saddam was a genius at doing evil, and for a time he transformed that nation into an evil empire. There is no question that Iraq had weapons of mass destruction, and without the intervention of American and coalition forces in 1991 and 2003, the world would eventually have suffered even greater disasters. The evidence of that is documented in these pages.

I heartily commend this important book to the American audience, and to the many others around the world who will encounter the life and legacy of General Georges Sada for the first time. This is a story you will not soon forget.

— David Eberly, Colonel, USAF (Retired)

One of Saddam's secrets was so incendiary that, had it come to pass, it would have set the entire Middle East ablaze, if not the whole world.

In November 1990 I made a frightening discovery: Saddam had ordered the air force to begin planning for a major aerial assault against Israel. If the Americans were going to attack and force him to give up Kuwait, he said, then our pilots would be ready to attack Israel as soon as the first rockets hit, and they would extract a heavy price. They would attack in two massive, back-to-back assaults with three types of chemical weapons: the nerve gas Tabun, as well as Sarin 1 and Sarin 2.

The mission was to deploy ninety-eight of our best fighter aircraft—Russian Sukhois, French Mirages, and the MiGs—fueled and equipped to penetrate the Israeli borders through Jordan and Syria, but without telling either of those countries that we were coming. Clearly this would be an unauthorized invasion of Syrian and Jordanian air space, with payloads of deadly toxins. I was shocked that such an order could have been given; but I knew that if this mission ever took place, crossing restricted air space would be the least of our worries.

A few days after I first learned about the plans, I got a call from the palace. They told me that Saddam was asking for me personally, and he wanted to see me in his office right away. So, again, I went to meet with the president, and I was surprised to see that the entire general staff was already assembled in the conference room when I arrived.

Saddam had checked me out many times, and I think he respected me. I know why he trusted me: he couldn't trust most of his generals to tell him the truth because of their fear of him and their allegiance to a religious or political agenda. Either they would say whatever Saddam wanted to hear, or they would say what was politically advantageous to their own people. So he would often say to me, "At least Georges will tell me the truth." And even Saddam occasionally needed to hear the truth.

I didn't know why he had called me that day, but I knew it was going to be something very important. Several of the officers in the room were of higher rank than I was, but it was prearranged for me to sit right in front of Saddam. By right, my place should have been on the second row, but he had instructed his aides to put me on the first row, so that's where I sat.

When everyone was seated, Saddam made a few remarks and then he looked at me and said, "Georges, do you know why you're here?" I said, "No, sir, but it's a great pleasure to be here." He said, "I've decided that the air force will attack Israel." Suddenly I knew what this was all about. Although I had no idea where the conversation would end up, it was clear that Saddam was look-ing for justification for a decision he had already made.

So I asked, "Attack Israel, sir?" and he said, "Yes, that's right." He gave me a moment to reflect on that, and then he began asking me all sorts of questions.

The first question he asked was surprising. He said, "Georges, who's stronger, Israel or Iraq?" I knew what he wanted me to say, but I had to be realistic. After all, the reason Saddam had called for me was because he knew I would answer him honestly and correctly. So I paused for a moment and said, "Sir, what you're talking about is the difference between men who are blind and men who can see."

He looked at me quizzically and said, "What do you mean, Georges?" I said, "Sir, there are two groups, one which is blind and one which can see, and they're preparing for battle."

"Yes," he said, "and which is which? Which ones are blind and which ones can see?" "Unfortunately, sir," I told him, "we're the blind ones and the Israelis are the ones who can see." With that, Saddam erupted. "Why!?"

Believe me, I knew I was on shaky ground. Many good men had died for words less offensive than the ones I'd just spoken. Saddam had personally shot and killed high-ranking officers on the spot, and he had ordered men to be executed for thoughts or actions he only imagined. So before I answered the question, I decided to make one more defensive maneuver, and I said, "Sir, if I speak the truth to you now, will you, according to the custom of the Arabs, give me permission to speak freely, with immunity?" In other words, I was saying, Will you promise not to shoot the messenger?

Saddam's eyes were threatening, but he knew what I meant. What I was asking for was a centuries-old tradition among the desert Arabs, an oath sworn by tribal leaders to allow a messenger to speak freely without fear of being killed.

As he folded his arms across his chest, Saddam said, "Yes, I give you immunity." Then, more forcefully, he said, "Now tell me what you mean!" I had no choice but to answer him. I knew full well that he had given immunity to others in the same circumstances and they were hanged, but I was honor-bound to tell the truth. So I breathed a silent prayer, Lord, give me the courage to speak, *and I spoke.*

From beginning to end, my answer took one hour and forty-one minutes. When I served as air vice marshal in the air force, I studied all these things in detail, so I had extensive knowledge of the military capabilities of the forces in our region, as well as those in Europe and North America. So I was able to cover those topics in detail. But the minute I finished, Saddam erupted once again in anger. Fortunately, this time the anger wasn't directed at me but at the others who had not told him the truth about these things.

Most of these men were eager to assure Saddam that two plus two is nine, because they knew that's what he wanted to hear. But, thank God, Saddam listened to me, and that was a miracle in itself. He never listened to anyone. He had his own ideas and he never wanted to be confronted by the facts if they would prevent him from doing whatever he had already decided to do.

When I told Saddam that attacking Israel would be like the blind attacking the sighted, we were surrounded by all of the members of the general staff, and Gen. Amir Rashid Ubaidi, who was deputy air force commander for technology and engineering, leaned over to his colleague and whispered, "Georges is going to be killed, now, right on the spot. His head will be separated from his body." I didn't hear the remark, but they told me later what he'd said.

Gen. Amir, incidentally, was a true genius. He had been number one in his class at the University of London, where he earned his Ph.D. in engineering. After the Gulf War, he was taken into custody by the Americans and imprisoned in Iraq. He had been in charge of the "superweapons" program but claimed that Iraq never had chemical weapons or WMDs of any kind; of course that wasn't true and he, of all people, knew it.

In any event, I told Saddam that the reason I had used that expression is because Israeli aircraft have very advanced radar with the capability to see more than 125 miles in any direction. On the other hand, 75 percent of Iraqi aircraft were Russian-made, and the range of the radar on our fighters was only about fifteen miles. This meant that the Israeli fighters could see our aircraft at least 110 miles before we would even know they were there. And that's not even the worst part. Their laser-guided missiles could lock on our fighters while they were still sixty-five miles away, and we'd have no idea that enemy fighters were anywhere around. Then the Israeli pilots could fire their missiles at a range of at least fifty miles and our pilots would never even know what hit them.

So at that point I asked Saddam, "Sir, don't you agree that this is a fight between men who are blind and men who can see?" Saddam just sat there for several seconds looking straight ahead. Then he turned sharply to his left where Gen. Amir was sitting and he yelled very loudly, "Amir, what is Georges saying?" In other words, Saddam was asking his weapons expert: Why haven't you told me this before now? This is your area, and I hold you personally responsible for telling me these things.

I didn't change my expression but continued to look at Saddam. But then I realized, Oh, no! Gen. Amir is not that brave. I'm afraid he will not tell Saddam the truth, and he'll try to put the blame on me or someone else. *So I turned quickly and looked Amir straight in the eye, and he could see that I was very serious. After the meeting he came to me and said, "I knew, Georges, when you turned to look at me that way that you were sending a message." And that's exactly what I was doing. Without saying a word I was telling him to speak the truth because we were both speaking directly to Saddam Hussein. If he disagreed with me or tried to lie his way out of it, I would have defended myself in the strongest terms, and Gen. Amir knew exactly what I meant.*

Well, God was with me that day because Gen. Amir said to Saddam, "Sir, what Brother Georges is saying about the difference between the Israeli aircraft with sophisticated American and European technology, and our Russian-made aircraft with Russian technology, which is not so sophisticated, is right." And then he began explaining it to him in very detailed engineering terms, telling Saddam everything about the technology of the different fighter aircraft. Amir knew that Saddam didn't care in the least about any of those details; he was just covering his own backside. But what it came down to was that he told him, Brother Georges has told you the truth about our fighters, and we're no match for the Israelis.

When he finished, Saddam just sat there, silently, staring straight ahead. For more than a minute you could have heard a pin drop in that room. And, believe me, a minute of silence in the presence of Saddam Hussein could seem like eternity. There were at least ninety people in the room, all generals and high-ranking commanders, and there wasn't a peep out of them.

At the end of the meeting, the only thing I could be sure of was that Saddam had listened to me, and he knew that to the best of my ability I had told him the truth. I had no idea what decision he would make, but at least he had heard me and he understood what I'd said. Then in mid-December 1990, less than a month from the deadline that had been set by the United Nations for Saddam to pull our forces out of Kuwait, I was told that the president was ready to announce his decision.

On December 17, we received the message we'd been expecting. Saddam's message was worded very deliberately, almost poetically in Arabic, to give the impression of a decree of great solemnity and importance. It said, "Uwafiq Tunafath Ala Barakatalah," which means roughly, "I agree to the attack, and we shall attack with the blessings of Allah." It was as if Nebuchadnezzar had spoken. But what he was saying was that we were being ordered to proceed with a massive chemical-weapons assault on Israel, in two waves, one through Jordan and the other through Syria.

A MAN OF THE PEOPLE

"He was not a man of the people or a friend of the Arab people.
The fact is, Saddam Hussein killed more Arabs than anyone in the history
of mankind. There was nothing he wouldn't do to secure his grip on the
country, and there were no principles he would not sacrifice
for the sake of his own power and greed."

In Iraq there was no leader, no general, no commander, no minister. There was only one man who claimed to be all things to all people, and his name was Saddam Hussein. During the dictator's thirty-five-year reign of terror, he transformed Iraq into a very small country—from twenty-seven million hard-working men and women to just one man.

And just imagine how this tyrant dominated everything in our lives: Saddam and the army, Saddam and the Party, Saddam and the Republican Guard, Saddam and the special guards, Saddam and the tribes, Saddam and the people, Saddam and the rivalries in the Middle East, even Saddam and religion, when he was anything but a religious man.

Saddam manipulated all of these groups, constantly playing one against the other, in order to expand his grasp and control over the region. His ego was so enormous he never even realized how ridiculous he looked to everyone else. Emotionally, Saddam was a child with a disturbed personality, totally focused on his own power and glory. If he hadn't been stopped by the grace of God and overwhelming military force, believe me, Saddam would not have been satisfied with Iraq alone. He would have used his ever-increasing power to turn the whole world upside down.

When the American-led coalition came back to Iraq in 2003 to liberate my country from the grasp of Saddam, they did us a great service. They were able to rout the enemies of freedom and destroy Saddam's corrupt regime by going after the leaders of the Baath Socialist Party. But they also took pains not to target the civilian population or destroy the infrastructure we needed so badly. During Operation Desert Storm in 1991, 147 bridges were demolished by coalition bombers and missile strikes. In 2003, by contrast, not a single bridge was destroyed.

Unfortunately, not everyone understands or appreciates what happened. Some people, both in the West and the Middle East, were strongly opposed to the decision to use military force against Saddam. But I'm not one of them. I believe it was the only thing that could have saved Iraq from utter ruin. Saddam's paranoia and lust for power were consuming everything and everyone, and no one was safe so long as he remained at large. Most people in my country are beginning to see that now, as they realize how things have changed since Saddam was driven out. And now that the liberation of Iraq is a fact, many who resisted in the past are beginning to say, "Okay, I guess they did the right thing after all, because things are so much better now."

A Unique Perspective

As an Iraqi pilot and ultimately as an air vice marshal of the air force, I have spent most of my life serving my country. My connection to this place is real and very deep. I am an Assyrian Christian, born and raised in northern Iraq, and a descendant of the original inhabitants of this ancient land. My people were making a living from the mountains, rivers, and fertile plains of the Tigris and Euphrates Valley long before Abraham made his historic journey from Ur of the Chaldees to the land of Canaan.

My ancestors were living in the ancient capital of Nineveh when Jonah arrived, having been sent by God to call our pagan forebears to repentance. At that time, Nineveh was the capital of the Assyrian Empire. The armies of Assyria were led by warrior kings with strange-sounding names such as Shalmaneser, Tiglath-Pileser,

Sargon, and Sennacherib, and they conquered much of the ancient world, destroying the nation of Israel five separate times.

The people of Assyria worshiped the gods of nature, but they did not know God. So God sent Jonah to tell them to repent, or else he would destroy the city as he had done to Sodom and Gomorrah. The Bible also says there were 120,000 people living at Nineveh, with all their cattle and livestock. It was a three-day journey to walk from one side of the city to the other. Jonah cried out for the people to repent, and when the king heard it he put on sackcloth and sat in the ashes. He commanded the people of the nation to fast and seek the face of God. So in the eighth century BC, the people of Nineveh repented and turned to the God of the Bible.

To this day we still celebrate a three-day fast called Bautha d'Ninweh, meaning the Fast of Nineveh. It's held each year three weeks prior to the first day of Lent and about nine weeks before the Easter celebration. In ancient times, the people did not eat or drink at all for three days. The Bible says the king of Assyria commanded that not even the cattle or livestock were to be fed during the fast. Today, however, we understand that the fast is symbolic and it is a way of recognizing our need for repentance and faithfulness to God.

Traces of that legendary city survive to this day. The modern Ninawa faces the city of Mosul in the province of Ninawa where I grew up. This "land between the rivers" known as Mesopotamia was once the home of Sumerians, Akkadians, Assyrians, and Babylonians. For more than seven thousand years our ancestors dominated the region, and they enjoyed a rich and thriving commerce that spanned the known world. And believe me, all this history still lives in the hearts of our people.

Like every ancient society, we've seen many wars. Under a succession of warrior kings, the empire expanded and contracted based on military conquest and its legendary trading caravans. In the time of Alexander the Great, the Assyrian legions formed the right wing of the Persian Army, and they fought like lions. Soldiers of the Assyrian Empire, which had fallen in 612 BC, fought with the Persians against Alexander. If the empire hadn't fallen, I suspect we would have sided with Alexander against the Persians. But such is history. Alexander died in 323 BC, near the city of Babylon in southern Iraq, but that would not be the end of conflict.

Christianity came to the region in the first century AD with St. Thomas, the disciple of Jesus, who passed through Mesopotamia on his journey to India. Subsequently, others were converted by Saint Addai and Saint Mari, who were also missionaries in the first century. These early converts included many from the Jewish Diaspora, and Iraq remained predominantly Christian until the Arab Conquest of 634 AD when Islam was imposed as the official state religion. In time, Islam would become the dominant religion of the entire region, and Arabic would become the common language.

Even so, not everyone converted to Islam. Today between 3 and 4 percent of Iraqis are Christians. Catholics in Iraq are generally known as "Chaldeans," while most Protestants are affiliated with denominations such as Presbyterian, Baptist, and Methodist, as well as the Ancient Church of the East, which is comparable to the Orthodox Church. All these people speak Arabic, and many speak other languages as well. The common language among my own people is Aramaic, which is the language of the New Testament—the same idiom that Jesus spoke. When I read my Bible today, I'm reading the very words that Jesus used.

Baghdad was founded as the Arab capital in 762 AD, and it served as the seat of the Abbassid Caliphate from 750 AD to 1258. The Abbassids were defeated by the Mongols under Hulagu, the grandson of Genghis Khan, who left the country in ruins. By the sixteenth and seventeenth centuries, Iraq was a perpetual battleground of the Ottoman Turks and Persians.

The Ottomans controlled Mesopotamia until the First World War when the British occupied the region and modern-day Turkey was established. Iraq remained a British Mandate until 1932; however, in 1921 the League of Nations and the British government named King Faisal I, a member of the royal Hashemite family, as the nation's leader.

King Faisal I was responsible for opening up Iraq to Europe and the West, and even after the Mandate ended, British influence remained strong. But this was an era of turbulent changes in the Arab world. Socialism was now the controlling ideology in Egypt and Syria. King Faisal I died of a heart attack in 1933 and his son and successor, King Ghazi, died in an automobile accident in 1939. Then, in 1958, Ghazi's son, King Faisal II, was overthrown by a military coup led by Gen. Abdel-Karim Qassem, who transformed Iraq into a pro-Soviet republic.

A Strange Relationship

As fate would have it, I became a cadet in the Air Academy that same year, and the new regime had very different ideas about training its officers. After graduating as a young flyer, I found myself involved in coups, wars, battles, battle-planning, and every other type of military operation that would shape the fate of the nation. So that's the perspective I bring to this book.

I was involuntarily retired from the air force in 1986, brought back by Saddam after the invasion of Kuwait in 1990, and then imprisoned by Saddam a short time later. I will explain all this in subsequent chapters. But so long as I wore the uniform of my country, I was a loyal soldier and I followed orders. I was a highly trained fighter pilot, educated in Russia, America, Great Britain, and other parts of Europe.

I flew the MiG-17 and the MiG-21, and I had a national reputation as Iraq's most daring aviator before I had earned the rank of captain. In time I rose to become an air vice marshal, a two-star general, and I was responsible not only for training Iraqi fighter pilots but also teaching courses on air power and military readiness at the War College, the Army Staff College, and the National Defense College.

These were things I was proud of; it's what I had worked my whole life to achieve. But I was not a member of the Baath Party. As an Assyrian Christian, I would have been a pretty poor candidate. For a long time now I've wondered how to tell my story to the American people. How would I explain my decision not to be a member of the Baath Party, and why I refused to be a part of Saddam's inner circle. In part, it was because I'd been told that the slogan of the party says:

"The body of the nation is Arab, and the soul of the nation is Islam." I was neither Arab nor Muslim and I couldn't have pretended to be.

For most of my life it has been costly to speak the truth in Iraq, because the regime demanded that everyone act and think and speak alike. Furthermore, I had a strange relationship with Saddam. It was apparent that he respected me because I was a capable and efficient officer, just as he was in his own way. But I refused to lie for him, and I was honor-bound to speak the truth without inappropriate concern for the political or personal consequences. And I'm sure he hated me for that.

Regardless how people may react, I'm committed to telling the truth, so far as I know it. And I would be dishonest not to be frank about what I've done. Israeli prime minister Ariel Sharon can't avoid talking about the fact that he led the Israeli Army's assault across the canal into Egypt in 1973. It may have been an action that made him less than popular in Palestine and other parts of the Arab world, but it's still a fact of history. So I, too, will speak candidly about the facts of my own life and career.

During my military service, I was involved in strategic operations, or in the planning of them, in three separate wars with Israel: the Six Day War of 1967, the October War of 1973, and a little-known attack that Saddam wanted the air force to carry out using chemical weapons in 1990. Some of my friends have urged me not to talk about any of this, because it could make some people think less of me.

I've been told that people in the West—and especially American Christians who have a close relationship with the people of Israel— would be angry at me because I once fought against the Jewish state. But to deny or simply fail to mention these facts would be less than honest. So in the interest of full disclosure I have chosen to speak fully and openly.

I also want to speak about my role in the Revolution of 1968 when Gen. Ahmed Hassan al-Bakr and Saddam Hussein came to power. I'll tell about my discussions with President Al-Bakr, as well as what Abdurazzaq al-Nayif said to me before he was killed in London, and how I led formations of Iraqi fighters into Iran at the outset of the Iran-Iraq War in 1980.

Saddam seldom based his military strategy on logic, national inter-est, or least of all, genuine national defense. As in everything else, his tactics were centered on whatever would benefit him personally or exalt his reputation and authority in the region. He was interested only in his own glory and power, which helps to explain another little-known secret: we were ordered to carry out an attack against Israel using chemical weapons. I will talk more about that, and I will also go into some detail about Iraq's weapons of mass destruction (WMDs).

Yes, we had them. We used them. And Saddam shipped them out of the country before coalition forces ever arrived. I will talk about how these WMDs were used by Saddam and the military on both sol-diers and civilian targets, how Saddam managed to hide them under the noses of U.N. inspectors, and then how he managed to smuggle them out of the country before the beginning of Operation Iraqi Freedom in 2003.

Saddam, The Crasher

These are some of the more difficult aspects of my story, but I'll be frank about what happened and how we did it because I believe these things need some explanation. I think it's important to talk about the events of July 1979 when Saddam came as a gangster and told President Al-Bakr to get out because he was taking over. I'll speak in more detail about the way Saddam manipulated people and events to increase his dictatorial power.

Saddam was a cunning and manipulative man: I've often said he was a genius. Like the communist leader Josef Stalin, on whom Sad-dam modeled himself, he was truly a genius at doing evil. He was a man without a conscience. He was ruthless and brutal, and there was nothing he wouldn't do to achieve his own ends. He killed many times and ordered the brutal murders of hundreds of thousands of our own people. He was a true Stalinist, inside and out, and this is why he had to be removed from power, once and for all.

In Arabic, Saddam's name actually means "The Crasher." It's a word we use whenever there's an auto accident—when two cars crash into each other. When people first heard the name, we were puzzled by it. We had never heard of anyone named Saddam before he came. But today, as you can imagine, there are many little Saddams in our part of the world. Adoring parents named their little boys Saddam, and there are even children named Uday and Qusay, for Saddam's sons, who were more evil than their father.

What Saddam did in Kuwait was appropriate for someone with such a name. He burst in, destroyed, raped, tortured, and took whatever he wanted. He was, by nature and training, an assassin, a thug, and a crasher from the beginning. His job in the Baath Party was to crash in and intimidate people or kill them. He had a reputation for being a gangster before he turned twenty years old, and he lived up to the name.

In 1959, Saddam led a gangland-style assassination attempt on Iraq's president, Gen. Qassem. When the attack failed he fled to Syria where he lived for four years. During that time he was introduced to Egyptian president Gamal Abdel Nasser, who had befriended many thugs in his own rise to power. But even Nasser, who was a belligerent pan-Arabist, could see the evil in Saddam Hussein, and he warned leaders of the Baath Party in Iraq to be wary of him. Nasser said Saddam was a dangerous man and a loose cannon, but no one in Iraq took the warning seriously until it was too late.

I knew Saddam and I knew what he was capable of. I don't hesitate to say that his decision to invade Kuwait was wrong. The way our forces did it was wrong; the behavior of our soldiers in Kuwait was not only wrong, it was immoral. Failing to withdraw the army immediately, as we were called upon to do by America, Britain, and the United Nations, was wrong as well; what happened to our forces was a disaster that could have been avoided.

This all happened because one man had all the power, and the entire mission of the army, air force, and navy of Iraq was to do whatever this wicked dictator demanded they do. I was not the only one who argued against the action in Kuwait—there were a few others —but there was no one with enough influence or enough courage to stop him. There was no system for objecting to Saddam's orders, and most of his commanders knew that if they did not obey he would have them hanged immediately.

The British scholar and historian Lord John Acton said famously, "Power tends to corrupt, and absolute power corrupts absolutely." But he also said, "Great men are almost always bad men." Saddam Hussein was a great man in the same sense that Adolf Hitler and Josef Stalin were great men. They were rulers with the power of life and death over other men, and they would stop at nothing to fulfill their wicked dreams of conquest and domination. And all of them were absolutely corrupt.

Losing the Peace

We all know the results of the Gulf War. Because Saddam was left in power for twelve more years, he was able to do much greater harm than he had ever done before the war. President George H. W. Bush was a career diplomat and not a natural wartime president, as I believe his son, President George W. Bush, to be. I believe he thought that the people of Iraq would rise up and drive Saddam from power; unfortunately, he didn't understand the absolute tyranny of Saddam in that nation or the control he had over us.

I know many, many Iraqis who were weeping on the day the Americans announced their withdrawal. They said, "Is it really going to end like this? Is Saddam going to win after all?" They knew what would happen. They knew Saddam would quickly regroup and rebuild his military and claim he had won after all, and millions of Iraqis would suffer. We were all terrified of what would come next.

If Gen. Colin Powell and Gen. Norman Schwarzkopf thought the cost of going on to Baghdad would have been too high, then I must say they were badly mistaken. There was no one defending Baghdad at that time. If their intelligence was telling them that the defense of Baghdad was too strong, I must say, "Sorry. Your sources were wrong." The closest thing to a defense of Baghdad at the end of the first Gulf War were a few hundred seventeen- to nineteen-year-old cadets at the Military Academy and the Air Academy.

If coalition forces had gone into Baghdad immediately after the liberation of Kuwait, Saddam would have been finished once and for all, and countless lives, including the lives of the thousands of Iraqis who were executed by Saddam over the next ten years, could have been spared. And, not least, American soldiers, sailors, and airmen wouldn't have had to come back in 2003 with the risk of losing another two or three thousand troops, as they're doing now. By not going on to Baghdad when they had the chance, the coalition forces created a disaster that will take years, if not decades, to overcome.

But that's not even the worst of it, from our view. When they left Iraq in 1991, American and coalition forces encouraged the pro-democracy resistance in Iraq to rise up against Saddam, and they did. Fourteen of eighteen provinces were freed from Saddam's control by our brave young men, but then the Americans suddenly left. At that point, Saddam mobilized his Special Forces and they went in and massacred tens of thousands of civilians. They murdered anyone suspected of participating in or sympathizing with the attempted coup. Men, women, and children were butchered by the thousands, and the world did nothing to help.

An Error of Judgment

If those pro-democracy forces could have had the support of America, the British, or any nation to supply them with arms and logistics, the resistance would eventually have taken all eighteen provinces. They would have cleaned them out the Iraqi way. By that I mean they would have left no one in power who could come back to make trouble later. There would be no insurgency, no resistance, no terrorism. They would have wiped the slate clean with a new regime, new laws, new order, and a new beginning for Iraq, without Saddam Hussein.

They only needed to take the four provinces in the Anbar region, known as the Sunni Triangle, where most of the Saddam loyalists were living. But when our bold young rebels tried to go in there, they were deserted by the West, and consequently they lost the momentum and the battle, as well as the lives of thousands of fine, brave men. All this happened because America didn't finish what they started. They may have won the war, but they hadn't won the peace.

Instead of solving a problem, for the next twelve years the world bickered with Saddam about nuclear and biological weapons, demanding that Iraq permit United Nations inspectors to come in. Believe me, Saddam was laughing the whole time, because he had made fools of them. He went on national television in Iraq and told the people he had won the Gulf War. By that he meant that he was still in power, and nothing had really changed in the way things would be done. He had billions of dollars in gold, currency, and high-tech equipment that our soldiers had stolen in Kuwait, and no one was going to intervene. The fact is, some of that booty was eventually returned to Kuwait, but Saddam made a fortune from it in the process.

Later, when America and the U.N. decided to punish Saddam by imposing sanctions on our country, once again they thought that economic pressures would force Saddam to capitulate or possibly even leave the country. Forgive me, but this was the stupidest idea of all. Saddam and his friends were not hurt in the least by sanctions. He already had dozens of palaces and had begun building more. He had hundreds of servants, and all the oil money anyone could ever dream of. Only the people of Iraq were hurt by sanctions because Saddam didn't care in the least if the people of Iraq starved to death as long as he was in control.

Because the first Gulf War ended so abruptly, America and the West now have problems that will be much more costly in the long run, for themselves and for Iraq. Until the Iraqi military can take over the job of safeguarding the country, multinational forces will have to stay where they are. And this means that more people will die on both sides, more equipment will be destroyed, and it will affect foreign policy in Iraq, the greater Middle East, and the West for years to come.

Although we went through hell in Iraq for twelve years because of the pullout in 1991, most Iraqis were happy to see the Americans return in 2003. But since they had not won the peace when they had the chance, coalition forces now have to deal with many new problems. For too long there was a great vacuum in security that led to more violence, looting, and armed resistance from the Sunni minority who realized that they were losing their superior position in Iraqi society. This can be stopped, but it will take time.

No Time for Compromise

Actually, I never set out to write a book about these things or to talk about the secret world of Saddam Hussein that I witnessed as a senior officer and member of the government in Iraq. I was only persuaded to undertake this project after a series of speaking engagements in America and a chance meeting with someone in the publishing business. But after much thought, prayer, and consultation with family and friends, I decided that such a book may help the people of my country and shed new light on our situation.

There were times when I wanted to speak up, and there were times when simply doing the humane thing—such as refusing to execute coalition pilots captured during the first Gulf War—did cost me my job and freedom. But now that Iraq has been liberated from the blood-stained hands of a dictator, with a new constitution and a new government of freely elected representatives for all people, I am finally able to speak. I'm still not out of danger; there are people in Iraq who would silence me if they could. But the world needs to hear from someone who will speak the truth, and that's what I've attempted to do in these pages.

The story I know best, of course, is my own, and that will be the thread that ties this narrative together. I had the good fortune to grow up around professional soldiers and fighter pilots, and then to become a pilot myself. For most of my adult life this was my passion, and you'll hear more about that. But since the mid-1980s, our lives have become much more complicated, so the drama of life in the Middle East will also be a persistent theme in these pages. I hope my own journey as a member of an ethnic and religious minority may offer a point of focus that will be useful in gaining a better understanding of what really happened to us.

Saddam Hussein was a tyrant, we all knew it, and he had many secrets. The chapters of this book, however, will not be infused with one amazing secret after another. Rather, I will discuss private conversations, little-known facts about certain individuals and events, and other aspects of life in the Middle East that are not widely known in the West. And of course I want to speak about the nature, deployment, and ultimate destination of Saddam's WMDs. But I will do all of this chronologically in the course of my story.

Looking back now, it seems like such a strange odyssey. King Faisal I, who ruled during the British Mandate of the 1920s and '30s, was by all accounts a wise and intelligent leader. His son and successor, King Ghazi, was educated at Harrow in England, and when he died in an automobile accident in 1939, he was succeeded by his son, Faisal II. The prime minister at that time was General Nuri es-Said, who was educated at Constantinople and became a good friend of T. E. Lawrence, the flamboyant British officer known as Lawrence of Arabia.

Like both of the monarchs, Gen. Nuri hoped to maintain strong alliances with Europe and America. Unlike most Middle Eastern countries at the time, Iraq was well positioned to build strong commercial and economic relations with the West. But the pro-Western government was overthrown by a military coup on July 14, 1958, and the new ruler, Gen. Abdel-Karim Qassem, transformed the nation into a pro-Soviet republic. Then in typical communist fashion, King Faisal II, the royal family and Gen. Nuri were murdered, along with many who had served in the cabinet.

Qassem's government wasn't to last very long, however. Five years later, on February 8, 1963, Col. Abdel-Salam Aref and the Baath Party mounted a coup to oust President Qassem; and five years after that the Baath Party leader, Ahmed Hassan al-Bakr, overthrew Aref. Al-Bakr seized power with the aid of Saddam Hussein, whose notorious brutality and efficiency had made him a valuable asset to tyrants. But, true to form, Saddam gradually forced Al-Bakr into a position of subservience, and on July 17, 1979, Saddam walked into Al-Bakr's office and told him that he was taking over. Al-Bakr capitulated immediately, and on that day "The Crasher" took over as Supreme Leader of the country.

When I served under him, military officers could only say what Saddam wanted us to say, and if we chose to say anything different from what was prescribed, it could be a fatal choice. We had to follow the party line, and it was often forbidden to speak the truth. Some people have told me I'm crazy to tell this story. The war is still under way. There are American and coalition forces on the ground in Iraq, and United Nations representatives are everywhere. On top of that there is an intense political battle taking place all around us that is every bit as hot as the war on the ground. When it gets this hot, they say, the right thing to do is to back away from the fire, but they think I'm jumping into the middle of it.

One man said to me recently, "Georges, you think you have to tell the truth all the time! Don't you know it's not safe to tell the truth so much!?" But I just said, "I'm sorry, this is the way I'm made. I can't be any other way."

Ever since Saddam seized power in 1979—and, really, for a decade before that—we knew that truth was whatever the leader said it was. If Saddam wanted two plus two to equal nine, then everybody would say it was nine. And more than that, it was nine with flowers and ribbons around it, because that's how Saddam wanted it to be. Even in the military, where you would expect men to have courage and stamina, it was considered indiscriminate and dangerous to speak openly. Unfortunately, I had a habit of saying that two plus two is four, knowing very well that speaking the truth could cost me my life. Ultimately, it almost came to that, but I'll come back to that in due course.

Our Infamous Friend

Oddly enough, I had a casual acquaintance with Saddam a couple of years before his ascendancy. At that time, Saddam and his wife, Sajida, were just ordinary people—or so it seemed to us. They didn't have much money and they lived in a modest house. I knew who he was. Saddam was a member of the Baath Party, and his wife was a teacher at our local school, Al-Massarah Athaniya. Sajida was from the town of Al-Mansour, which is a nice suburb of Baghdad, and this is also where my wife was from. Both of them were teachers there, so we were familiar with Saddam and Sajida before his more-celebrated exploits began.

Sajida would eventually go on to become head of that school, but during those years she was very much the traditional Arab woman. She wore the long dress, the Abaya, and she was friendly to us. I was a young officer, but I had recently returned from advanced flight training in Texas and I brought with me a brand-new 1965 Chevrolet coupe, with Texas plates. I would drive to school each day after work and pick up my wife. Since Sajida generally walked to work, my wife would say, "Georges, let's give Sajida a ride," and we were happy to take her home. At that time my Chevy was the nicest car in Iraq—the president had a 1964 Chevy and mine was a '65—so that was fun for all of us, and we were glad to help them out.

I would see Saddam from time to time, especially on social occasions at the school, and he'd show up wearing a casual shirt and his lounging slippers. Afterward he and his wife would walk home together and everything seemed normal. I spoke to him briefly on a few occasions—it was not a close friendship by any means, but I can say that we knew Saddam before his rise to power. I would come to know him much better in time.

In those days we thought Saddam was like everyone else. He had a reputation, it's true, and we knew his name because of the assassination attempt in 1959. But that was years earlier and most people thought of him as a rebel, or a somewhat overzealous politician. He had been an assassin, but he was brought back by the administration and given amnesty for his past actions. After that he seemed to be living a normal life.

Little did we know.

PART I

CHAPTER 1

A WORLD OF CHANGE

As far back as I can remember, I have been in love with flying. By the age of twelve, I knew everything about the airplanes that flew out of the Royal Air Force Base at Habbaniya, which is located about fifty miles west of Baghdad. My father, Hormis Sada, served in the Royal Air Force in those days. He was stationed at Habbaniya, and that's where I grew up. That's also where I discovered my passion to become a military aviator and a top-rated fighter pilot.

I knew all the maneuvers our pilots would perform. I memorized the names of their planes and equipment, and I would go to the airfield every day after school to watch them take off and land. I could tell you when a pilot was going to do an undershoot or an overshoot. I knew the difference between high-speed and low-speed landings, and I became acquainted not only with the pilots, but I even learned the terminology and tactics they used. It was easily the most exciting part of my life during those years.

My father served for more than thirty years under the British flag. Our family traveled to England when he was stationed there for a time, and I learned more about flying each day as I watched the British pilots take off and land. Father eventually retired from the Royal Air Force with a pension from the British government, but for many years this was my life. I spent so much time hanging around the flight line making a nuisance of myself that one day an old sergeant major stopped me and said, "Georges, you know you ought to be working for me, you spend so much time down here."

My eyes lit up when I heard that. "Really?" I said. "Would you give me a job?" I'm not sure he really meant it at first, but he thought about it for a second and said, "Sure. Why not? Can't pay you much, but you can help out around here as much as you like."

That was all the encouragement I needed. Every day during my summer holiday I was there first thing in the morning. Except for lunch and dinner breaks, I was on the job until the sun went down most days. It was the best job any boy could ever want, and in some ways it was like a college education. I was in and out of the office all day long, observing how business was done, how the orders came in, how the pilots got their assignments. I carried messages all over the base, and I got to spend a lot of time on the flight line, which I loved best of all. Watching the technicians working on the planes and seeing the pilots climb aboard those shiny new fighters and zoom off was thrilling.

On top of that, I even got a little money each month, and that was great too. Suddenly I had more cash than any of the kids I knew, and I could buy just about anything I wanted. But the best part was the feeling that I actually had a small part in keeping our fighter pilots in the air. I decided then that as soon as I graduated from high school I was going to become a pilot myself, and that's just what I did. I applied to the Air Academy my senior year and was accepted as a cadet in 1958.

Changing Alliances

Before we actually began classes, however, the country was shaken by a major military coup. Overnight it seemed we had a new government, a new president, and a new set of strategic alliances. Up until that time, Iraq had been closely allied with Great Britain. King Faisal I, his son, Ghazi, and Ghazi's son, Faisal II, were pro-Western and genuinely peaceful monarchs. But with the overthrow of the monarchy by a military coup, Iraq became a socialist republic with new leaders who favored the Soviet system.

This sudden change of direction also changed the way the military was run, and it changed the way students were trained in the academies. Most of the cadets in the Air Academy ahead of me had gone to America or England for flight training, and that's what I had expected to do. I spoke pretty good English and I knew a lot about both those countries. But as it turned out, we were to be the first class of pilots under the new republican regime, and nothing had prepared me for what was to come.

When we arrived for the first day of classes, we were divided into groups and introduced to our instructors. We were given a basic overview of the program and informed about what we would be doing the next few years. But when they told us about the procedures for flight school, they said we wouldn't be going to England or America this time. We were to be the first class to go to Russia. That was a big surprise, but I don't think we were terribly disappointed. We had heard a lot about Russia, and it sounded interesting and exotic. So we completed the basic classes. We had to pass a battery of physical exams and aptitude tests, and when that was complete, on February 9, 1959, we were loaded up and shipped off to our new quarters in Russia.

Unfortunately, nobody had told us about the weather in Russia in the month of February. We were boys from a warm country and we assumed that everywhere was about the same. So you can imagine our shock when we stepped off the plane in Moscow and the temperature at the airfield was hovering around twenty below zero! We weren't just freezing; we were freezing and terrified. We had no warm clothes, and nothing heavy enough to protect us from the extreme cold. If we had put on every piece of clothing in our luggage, it wouldn't have helped. I had never felt such bone-chilling cold in my life, nor even imagined it could exist.

The Russians who came to get us were as shocked as we were that we hadn't been warned about the weather. So they immediately loaded us on trucks and took us down to a large government store, built deep below ground, and they told us to pick out whatever we needed—especially warm clothes, overcoats, and heavy boots. So that's how it all started.

Our next major problem was that we didn't know a single word of Russian—we'd all been expecting to go to England or America. But, fortunately, there were translators who could speak to us either in English or Arabic. So we soon found ourselves in a Russian immersion program, and we had to learn the language very quickly. We spent the first few days in Moscow becoming acclimatized, and then we were taken to the Alma-Ata Air Base—located in the Kazakhstan region of the USSR—and that's where we actually went to school.

To say that this was an eye-opening experience would be an understatement. Within days of our arrival in the Soviet Union we were seeing and doing things we never could have imagined. All our ideas and beliefs were challenged, and none more so than our religious beliefs.

A Close Call

Along those lines, there's one story from those days that's very important to me now. As I indicated briefly in the preceding pages, I come from a Christian family, and my father was very serious about his faith. He was the head of our family, and he was also the leader of deacons in our church, which was the Ancient Church of the East at that time. I was going to be gone for nearly four years, and Father wanted to be sure I wouldn't forget my faith while I was away.

As I was about to leave the house on the 9th of February for the flight to Russia, Father said to me, "Georges, you're going to be away from the family for a long time. Do you have your Bible with you?"

Suddenly I was embarrassed. I said, "No, Father, I don't. I forgot to pack it." So he said, "Why don't you go and get it, son?"

So of course I did. I ran back to my room and grabbed my Bible. I quickly opened my suitcase, which was packed and ready to go, and I just laid it inside—right in the middle—totally forgetting that I was going to a communist country where the Holy Bible was a forbidden book! If I had thought for even a moment, I would have known. If the security officers in Russia found me with a Christian Bible, they wouldn't only burn it, but they might wash me out of the academy and ship me back home on the first plane. But the thought never crossed my mind until we arrived at the Intourist checkpoint in Moscow.

When we got there, a group of security officers checked us in and they looked through everything in our luggage. A tall, muscular Russian, obviously a KGB officer, opened my bag and immediately spotted the Bible lying on top of my clothes. It said "Holy Bible" right there on the cover, but it was written in my native Assyrian language, Aramaic, which is actually the language that Jesus and the disciples spoke in the first century. Of course the officer couldn't read it, so he asked me, "What's this?"

Suddenly I realized what I'd done. I thought, *My God, this is Russia, a communist country! And this is a Bible!* I hesitated for a second and then somehow managed to answer him. "Well, this is a book; it's a story." He looked at me and said, "Oh, yes? What kind of story?" So I said, "It's a story about a very good man." I was thinking as fast as I could, but of course I didn't say the name of the good man. Still, I wasn't lying to him.

He thumbed through the pages a bit more, and then he asked me, "A good man, huh? Where from?" This time I said, "Well, he was a good man from our area," meaning the Middle East. Again, I was being accurate but not too precise in my reply.

At this point, the security guard asked me, "What language is this?" And I told him it was written in the Assyrian language, which is the language of the Assyrian Empire. He thumbed through it again briefly, then laid it back in the suitcase, shut the top, and he said, "Okay, you can go."

I thought, *Oh, my, that was close! But my Bible is safe for now!*

That was the only time they checked us, so I went from there to my base and placed the Bible out on my nightstand where I would see it and remember to read a few verses every day. Since it was written in the Aramaic language, no one else could read it, and none of the Russians had any idea what was inside those pages.

On weekends we were given passes to go into the city of Alma-Ata, and on one of those trips I drove in with a group of my friends. So long as our grades were good, we had passes every weekend and we could go wherever we liked, so we would go to places where we could meet the Russian girls and dance with them. I had met a girl who was a student at the college of languages, so I would go there, while my best friend, Samir, would usually go to see another girl who was a student at the medical college.

Divine Appointment

Samir struck up a conversation with a young woman on one occasion, and right away she asked him where he was from. He told her he was from Iraq, and she got very excited. "You're from Iraq?" she asked. "That's my country! My parents and grandparents are all from Iraq. Those are my people too!" And then she asked, "Are you Assyrian?" And Samir said, "No, I'm not, but I have an Assyrian friend, and his family is from that part of the country."

This young woman told him that her family had come to Russia after the First World War, and this was the first time she'd ever met anyone who actually lived in Iraq. She said, "Are there any Assyrians at your base?" Samir said, "Yes, my friend is Georges Sada, and he's a cadet at the Air Academy with me." She said, "Oh, yes, Georges!" Then she pronounced my name the Assyrian way—Gyorgyes. "That's an Assyrian name," she said. "I recognize it."

Samir asked her, "Would you like to meet him?" and she said she would. So Samir told her he would arrange a meeting for the next day. We would rendezvous at the opera house in the town near our base. It didn't take me long to warm to the idea and I got a ride back into town the next day, making sure I wasn't late for the meeting. When I got to the opera house, the young lady was already waiting for me, and I was impressed to discover that she was so beautiful.

I recognized her as Assyrian by her features and her eyes, but she spoke first: "Are you Gyorgyes?" she asked excitedly. I said, "Hello, yes I am," and I asked if she was the one I was supposed to meet. She said yes and gave me a big hug as if she'd known me forever. And she said, "Come on, Gyorgyes, I want you to go to my house. I want you to meet my family."

I thought that was unusual, but I went with her, and when we arrived at her house it was packed with Assyrians—young people, old people. Men, women, and children of all ages. It was amazing, frankly, and they all wanted to speak to me in the Assyrian language. It was incredible, but I was apparently the center of a big celebration.

We talked and laughed and got better acquainted, but after a little while, an old man came over to me and whispered, "Gyorgyes, do you have a Bible?"

"Bible?" I said. "Why, yes, I do. I keep it on my nightstand back at the Air Academy."

To say his eyes lit up wouldn't do justice to the expression that came over his face. "You do?" he exclaimed. "You have a Bible?" But then he said, "Oh, my God! You left your Bible back at the Russian base? On your nightstand?"

I said, "Yes, I read it every day." The book was written in Aramaic, so only an Assyrian who knew the ancient language could read it. But the old man was clearly worried and said, "Look, we must go and get it now." He immediately called three young men and told them to get their car. He said they would have to drive me back to the base to get my Bible before someone came and took it away.

I was embarrassed by all the commotion and I said, "Sir, it's very far from here. As you know, the Alma-Ata Air Base is at least thirty miles away." But he insisted. "No, listen to me. I'm sure of this. We can't leave that Bible there for another minute."

With that, I joined the three young men and we drove to the base as quickly as we could. I went down to my room to see if the Bible was where I left it, on the nightstand, and sure enough it was. Actually, this was the first time I'd worried about it. It had never crossed my mind that someone might take it. So I took the Bible with me and we drove back to the city.

When I handed the Bible to the old man, he immediately opened it. His eyes shimmered with tears as he held the book in his weather-beaten hands. And when he began to read aloud in the Aramaic language, I could feel his emotion. Tears of joy flowed gently down his wrinkled cheeks, and everyone in the room crowded around to see for themselves. I couldn't believe they were all so happy.

But then I thought, *You know, it's really a miracle that this Bible is here at all. I only put it in my suitcase at the last minute because Father had asked if I remembered to pack my Bible. And then the KGB officer had gone through my luggage at the airport, and if I hadn't been very careful in the way I answered his questions, he would have taken the book away and destroyed it. And now, here I am, with a Bible that only these people can read, in their native language. And they're filled with such joy to be able to put their hands on this forbidden book after so many years.*

As the thoughts were racing through my mind, I remembered the passage in Isaiah which says: "'For My thoughts are not your thoughts, nor are your ways My ways,' says the LORD. 'For as the heavens are higher than the earth, so are My ways higher than your ways, and My thoughts than your thoughts'" (Isaiah 55:8–9 NKJV).

I was humbled to realize that when God wants his Word to reach a particular group of people, even if they're thousands of miles away, he has his ways of doing it. And in this case, I was chosen as his messenger, to take that precious book to people who hadn't seen a Bible in many, many years. I was so happy I'd managed to bring the book from Iraq to Russia, and to put it in the hands of people who wanted so much to read it. They were afraid that the police might come and confiscate it, so they came up with a plan. They decided that each man in that group was to take the Bible for a week, and one at a time over the next several months each one would copy ten pages by hand.

In time they would be able to copy the entire Bible in their own hand. And then, when they had one complete set, with all the verses and chapters of all sixty-six books, they could pass the handwritten copy around and each family could make their own copy. It would have to be kept in a safe place, but this way every one of the Assyrian families in that area would be able to read and memorize the Scriptures. And once again, for the first time in a very long time, they could worship God as they had done in their native land.

In reality, I suppose, we were smuggling Bibles into Russia, but I must say that it was done innocently enough. As you might imagine, this experience had a profound influence on me, and I was humbled to know that God had chosen to use me in this way.

Something to Prove

I was in Russia for three years, and during that time I qualified as a fighter pilot and graduated from the Academy as a 2nd lieutenant in the Iraqi Air Force. That's how my life as an officer began. At that time the hottest plane in the sky was the Russian-made MiG fighter, and I was excited to learn that I would be flying the MiG-17F, which had a very sophisticated afterburner system. When I began flying regular missions, I felt like I owned the sky—and for all practical purposes, maybe I did. That plane was incredibly fast. It carried a standard payload, and it was a thrill to fly.

From 1961 to 1963, I was gaining a lot of experience as a fighter pilot, and I was eventually transferred to a MiG-21 squadron at Al Rashid Air Base in Baghdad. But all this happened just in time for the next big surprise from the Iraqi government. On the same day I arrived at my new unit, there was another revolution. This time it was a coup d'état staged by the Baathis, who overthrew the government of Prime Minister Abdel-Karim Qassem.

President Qassem was driven from power and executed on February 8, 1963, and the Baathis—led by Col. Abdel-Salem Aref and supported in turn by Gamel Abdel Nasser and the Arab Nationalists in Egypt—took over the government. For the next three years the country would be run by a group of socialists who happened to be anti-communist, which meant that there were all sorts of new tensions between Baghdad and Moscow.

After the coup, President Abdel-Salem Aref managed to hold on to power for three years, until his death in a helicopter crash in 1966. Someone had sabotaged his helicopter, but at that point his brother, Abdel-Rahman Aref, who had been chief of staff of the army, succeeded him as president. That government only lasted until 1968, when a different group of Baathis, led by Ahmed Hassan al-Bakr, rose up and forced Abdel-Rahman Aref to flee the country and go into exile in England.

In 1964, in the middle of much confusion and uncertainty in Iraq, I received word that I had been selected for advanced training in night flying, instrument flying, and bad-weather flying. But I was doubly surprised when I found out that I was going to Randolph Air Force Base in San Antonio, Texas, to get my instructor's rating, and to work with some of the best trainers in the world. Randolph is connected to Lackland Air Force Base, and those two installations were widely recognized at the time as having the most advanced pilot training in the world.

Not only was I glad to be getting away from the mayhem in Iraq for a while, but it was a great honor to be allowed to go to the United States to take advanced instrument training. I'd learned a lot during my basic flight instruction in Russia, and the hours I'd already logged in the MiGs would soon prove to be very important. But the thought of going to America for my instrument rating was the best news I could have gotten.

By the mid-1960s, relations were getting somewhat better between Iraq and America, and I was able to go to school over there with a double salary—I not only received my regular officer's pay from the Iraqi government, but I also got a nice stipend with flight pay from the American government. So I was well paid during my time in Texas, and that made it possible for me to see and do a lot of interesting things while I was there.

The first thing I had to do, however, was to gain the acceptance of my fellow officers. As it turned out, I was the only student pilot from the Middle East, and most of these guys had never met an Iraqi before. They were convinced I couldn't tell one end of a jet fighter from the other. A few of them teased me, asking if I'd left my tent back home in the desert, and some of them called me "Camel Jockey" behind my back. This surprised me because I had never ridden a camel.

But one day the chief flight instructor called me into his office and said he wanted to check me out in one of the new trainers. There were planes at the base, including the T-38 Talon and the T-39 Saberliners that were being used by the air force and navy. I'd never flown either of those planes before, but I was pretty sure I could handle it. So I told him I'd love to go up with him. The next day when I reported for duty, he had a dual-seat trainer warming up on the flight line, so we both put on our flight suits and helmets and climbed aboard.

The instructor handled the takeoff, and once he got her up to a good altitude, he started showing me the controls and gauges, pointed out how the lights and instruments worked, and then he made sure

I knew about the canopy controls and the ejection system. I was sure I had a good grasp of all that, so after about ten minutes I said, "Sir, I think I've got it. Can I have control?" I guess he thought I was being a bit hasty—after all, to him and the others I was still the unproven camel jockey—so he asked if I was sure I was ready, and I told him I was.

At that point he let go of the stick and said, "She's all yours." That's all I needed to hear. For the first couple of minutes, I made a series of banks and turns, getting used to the controls, and I increased and decreased speed to get a feel for the way she accelerated. Before long I was sure I had it down and I asked the instructor if I could go ahead and try a few maneuvers. He said, "Are you sure?" Again, I said, "Yes, sir, I'm sure."

Making an Impression

The trainer we were flying was a very good airplane, but, honestly, I could have run circles around it in my MiG-21F. With all due respect for the plane and the pilot, however, I made a few turns and banks to get the feel of it, and then I proceeded to put that airplane through her paces. First I took her into a steep dive followed by a gentle climb and a series of hard-left turns and a roll at the end.

Each maneuver was a little faster than the one before, and it gave us a strong gravitational pull, which was something else I needed to experience in that airplane. At that point I took her into another dive and leveled out into a slow roll and turned back to the right. It was a good ride, and the plane handled perfectly. But after about fifteen minutes, the instructor keyed his headset and told me, "Okay, Georges, take us home."

As we approached the airfield, I was sure the instructor would be expecting to take the controls and bring her in, so I said, "Sir, if it's okay with you, I'd like to do the landing." He hesitated briefly but gave me the go ahead, and I made the approach and touched down very nicely. Then I just taxied back to the same spot on the flight line that we'd left from. As soon as we stepped down from the cockpit onto the tarmac, the young officer nodded his head toward the head-quarters building and said, "Follow me."

That's all. No word of satisfaction or disappointment. Just, "Follow me." For a minute I wasn't sure if I'd passed or flunked, but once we got inside the building he led me down the hall to the commander's office, tapped on the door, and then both of us went in and reported to the commanding officer. Looking over at me, the flight instructor said, "Sir, this man can fly. He just took me on one hell of a ride, and I can tell you, we've got nothing to worry about with this guy." Then he reached over and shook my hand and said, "Georges, welcome to Texas." It was such a great feeling to be accepted so quickly, and in that way. And that was only the beginning of seven incredible months in America.

By the time I got back to Iraq at the end of my training, I discovered that I'd been transferred to a new squadron that was just being formed to fly the new MiG-21FL. These planes were faster, more powerful, and much more sophisticated technically than even the 21F I'd been flying.

The Tactics of a Monster

It was after the revolution of July 17, 1968, that Saddam began moving up in the party. He still had very little power, but it was clear that he was making his move. His job at the time was that of chief bodyguard to president Al-Bakr. But because of his efficiency and determination, he rose quickly and before long Al-Bakr named Saddam as his deputy.

This was all the encouragement Saddam needed, and soon he demanded to be given officer's rank in the army. A short time later he was appointed to the rank of four-star general without ever having served a single day in the military. Career officers like me were required to attend the National Staff College for three years and pass a rigorous set of examinations before they earned the rank of a field grade officer—meaning major or higher. But Saddam became a four-star general overnight, with no effort at all.

By this time, most of us knew that Saddam was a brutal and treacherous man. He had a hair-trigger temper and wouldn't think twice about killing you if you got in his way. This made him very useful during the revolution, but it also made him very dangerous to both his friends and his allies. Everybody was afraid of him. He killed for nothing, and he collected people who were loyal to him and kept meticulous notes on those he distrusted. He started his climb to power in the Intelligence Service, which is known as the Mukhabbarat in Iraq. This was a mostly secret division of government that was styled on the order of the KGB in Russia.

Mukhabbarat actually means Civil Intelligence, although they didn't call it that at the time. They gave it the more innocent sounding name of Public Affairs. And in that capacity Saddam was able to bring in all sorts of thugs and gangsters to help him carry out his plans. And he had big plans.

In America, the Central Intelligence Agency (CIA) is not allowed to spy on private citizens. If they suspect that foreign terrorists or spies are operating within the country, they can go to a federal judge and get specific permission to conduct covert surveillance, but there are strict limits on the intelligence services in the United States. In my country, however, that was not the case until recently. Especially under Saddam, the government could spy on anyone, anytime, and anywhere. And believe me, they did it with a passion.

Part of the problem since the liberation of Iraq in 2003, in fact, has been that many Iraqis who grew up under the old regime want to revert to those tactics. They want the government to be able to spy on private citizens. I have a role in the new defense ministry now, and one of the things I have to keep telling people is that those old cloak-and-dagger procedures are no longer legal. They're against the law. We're not permitted to spy on our own people any longer, and if there's to be law enforcement in the country, then the police will have to handle it.

But no such restrictions were there to hamper Saddam Hussein, and he wouldn't hesitate to spy on anyone, or to order the execution of his political enemies. On one occasion, Saddam called me in to his office with Gen. Adnan Khairalla, who was minister of defense. He said, "Look, Georges, if my sons Uday and Qusay step one millimeter over the line and don't behave exactly as I want them to, I won't hesitate to chop off their heads." That was his first sentence to me, and that tells you the type of obedience he demanded.

He recognized no restrictions on his authority, and he would take drastic measures with anybody, any time, whether they were Sunni or Shia, Tikriti or non-Tikriti, Arab or non-Arab, man or woman, adult or child. Saddam would never hesitate to punish anyone who stepped over the line or who refused to obey him. When he threatened Al-Bakr and forced him to step down, there was a strong negative reaction by some high-ranking members of the Baath Party. They said, "Why should Saddam Hussein be in power? Why shouldn't we vote for a new leader instead of just letting Saddam take over with a gun?"

When Saddam heard about those comments, he brought all the members of the party to a large auditorium in downtown Baghdad. When he arrived, everyone was in their seats, but Saddam lit a big cigar and casually began calling each of those dissenters by name, sending them outside where they were executed by their own party members. And some of them were killed in the most dreadful ways you can imagine. Actually, they were killed in ways you could probably never imagine because his tactics were so evil. I've never heard of anything like this anywhere else in the world in my lifetime, except in my own country.

Years later, a film re-creation was made of those events, and even knowing how and why it happened can't lessen the feeling of revulsion I get whenever I've seen it. Some of the men he killed that day were members of the central committee of the Baath Party. I knew many of them, and they were all very capable, intelligent, and distinguished people. But he had them killed systematically, one by one. When they stepped outside, the Mukhabbarat were already waiting for them. Saddam didn't actually know if the names he called out had said anything bad about him. But, as he said to me, if he thought that at some time they had stepped even one millimeter over the line, he wouldn't think twice about chopping off their heads.

Internal Corruption

In this way Saddam screened out anyone who could make trouble for him in the future. He was a genius at doing evil, and he gathered around him a large group of men who had gone to Yugoslavia, Bulgaria, and East Germany to learn the most efficient methods for eliminating one's political enemies. I met some of those men. They were little better than savages who had gone to Russia to learn how to interrogate prisoners and get every last bit of information out of them before killing them. They were trained how to use some of the most diabolical forms of torture ever devised. And they wouldn't think twice about using them.

Even if there were no other reason to drive Saddam from power and change the regime in Iraq, that would be reason enough. His brutal repression of dissent, his murders and torture of political opponents, his barbaric treatment of the good and innocent people of Iraq, and his manipulation of people, turning one against the other for his own political advantage—these were clearly the work habits of a monster. And, thanks to America and her allies in the coalition, we are finally rid of that monster today. It's true he had weapons of mass destruction, and he used them. But there was something even worse than WMDs—the mind of Saddam himself.

With so much evil inside his head and so much wealth in his hands, God only knows what he would have done if the Americans had not come in and stopped him.

The decision to remove Saddam was the right thing to do. It was done at the right time and, I believe, in the right way. If you only hear what the news media say about the situation in Iraq, you would probably get the impression that nothing is going right and that the decision to use military force was a bad one. But this is not true. Many things are going very well now, but I've never heard anyone on the evening news saying that the new government is doing well. No one is telling you that we've built 12,500 new schools, that we have electricity and telephones again, and that roads and other infrastructure are being rebuilt better than before. No one is telling you that teachers, who were earning less than $3.00 a month under Saddam, are now being paid $350 or more a month, which is a respectable living wage in Iraq.

Several years ago, teachers in Iraq were very well paid. They could afford to travel in the summer and take trips abroad. They could afford to give little gifts to their students. When my wife was a teacher, I used to go with her to the shops in Baghdad to buy presents for the children who were earning high marks in her classes. But when the inflation was so bad, teachers had to ask their students for food—they would ask those from well-off families to bring them an egg, a potato, a tomato, or whatever they could spare from home. Teachers are the most numerous profession in Iraq, with nearly a million men and women at all levels, and this large group of people was forced to beg for food.

Under Saddam, the entire system was corrupt, and the military was the most corrupt of all. For example, if a soldier wanted to go on leave, he would have to bribe his commander to let him go. Seven days leave might cost him two-hundred dollars. Or if a soldier wanted to transfer to another base, to be closer to his family, his commander could demand that he pay him five-hundred dollars or more. The whole system was corrupt, and everybody knew it. In time our people became artists at using bribes and corruption to get whatever they wanted.

There have always been certain people who would demand bribes and kickbacks, but in Iraq this became the rule. If you went to the police, you had to give them a bribe to get help. If you went to the post office to mail a package, you had to give the teller a bribe. Even if you only wanted to pay your electric bill, you had to pay a bribe. If you couldn't afford it, you'd have to go stand in line for two or three hours, or perhaps longer, to transact even the simplest business.

We're not beyond that entirely, even now, but it's getting better. The problem is that Iraq now has a very young government. And in some ways you can say that we're a young nation. The government is young and our military is young, but also the average age in Iraq is very young—around fifteen to sixteen years of age. Even the parents of our young people have never known any other way of life.

Fear, anger, suspicion, and corruption is all they've ever known. And the idea that you must distrust everyone and cheat in order to get ahead is embedded in their consciousness. So the question now is, how do you change the habits of people who have known no other way of life? I believe it can be done, and it's happening, little by little. But it's a slow process. The miracle is that it's happening at all.

Working for Change

I recall one day shortly before the war, in 2002, when I was in my office in Baghdad, and we were visited by two young women. One of them was from Sweden and the other from Holland, and they had come to Iraq as reporters for the Christian organization they worked for in Europe. They came to my church, and since I served as president of the Evangelical Presbyterian Church in Iraq, I had agreed to meet with them. They were asking about Christians in our country, and they especially wanted to know about prisoners of war coming back from Iran.

They had spent several days looking around the country, and this was the last day before they returned to Europe, so they still had several questions for which they needed answers. One of the young women said, "General, I will tell you one thing. We visited hospitals and families all over this country. We visited soldiers, former prisoners of war, and many others, and we think that the whole population of Iraq should be in the hospital, because everybody here is sick."

Those words really struck a nerve, but I said, "You know, I agree with you. And even the man who is speaking to you now is sick. We will need a miracle to change the lives of these people, or at least a prophet who can speak to them and change their hearts." That's not to say that good things aren't happening in Iraq today, because they are. But nothing can change the hearts of the people overnight. Neither Prime Minister Al Jaafari nor Dr. Ayad Alawi nor President Jalal Talabani could change them immediately. None of us has a magic wand. It will take time and good influences from abroad, I believe, to help us accomplish so much. Our needs are simply too great for change to come in a day. But, God willing, change will come.

One day after liberation in 2003, an American official came to me and said he wanted to find out about the condition of the police in Iraq. At that time our records indicated that we had approximately 150,000 police on the payroll in the country. But he wanted to see how many were actually showing up for work on any given day. So we did an exhaustive study and found out that there were, at most, thirty-seven to forty-thousand policemen ready for duty. The rest were based on falsified employment records. Someone—or more likely a group of someones—was stealing all that money. As I said, the Iraqi people had become experts in finding ways to cheat the system. They had no loyalty and felt no guilt, and that's perhaps the worst part of all.

For many months there have been stories about the terrorist attacks on police stations in Iraq, and in most cases scores of policemen are killed or wounded, and many more just run away. You have to ask yourself, how can this happen? A half dozen terrorists come to a police station and shoot ten or twenty police officers. They blow the place up and set it on fire, and immediately all the policemen run away and hide. So then the same terrorists go on to the next police station and do the same thing, again and again, maybe five or ten more times. What's going on? How can five or six terrorists be so powerful that they can shut down the entire police force of Baghdad or Karbala or Ramadi?

The only answer is that the police force is corrupt. Until recently they haven't been able to hire men to serve who care about justice and protecting the people, mainly because these traits were never encouraged by the government under Saddam Hussein. So they hire anyone who's physically fit and willing to wear the uniform. Some of these people may want to be policemen because they think the uniform will make them more powerful. But they don't have the character for the job.

I don't mean to say that this is true for all of them, because we have many fine and capable police officers in Iraq today. But it's true far too often, and you will find that many of these men are not really interested in law enforcement. They just want a good job and a nice uniform.

The police in Iraq are being trained today by the British, and the military is being trained by the Americans. So far, the military is doing a better job of selecting and training new recruits. And I think it will all get better when the people begin to care about doing a good job. They will have to care for their country and its security, and they will have to learn that there are times when a public servant must be willing to stand and fight to protect his city and his nation. In Europe and America, the police have pride in their job. They don't run from trouble, but that's not always true in my country. At least, not yet. So this is something else that will have to change.

Facing the Opposition

The terrorists are committed to their cause. You can say they've been brainwashed, because the radical clerics have been filling their heads with hate for decades. Once they have agreed to carry out an assault, these young martyrs (called *Shaheeds* in Arabic) will do it or they will die. Sometimes they will come and attack a group of policemen with guns and grenades. At other times they will set off a car bomb by remote control. Or if that's too difficult, they will just drive a car full of explosives through the side of a police station or public building and explode it. The most difficult crime to prevent is one in which the perpetrator is willing to die in that way. What can you do to stop a suicide bomber? Even if you stop him before he gets to his target, he will set off the bomb and somebody will die. This is another reason why the police are afraid.

The Americans and the British are working on ways to prevent these kinds of attacks, to spot terrorists and their equipment before they can enter an area and detonate a bomb. But they don't have all the answers yet. Police dogs are very good at detecting terrorists. They can smell explosives, and they can sense when something is not right. The dogs can often tell at a distance if someone is wearing an explosive vest. Each day when I go to my office in Baghdad, I'm checked out by two police dogs before I go in. They know me because they see me every day, but they still check me out before I'm allowed to pass. So the dogs are doing a very good job.

The problem we're having now is to change the hearts and minds of the people, to make them love their country, to make them care about the safety of other people, and to make them stop killing other people simply because they're different or because they may worship in a different way. How will we ever do this? Honestly, I don't know the answer, but it's something I think about and pray about every day.

I spoke to a taxi driver in Baghdad not long ago who told me a very frightening story. He said that one day he stopped to pick up a nice-looking young man, and when the passenger sat down in the cab, the driver asked him, "Where to, sir?" The young man said, "Anywhere you like. I have some time to spare, so just drive around for a while and I'll pay the fare." This sounded like a good deal to the driver. He could just drive around the city with a passenger and he'd be well paid. What could be better than that?

Finally, after a half hour or so, the passenger said, "Okay, that's enough. Stop here." He took money from his pocket and paid the fare, and then he said, "I'm sorry it didn't happen today. You and I were supposed to have lunch today with Mohammed, the prophet." With that, he pulled back the top of his shirt and the driver could see that he was wearing an explosive vest. If they had seen a group of police officers or an American patrol on the streets, he would have set off the bomb and killed them all. And his only disappointment was that they didn't have lunch that day with Mohammed. You can just imagine how that driver must have felt.

This is the mindset we're confronting in parts of Iraq today, but I must say that things are getting better. Yes, there's still an insurgency, and yes, there are still people willing to blow themselves up for religious and political causes. But freedom and democracy are very powerful incentives, and the people are beginning to discover that freedom is something worth living for too.

Living with Freedom

Imagine the surprise of people who find that they can speak openly against the president and the prime minister. They can write letters to the editor of the newspaper and say whatever they like. This is a wonderful thing, and this is what America has given the people of Iraq. They're beginning to realize it now, and they like it very much.

I believe this was also what happened in the Soviet Union and Eastern Europe during the 1980s. The people of those countries were seeing people on television who were free to say and do whatever they liked. They saw American movies and listened to American music. They liked the blue jeans and stereos and rock music, and they wanted to have those things too. They thought that if this was what freedom and democracy could give them, then they wanted more of it. And once they made that discovery, it was only a matter of time until they were demanding to be free. After that, it was only a matter of time until the Berlin Wall came down.

Something very interesting is happening in the Iraqi military. Our young soldiers are beginning to act like American soldiers. When an American military policeman puts his hand up to stop a car, he does it forcefully and with authority. There's no doubt he means, "Stop now!" This is very different from the way Iraqi policemen were doing it before the war. But now the Iraqi MPs are beginning to act like American MPs. They're wearing the aviator sunglasses and fatigue trousers that have been tailored to fit just like the GIs, and spit-shining their boots. Suddenly they're looking and acting more like real soldiers, and it's really fun for an old soldier to watch.

Most noticeable, of course, are the crowds of teenage and pre-teen boys who are hanging around with the soldiers on the street. The GIs are very friendly; they give the kids candy and soda and chewing gum. Sometimes they send the boys down to the shop to buy something for them, and they always give them a nice tip when they get back. So you'll see these twelve- and thirteen-year-old kids counting out their dollars, and they're so proud to have money of their own. Anywhere you see two or three Americans on patrol, standing guard or just relaxing around their armored vehicles, you'll usually find a dozen or more Iraqi boys talking to them—and in surprisingly good English.

The boys are learning English so fast, but, unfortunately, they're also learning the dirty words as well. I've told the American generals, "We're very glad for the boys to be learning English from the soldiers, but please tell the guys not to be teaching them the bad words!" Of course, that's the way it always has been around soldiers. But these youngsters are learning the value of their own life. They're learning to like and respect people who are different from them. And, best of all, they're learning that no religious or political ideology is worth blowing yourself up for.

Most of these young people are attracted to the Western lifestyle. We have television and radio stations now that are run by the Voice of America, so they see these things all the time and it's having an influence on what they think and believe. It will take time for the transition to take place fully, but it's obviously coming. And even a culture like ours, which has so little experience of freedom and democracy, can be changed for the better.

It's shocking to me how quickly our people have gotten satellite TV into their homes. You see the dishes everywhere in Iraq now. And for the first time in their lives, these people can sit in their own living rooms with a remote control and go from channel to channel and see how the rest of the world is living. News, sports, dramas, comedies, you name it—some good and some not so good. And, by and large, they're not watching the Al Iraqiya Television Network or Al Jazeera. There are some people who are more anti-Western, of course, and they watch those channels, but they're in the minority these days.

In general the people are on the right track, and now it's time for them to choose which way they will go. This was what happened to me when I first came to America as a young aviator in 1964. I discovered that America is first in everything. They are first in military might, first in science, technology, art and culture, and all those things. They are also first in drugs, violence, and sex. So the real test of character is knowing what to choose and what to avoid.

A young boy in America today can choose to join a gang, sell drugs, commit all kinds of crimes, and then get caught and end up in jail for the rest of his life. Or he can work hard, study hard, learn a profession, have a nice family, and be a millionaire one day if he tries hard enough. Every boy and girl in America can make such choices. Until recently, boys and girls in Iraq have not been able to choose such things, but now they can. So these options are beginning to be available to our people, too, and I would have to say that's a miracle.

The Things That Matter

There are a lot of good things that the Iraqi people can learn from the Americans, but there are also bad things we should avoid. I want our people to make wise choices, but I also want them to hold on to their own culture and to respect our unique history and traditions. For example, we have a deep respect for our mothers and fathers in Iraq. We should keep that. I'm sorry to say that this is not always true in America—not like it used to be, anyway—so our young people have to recognize that this is a wonderful Iraqi tradition and we should keep it.

We have a tradition of respecting the feelings of others. My brother is a smoker, but he never smokes when I'm around, because he knows I don't like it. Also, we're more conservative about matters concerning women and girls, especially their clothing. Not very many women in Iraq wear the veil anymore—we're already more Western in that way than many countries in the Middle East. But why should a young woman walk around with half her body exposed, as teenagers in America do? Any teenage boy would be glad to see a girl dressed that way, but our culture is not prepared for it. Modesty is a good thing, and I hope we never lose it.

Another important tradition is that we respect our neighbors and relatives. I love my neighbors, and I would do anything for them, even die for them if it came to that. In Iraq, we're very close to the people who live near us, just as we're very close to our relatives. If a member of our family gets sick, fifty people will come to visit. And we do things to help them—take care of their children, look after their property while they're away from home, or whatever is needed. That's just how we are, and we don't want to lose that either.

We want to learn more about technology. We want to improve our skills, our military, our police, our civil servants, and all the professions. We want to improve in many areas, but we don't want to lose the traditions and values that are unique to our culture. Both in Iraq and America, people need to have the moral judgment to make good choices. Some of the choices that people can make today will destroy them, and we would be foolish indeed if we let freedom of choice become the Trojan horse that will one day destroy us.

Whether we like it or not, we have more freedom in Iraq than we know how to use properly at the moment. With satellite television in millions of homes, the people are seeing things they never imagined they could see on TV. From Europe and America we have programs that are vulgar and coarse. How do you stop that? You can't get rid of it, so you have to learn how to deal with it.

Even if you try to get rid of the vulgar images, some people will always find a way to look at those things because they're tantalizing, and because they've been forbidden in the past. So with freedom, we also need to have character and good, moral judgment, and these things can be taught in the home and encouraged in the schools. That will be another challenge we'll have to face in the days and years ahead.

In my church, we're proud of the job we're doing to teach modesty and moral judgment to our children. We're the smallest denomination among the Christian churches in Iraq—the Chaldeans and Eastern Orthodox churches are much larger—but we have the largest Sunday school, with more than 430 young people attending class each week. We have twelve church buses, which the American churches helped us to lease, and it seems the young people are always going somewhere. It's fun for them, and these kids come from many different backgrounds. Some are Chaldeans, some are Orthodox, some are Ancient Church of the East or other denominations. But they're all welcome, and they learn to show respect for others.

It's beautiful to see. They sing all the songs. They memorize verses. They know Jesus, and they have a wonderful time doing things together. Sometimes the leaders of the other churches complain that we're stealing their children, but we're not doing that. We don't ask them to join our church or change denominations, and I've received many letters from parents who've written to thank us for teaching their children in such a wholesome way.

One father wrote to me recently. He said, "Sir, my family and I are Chaldeans, and we love our church. But I'm very happy that my son is coming to your Sunday school. He's learning so many things and having a wonderful time. So thank you for what you're doing." This is the kind of response we get, but we're not the only ones who should be doing it. All the churches and mosques should be reaching out to the children. We should all be doing it—teaching our children the things that matter. We have so much to worry about already.

CHAPTER 2

SADDAM'S RISE TO POWER

Saddam Hussein was making a name for himself as a tough guy long before he began his calculated journey from poverty to the seat of power. He had been working his way up, primarily as a thug, ever since he was a boy in the village of Al Oja. He wasn't a very good student and his family background was very rough. His father, whoever that may have been, died while his mother was pregnant with Saddam, and the boy was raised as an orphan. He started school later than the other kids, so he was always the biggest and oldest in his class. Eventually he was just turned loose on the streets of Tikrit where he gained a reputation as a bully and a gangster.

The city of Tikrit is still known as a rough part of the country, and the people from that district are tough as nails. They're good fighters, and as far back as the Ottoman Empire, the city produced some of the fiercest warriors in our part of the world. At one time I served as commander of the base at Tikrit, and even then I heard stories about Saddam and his family. He was a gangster, a punk, and people who lived in the area would go out of their way to avoid him.

Saddam's uncle, Khairullah Tilfah, was also known as a violent and dangerous man, and he looked after Saddam until the boy was grown. Saddam grew up with his cousin, Adnan Khairallah, who would eventually serve under Saddam as minister of defense. Saddam was considered to be a clever and daring young man, but he was also universally feared. He had an unpredictable temper, and he thought nothing of torturing or killing someone if they stood in his way. We knew then that, one way or the other, Saddam would leave his mark on the world.

Such a man could be a valuable tool for ruthless people like the leaders of the Baath Socialist Party who were always plotting acts of revenge or mayhem. They brought Saddam in as an enforcer while he was still in his teens, and that's how he was picked to lead the attack on President Abdel-Karim Qassem in 1959. Saddam was supposed to be a student in the secondary school when he was asked to carry out the assassination. He hadn't graduated, and it's not likely he ever would have since his attendance and grades were so bad. But he had other, more useful talents.

When Saddam and his gang of thugs opened fire on the prime minister's car on Al Rashid Street, in the center of downtown Baghdad, they sprayed the vehicle with bullets, firing hundreds of rounds with automatic weapons. To make sure Qassem was killed, Saddam ran up to the car and blasted away with a machine gun, inside and out. But by some miracle the president was not killed. He was wounded, but he survived the attack and remained in power for three more years.

Qassem's bodyguards and the police had fired back, and several members of the security detail were killed. But they managed to stop the assassination, and as the attackers were running away, Saddam was struck in the leg by a single bullet. The attackers ran away to a prearranged hideout. But Saddam needed to find a doctor quickly, to remove the bullet from his leg. They were fugitives now on the run, so they couldn't just go to the hospital, and they couldn't find a doctor who would do the job. So finally Saddam took a knife and cut the bullet out himself.

As soon as he could walk, Saddam escaped across the border into Syria, where he stayed out of sight for the next four years. Despite the attempted coup in 1959, Qassem managed to hold onto power until February 8, 1963, when he was finally overthrown by the Baathis with Abdel-Salaam Aref and Ahmed Hassan al-Bakr. Al-Bakr had been a brigadier general in the army, but he was general secretary of the Baath Party, and Saddam Hussein was one of his closest allies. Both men came from the same city, the same tribe, and the same family in Tikrit. Al-Bakr believed he could depend on Saddam because he had a reputation for being courageous and ruthless. But he had no idea just how ruthless Saddam really was.

Unreasonable Demands

Unreasonable and dangerous demands were common in those days. On March 8, 1963, I had another early morning surprise when I was awakened by soldiers pounding on my door. I couldn't imagine what it was, but I heard men yelling at me, "Sir, you must come with us. The base commander wants to see you now!"

I dressed quickly and ran over to the headquarters to see Gen. Hardan al-Tikriti, who was my commander at our base near Mosul at that time. When I walked into his office, he was clearly very tense, and he said he wanted me to fly an unusual mission. I was to be the flight leader for an attack at Aleppo, in the far northwest corner of Syria.

When he told me what he wanted, I said, "What? You want me to attack Aleppo?" He said, "Not the city, Georges, the air base. I want you to hit the airfield."

"But why?" I asked. "We're not at war with Syria, are we?" He said, "No, it's not that. There's been a revolution in Syria. Half the airfield is in the hands of the Baath Party and the other half is still controlled by the old government. There's a battle going on now to see who will control the airfield, and they've asked for our help."

I asked him, "Sir, which part are we going to attack?" He said, "The western half is in the hands of our friends (meaning the Baath Party), and the eastern half is held by the opposition. So I want you to hit the eastern part."

I started thinking about the risks of a mission like that, and after a little quick calculation I realized it was going to be at least four hundred miles from Mosul to Aleppo, and it wasn't very likely that our formation could make it there and back. So I said, "Sir, I don't think we can make it back to base with the fuel in the MiG-17s." At that point he barked at me, "I don't care if you make it back or not. When your engines flame out, you just eject!"

I knew then that there was no room for argument, so I saluted and said, "Yes, sir." I went over to the telephone and called the scramble room and told them to get the planes ready. And I also said to tell my number two pilot to be prepared for a mission. When I got to the flight line to check out the airplanes, I told the technicians to load high explosive, and I made sure our drop tanks were full. My number two, Lt. Ahmed Khairi, came running up to me and I told him what was going on. We had been classmates at the academy, but I was senior to him, so I led the formation, which would be called the "black formation."

As soon as everything was ready, we took off and climbed quickly to cruising altitude. But just as we were setting our course for Aleppo, the flight controller came on the radio and said, "Black formation, return to base. Our friends have taken the airfield." I couldn't believe it! We were ready for the mission, and there's no way of knowing whether we could have completed it or not. But now we didn't have to go, and I just whispered, "Thank you, Jesus!"

Doing the Impossible

At the time of the 1963 revolution, we had one squadron of MiG- 21s in Iraq. We had ordered eighteen of the new jet fighters, but only six had arrived in the first shipment. As usual, Russian technicians came with the shipment and they had already taken two of them out of the crates and managed to get them reassembled and ready to fly. Both planes were checked out by a Russian pilot and parked on the flight line, but none of the Iraqi pilots had been checked out in the 21s, and these planes had sophisticated new avionics and hydraulics that we'd never seen before.

The plan was for the technicians to assemble all six planes and have them checked out, one by one, and the Russian pilot would make the first flights and decide if they were ready to be turned over to our flight instructors. Eventually, of course, they would repeat this process for all eighteen, and our squadron of MiG-21s would then be complete. They hadn't made an instructor model with two seats at that time—one seat for the student pilot and one for the instructor —so the instructors would have to teach us about the planes using the older MiG-15s.

But before this process was complete, and before any of our pilots were trained to fly the new 21s, the revolution came and the Baathis, who were fiercely anti-communist, took over. This meant that all the

Russian pilots and technicians were immediately sent home to Russia. So there we were with two brand-new highly sophisticated jet fighters sitting on the runway, but no pilots trained and ready to fly them.

When the Baathis took control of the government, Gen. Hardan al-Tikriti, the same man who had ordered me to make the raid on Aleppo, in Syria, was promoted to commander of the air force, and he was determined that one of his pilots was going to fly the MiG-21. He wanted to be able to boast that our Iraqi pilots didn't need Russian help: we could do it ourselves. So he ordered that the two best pilots in the air force be brought down to Al Rashid Air Base in Baghdad where the MiGs were kept. That order resulted in my sudden transfer to Baghdad along with my colleague, First Lieutenant Hamid al-Dhahi.

We arrived at the new base on a Wednesday morning in April 1963, and checked in with the base commander as we'd been ordered to do. I had been flying MiG-15s and 17s, and Hamid had been flying the British Hawker-Hunters up to that time. But the air force commander told us, "By Saturday I want to see this plane in the sky. And I expect one of you boys to be flying it." That was it. He dismissed us and a non-commissioned officer took us out to the airfield.

When I heard the commander's words, I didn't know what to think. I was just a young lieutenant. I knew I was a good pilot; I'd been trained in MiG fighters in Russia. But this airplane was so much more powerful and more sophisticated than anything I'd ever seen. Compared to the planes I'd been flying, it looked like a rocket ship sitting on the ground. It was entirely different, huge, shiny, intimidating. Hamid and I walked around the plane and looked it over, inside and out, but we didn't have any idea where to begin.

I asked a non-commissioned officer on the flight line if there were any instructors for the MiG-21 and he said no, that if there were any they were in Russia. I asked if there was a dual-seat model and again, he said no. When I went and sat in the cockpit and looked at the instruments, I realized this model was entirely different from the MiGs I'd flown. Some of the gauges were similar to the MiG-17, but they were positioned differently or they had new features I'd never seen before.

When Hamid looked at the airplane, his reaction was totally different from mine. He said, "This is a MiG-21." They said, "Yes, sir, that's correct." He said, "I'm not a MiG pilot. I fly Hawker-Hunters." They said, "Yes, sir, but the commander said. . . ." But Hamid interrupted the sergeant and said. "Look, I'm not going to kill myself in that plane. Sorry, but Georges can do it. I'm going back to my base in Habbaniya." And that was it. Hamid left me there, and for all I knew there was no one to help me. In just three days time I would have to learn everything I needed to know to take off and land this incredible machine. But God only knew if I would be able to do it.

Well, I breathed a silent prayer and asked the duty sergeant, "Sergeant, how many of your technicians have been to Russia to take the maintenance course on the MiG-21." He said, "All of them, sir." Well, at least that was a start. So I said, "Bring them all here." I didn't know if this would solve my problem, but it would certainly help to meet with the technicians and mechanics responsible for fuel, hydraulics, engine repairs, avionics, airframe, instruments, and everything else. If they could tell me what all the equipment was for and how it worked, at least I'd know something. So they brought those eight men to see me, and before long class began.

For the next two days I participated in one of the most unusual classes I'd ever seen. The eight students became my teachers, telling me everything they knew about this airplane—or at least enough to show me how the instruments and controls operated, how the oxygen and ejection systems worked, and what all the buttons, switches, and lights were for. All day long, from early in the morning until late at night, I listened and learned. When I wasn't asking questions I was reading manuals. And we were constantly going back and forth to the plane to look at the instrument panels and to get the feel of it.

In a jet fighter, the pilot has control of an enormous amount of power. He needs to know so much, not just about weapons systems and fuel capacity, but also about how to control that power in takeoff and landing. How much power does it take to lift off? What's the recommended air speed for landing, and what are the systems for breaking and stopping on a medium to short runway? These are all life and death matters.

In an aircraft like this one, takeoff speed is less critical than landing speed, but none of my teachers could help me with that. But it turned out that there was another pilot on the base who had actually taken pilot's training on the MiG-21 in Russia. He failed the course and was sent home, but surely he would be able to tell me something. I had them send that man to me, and when he arrived I asked him about takeoff and landing speeds and he gave me a pretty good idea of what I'd need to be doing at liftoff and touchdown, and how much runway I'd need. With a runway of only 3 kilometers (or 1.8 miles), and a high performance aircraft, these were all vital questions, as I discovered only too soon.

Going on Adrenalin

If you can just imagine my mental state during all of this! I must have looked like an alien from another planet. I was going up and down, back and forth, all over the aircraft, and my eight young teachers were doing their best to keep up with me. I was exhausted, living on coffee, and at times, I'm afraid, I must have been as irritable and short tempered as a Russian bear. But when Saturday came, I decided I could delay no longer. I got up early, showered, put on my flight suit, drank one last cup of coffee, and walked down to the flight line.

Everybody was there waiting for me when I arrived. The ground crew, the technicians, the sergeants, and many of the other pilots. I made a quick inspection of the plane, put on my helmet, and then I climbed the ladder and took my seat in the cockpit. Instruments awake? Check. Fuel? Check. Canopy down and locked? Check. And step by step I went through my procedures, ignited the engine, and then I released the brake and made my first taxi down the runway and back. By some miracle everything worked and I was in control of the airplane.

At that point I went to the line-up area at the far end of the runway and put my nose wheel right on the line, ready for takeoff. I was trembling like a leaf, but before going, I paused and said a quick prayer: "Jesus, you make it fly. I can't do this alone. You know I don't know what I'm doing. So please help me." That's all I said. I mumbled a quick "Amen," pulled down my visor, pushed the throttle forward, and gave her full power.

The technicians and the failed pilot had told me I would need to hit 135 miles per hour in order to get liftoff, so I was watching the gauge as I was accelerating rapidly down the runway. When she hit 135 I pulled back on the stick and nothing happened. When you pull back on the stick, you can tell if the plane is going to take off; but when I pulled back hard and the nose didn't lift, I realized I wasn't going to make it and I was quickly running out of room.

To make matters worse, there was a huge earthen embankment at the end of the runway; if I hit that, it was all over anyway. I said, "My God, I'm going to hit the end of the runway!" So I decided I had to stop the aircraft.

I released the drag chute from the rear to slow the plane and pressed hard on the brakes. When I finally came to a complete stop, I was no more than thirty or forty feet from the embankment. I don't know how I made it, but I collected my wits, slowly turned the plane around, and headed back to the other end. My hands were really trembling this time and there was sweat rolling down my face. Worst of all, I was humiliated that I hadn't been able to get the plane up in the air. I could have stopped there and gone back to the tarmac, but something inside me said, *No, Georges, you can do it. Go back out there now and try again.*

So I decided I had to go back, and I'd make it fly if it killed me. Before I could try another takeoff, however, I needed a new parachute installed since I'd used the first one on the first takeoff attempt. So as I was coming back, I called the tower and said, "Tell the boys to get me another drag chute." A couple of sergeants came running out with the chute, and as soon as the plane was ready, I went back to the line-up area. As I sat there, I gave myself a little pep talk. I said, "This time, I will take off, and nothing will stop me!"

So once again I released the brake and gave it full power and headed down the runway. This time when I hit 136 miles per hour, I pulled back hard on the stick and the nose hesitated briefly and then up she went like a rocket. I immediately put up the landing gear to reduce the drag, and she began to climb like a tiger. When I looked down to check my air speed, I couldn't believe my eyes. Within seconds I had already surpassed the top speed of the MiG-17, and I still had power to spare.

When I looked around at my instruments and gauges, I realized I was shaking like a leaf. My legs were practically dancing. So I said, "Georges, shame on you. You're a fighter pilot. Get a grip on yourself," and I tried my best to do that. But when I circled back around and began to approach the base, I looked down at that tiny strip of concrete and asphalt and thought, *Oh, my God, how am I going to land this thing?!*

The 21 Has Flown

The view from where I was sitting was unbelievable. The sky over Baghdad on that April morning was crisp and clear. When I climbed to six thousand feet I could see the whole city sprawled out before me—the rolling countryside, the Tigris River, and the deserts far to the west. All around me in every direction was the incredible dark purple horizon that encircles us, and I was overwhelmed by the joy of it, and the very strange privilege I'd been given.

Every pilot knows such emotions, but as a young aviator with so few hours in high-performance airplanes, I was out of my league and I knew it. It was wrong of my commander to send me up in that plane with no instructors, no briefing, no real technical knowledge of the plane, and only his own bravado and vain pride forcing me to risk my life in this way. But there I was, and perhaps I was too young and too inexperienced to worry about it for very long. For now, somehow, I had to get that MiG back down in one piece.

As I approached the base and caught sight of the airfield where I was supposed to land, all I could see was a tiny black line. From the air, the landing strip, which was barely 150 feet wide, looked like a thread. Once again I knew I had to find a way to get control of my nerves and prepare for the descent and landing. I said, "Okay, I'll try some rollovers." So I pushed the stick to the right and, quick as a flash, I did a complete 360-degree roll. I was shocked. It never worked like that in the MiG-17. In that plane I had to press hard on the stick and practically force it to roll over. But this MiG-21 rolled like magic. It was like a sports car in the sky.

I tried this three or four more times, and it made me feel much better because I realized I had control of the plane and I'd done some very nice rolls. I wasn't thinking at that time about what anyone on the ground was seeing, but I discovered later that all of Baghdad was watching me, and when I rolled the plane the crowds went wild. They were beating themselves on the chest, saying, "That's our pilot! That's our plane! That's an Iraqi pilot!"

When I checked the fuel gauge this time I realized I didn't have much time left, so I took her down closer to the airfield. I was feeling much better now, but I realized that before landing I was going to have to reduce my air speed, and I needed to know what it was going to feel like with the undercarriage down. So I put down the landing gear to get a sense of the drag, and once I was comfortable with that, I came in on approach.

I tried to remember what the technicians and the failed pilot had told me, but when I came in I still had too much speed. I was too far down the runway by the time I was ready to touch down, and there was no way I'd be able to stop. So I went around again and the same thing happened—three more times, in fact. On the last one, the red fuel light came on telling me I had no time to go around again and I had to land, one way or the other.

So, once again, I said, "Jesus, please help me," and I put the aircraft in landing attitude and brought it in with flaps down. As soon as I felt the wheels hit the pavement, I popped the drag chute and then, just in time, I hit the brakes and brought her to a stop. It wasn't the world's best landing, but I was alive, and from all sides of the runway I saw people running out to congratulate me. They were ecstatic, and within minutes I would be too.

In that short thirty-five-minute flight, I basically taught myself how to fly the MiG-21. It was a task I was not prepared for. But if not for the grace of God, I could have died at any point. Yet, somehow I did it, and from that moment on my name was known all over

Iraq. "Lt. Georges Sada has flown the MiG-21, and he didn't need the Russians to teach him anything!" That's what they said, and they were all very proud of me.

But it was even better than that. When I made the false start on my first run, nobody realized I had simply failed to get enough speed. And when I made the four false landings, the people were thrilled. They thought I was doing it for their sake, putting on a show! But if they had only known the truth, it might have been a different story.

Of course, the biggest surprise came later when I found out that it was forbidden to take off in a MiG-21 without using the afterburner. I had asked the technicians and the failed pilot if I needed to use the afterburner, and they said they weren't sure. They asked me, "Do you use it with the MiG-17?" I said, "No, I don't need it." They looked at each other, shrugged their shoulders, and said, "Okay, well don't use it with the 21 either." But that turned out to be very bad advice. If only I had known! It was only because I had used up so much fuel in my first attempt and reduced the weight of the plane that I was able to take off at all.

By the time I parked the plane, the flight controller had called the air force commander, General Hardan, and he came over and congratulated everybody. He barked to the crowd, "The 21 has flown!" as if he, too, were a hero. But they had no idea what I had been through for this to happen. When I stepped down from the plane, everybody was there to greet me: the base commander, the chief of the air force, and many other officers and pilots from the base, as well as all the technicians and the failed pilot who had taught me everything they knew.

After I rested for a few minutes and savored the congratulations of all the people crowding around me, I was feeling so confident that I told the crew chief I was ready to go up again. But he said, "Sir, there's no need to go up in that one. The other 21 is fueled and ready, so you can take that one up and see how she flies." I said, "Good idea." So I took a few minutes to drink a small glass of strong Arab tea, or *stikan* as we call it, and then I went back for my second flight of the day.

Defying the Odds

The next day, on Sunday, I made two more flights and on Monday two more. By the time I made the first five flights, I had control of the plane. By the sixth, I started playing around. A short time later, they assigned more pilots to our squadron and the Russian instructors were finally allowed back into the country. When they found out that I had flown the MiG-21, the instructors were shocked.

They said, "How did you do that? No one can fly the MiG-21 without training!" And they asked the base commander why he let a green lieutenant with so little flying time take the controls of a supersonic jet fighter. And when they found out I'd been taking off without using the afterburner, they were doubly shocked. "What! That's impossible!" they said. "No one should fly a MiG-21 without using the afterburner."

Despite all their bluster, the instructors recognized that I was a good pilot, and I think they came to respect me a lot. We became good friends and they taught me about all the things I hadn't learned from the technicians. In particular, they taught me what to do in case of an emergency. In those first six flights, I hadn't even considered what to do if something went wrong, and maybe that's a good thing. I might have been tempted to try something. The shame, of course, is that the commanders only wanted the privilege of boasting that one of our pilots had flown the MiG-21, never thinking that the plane could crash and the pilot would be lost. To them, I might as well have been driving a car—it was as if I had been driving a Buick and they just wanted me to switch to a Pontiac.

That's how unrealistic their thinking was. But, thank God, he helped me fly the plane and bring it back in one piece. And because of that very strange request so early in my career, everybody in Iraq knew my name and I became known as the father of the MiG-21. I'm sure much of my later success was inspired by that event, and I was able to continue flying throughout my career, from lieutenant all the way to major general.

The Revolution of 1968

The leaders of the Baath Party were unscrupulous men. Al-Bakr and Saddam knew they couldn't carry off another revolution by themselves, so they just took their time, watching for opportunities to come against Aref and his supporters. Eventually they were able to persuade the chief of military intelligence, Abdurazzaq al-Nayif, the commander of the Republican Guard, Col. Rahman Ibrahim al-Daud, and the commander of the palace guards and armored units, Col. Sadun Ghaidan, to join their cause.

These three men would prove to be very important to the coup since they were the only ones who could make sure the army did nothing to resist. Saddam was present at those meetings, and it was decided that Ahmed Hassan al-Bakr would be president and Abdurazzaq al-Nayif would be prime minister. Ibrahim al-Daud was selected to serve as minister of defense.

The revolution took place in the pre-dawn hours of July 17, 1968, when I was the senior duty pilot at Rashid Air Force Base. I was assistant commander of Squadron 11, which was a unit of MiG-21s assigned to protect Baghdad. I was a twenty-eight-year-old captain at the time, but I was the most experienced pilot and I'd been flying the MiG-21s since early 1963. The squadron commander had only recently transitioned from the British Hawker-Hunters and wasn't nearly as experienced as I was.

It started out to be a quiet morning, but around 3:00 a.m. six tanks and armored personnel carriers (APCs) pulled up at the front gates of the base. They didn't threaten to use their weapons, but they ordered the guards to stand aside and drove straight to the base headquarters where I was working. They had been instructed to block the runways so none of our aircraft could take off. They knew that if they put tanks and APCs on the runways, nobody could fly. And they told us that if anyone tried to fly without permission they would shoot them and destroy the airplane.

I was sitting with a fellow officer, Captain Hamza, a pilot with a squadron of MiG-17s, when the phone rang. Hamza answered it, and it was President Abdel-Rahman Aref on the line. As soon as the president identified himself, Hamza said, "Sir, I need to let you speak to my senior officer, Captain Georges." And he quickly handed the receiver to me.

I greeted him: "Yes, sir. This is Captain Georges." And the president said, "Tell me, Georges, what's happening at your base?" I said, "Sir, six tanks and APCs entered the base a short time ago and they told us that if anyone tries to fly they'll shoot the pilot and destroy the plane." Aref said, "No, no, son. Why should you risk being shot and letting the aircraft be destroyed? Don't go to the aircraft."

Then he said, "Didn't the air force commander call you?" And I said, "No, sir. No one has called tonight." So he said, "Okay, I'll contact the air force commander and he'll be calling you right away." So I thanked him and hung up the phone.

Ten minutes later the phone rang again, and this time it was Major General Jassam Mohammed al-Shahir, the air force commander. He said, "Hello, Georges, how are you?" There were only two squadrons of MiG-21s in the Iraqi Air Force at that time, and they were our best fighters. So General Jassam knew me very well because I was a MiG pilot. He said, "Georges, what's going on down there?" So I repeated what I'd just told the president, and he said, "Are the soldiers there now?" I said, "Yes, sir, two of the officers are here in the room with me now." So he said, "Tell them the air force commander is in his office now. If they want to speak to me, tell them to come here. I'm ready to talk to them."

The two officers, Warrant Officer Kamel Yassin and Major Daud al-Tikriti, had been watching me as I spoke to the commander. So I signaled with one hand to see if they wanted to speak to the commander. But they signaled back, No, not now! So I said to Gen. Jassam, "Yes, sir, I will tell them what you said." And Gen. Jassam said, "Okay, Georges, thank you. Now I'm going to have the base commander call you."

Heroes of the Revolution

The base commander was a very famous officer named General Hassan Arem. He was an older officer and a very colorful man, full of great stories, who could keep me laughing for hours. He called about ten minutes later and asked what was going on at the base, so again I repeated the whole story and he said, "Okay, Georges. I'm coming now." But he never came.

Later that morning before the sun was up, the phone rang once again and I picked it up. It was Abdurazzaq al-Nayif, who was soon to become the new prime minister. He said, "Hello, who's speaking?" I said, "This is Captain Sada." He knew me very well so he greeted me warmly, and then he told me he needed one thing to be done immediately. He said, "Georges, I need a formation of MiG-21s to fly for the revolution." I said, "What do you mean, sir? What do you want them to do?"

"You know," he said, "make a nice formation and fly over the city of Baghdad so everyone can see that the air force and the army are with us." I said, "Yes, sir. I understand. But, sir," I added cautiously, "these pilots are new guys and they've never flown the MiG-21 in formation before. Will it be okay if I do it by myself?"

He said, "Oh, no, Georges. We want a nice formation to fly over the city." At that point I knew he was serious, so I said, "Okay, sir. Somehow we'll manage to do it."

I had two guys, Lt. Shihab Ahmad and Lt. Mohammed Abdulaziz, who had flown with me before, but they were inexperienced in flying the 21s in formation. It takes practice and experience to know how to hold position in a fly-over. Also, the pilot needs to know how to key in on his leader and keep his eyes open any time he's flying at low altitude over a big city. There was no telling on that day who might want to take a shot at us. So I was a bit nervous about the whole thing.

Furthermore, I didn't know who might be in charge when we returned to the base for landing. I knew that Abdurazzaq al-Nayif had been the chief of intelligence, so he spoke for the government. The two officers who had come to the headquarters during the night, and who were still there, were both members of the Baath Party. So I wondered, *Are all these guys in it together? Do they all want us to fly in formation over the city? Or will they kill us the first chance they get?*

I considered the options and finally decided it was best to obey a military order and fly the formation. But I also decided we wouldn't use aircraft that were armed. Most of the time the MiG-21s were armed with missiles and rockets, but I thought it would be much better for a demonstration flight not to have dangerous weapons on board. No one would know whether they were armed or not, of course, but with inexperienced pilots, this would be safer.

I gave both pilots, who were young lieutenants, careful instructions on the maneuvers we were going to fly and I told them that they were to follow my explicit commands. When we took off, we got into formation to fly over the city and I switched my radio over to Radio Baghdad on the civilian band to hear what was being said. As we came in over the river, from west to east, the announcer was telling everyone to look up and watch the heroes of the air force flying for the revolution. They wanted everybody to know that the military supported the coup.

But as soon as I heard that announcement, I heard another click on the military frequency, meaning that someone else was flying nearby. It wasn't one of my young pilots, so I said, "Hello, who's there? Who's in the air?" I didn't know if it was going to be friend or foe, so I repeated the challenge again, a little louder: "Who's flying? Please identify yourself!"

Finally, on the second try someone responded, "Who is that?" I replied, "Who are you?" And he said, "Who are you?" This was going nowhere. This guy was afraid to identify himself. I was in a MiG-21, the fastest plane in the sky so I didn't need to worry, whoever it was. So I decided to identify myself. I said, "This is Captain Georges Sada, flying out of . . ." and before I could even finish the sentence he came back on and said, "Hello, Georges, how are you? This is Lieutenant Colonel Hamid Shaiban."

Hamid was a good friend. He was the base commander at Habbaniya and very much my senior officer. But I said, "Hello, sir. Thank you very much, but I had not been told there was another formation in the air. Will you go and land please?" He must have known this was a serious matter, because he didn't argue with me. He was a Tikriti, and he had been told to fly by Al-Bakr. That made two formations, one from the Baath Party and one from the air force, but Colonel Hamid was only too happy to land.

We finished our flight and circled the city one last time. Just for fun I made a low-level pass over my house in Al Mansour, just to let my wife and family know it was me, and then we returned to base. Altogether, we were up for about an hour. But before landing, I took a good look around the airfield, because in a situation like that you never know when someone might jump out and start shooting at you. The best jet fighter in the world is helpless on the ground—anyone with an AK-47 can ruin your day. But I didn't see any problems, so we landed and as soon as we shut off the engines people came running out to greet us. They wanted to thank us for the fly-over, and they were cheering like we were the heroes of the revolution.

Later we learned that the revolution took place without a single shot fired. There was no resistance. Today they call the 1968 coup the White Revolution because of that. The army and the air force supported the coup, and the only thing that changed was that we had a new president and a new air force commander. And our base commander, General Arem, was replaced as well. That's why he never got back to me.

The next time I saw General Arem was more than ten years later, after I had become a general myself. When he saw me he came over and gave me a warm greeting, but I looked him in the eye and said, "Sir, in 1968 you said you were coming to the headquarters to see me, and I'm still waiting for you!" He said, "Okay, stop it, Georges! You know what happened." Indeed, I did.

Treachery and Deceit

The Revolution of 1968 only happened because three high-ranking officers and a common thug were persuaded to go along with Al-Bakr and Al-Nayif to carry out the coup. One commanded the palace guard, the second was with the republican army, the third was the chief intelligence officer, and Saddam Hussein came like a gangster. So why did these men agree to cooperate? Because the leaders of the Baath Party knew they couldn't do it without the intelligence service and the Republican Brigades. For any of these groups to try to take over the government without the others would have been suicide.

None of them knew it at the time, but for men of such stature to join forces with a villain like Saddam was sheer madness.

They knew the kind of man he was, but they were hungry for power and didn't stop to consider what could happen in the future. Abdel-Salam Aref had been president, but his helicopter was shot down and burned. After that, his brother, Abdel-Rahman Aref was able to succeed him. But it was clear from the first that he was not the right man for the job. He was a gentleman and a good man, but he was also a weak man and totally unprepared for the demands of such a job in a place like Iraq.

So Saddam made a deal with the Republican Guard, and that's the real background of the coup of 1968. The problem was that these groups were all very different, with different plans and ideas, and it was going to be impossible for them to work together. Saddam saw this weakness as his chance to make a move, so he stepped up and took command. On the thirtieth of July, just thirteen days after the first coup, he overthrew his own allies, making Al-Bakr the president and himself the deputy.

There was an attempt to stage a counter coup at the time. If it had succeeded, the history of Iraq would be very different. But, sadly, it didn't happen. Gen. Ibrahim al-Ansari, who was not a member of the party, was the chief of staff. He was a good man and he could see that Saddam and his allies were going to be a disaster for Iraq, so he went secretly to Hardan al-Tikriti, who had recently been the air force commander but was named minister of defense in the new government, and he said, "Now's the time to catch these guys and get rid of them." He said, "I only need three battalions from my brigade and I will catch Saddam, Al-Bakr, and all the others. We will make a much better system, but now is the time to act."

Hardan, who was a Tikriti and a Baathi, was a friend of Al-Ansari, and I believe he agreed with the idea. But he was suspicious and he feared that Saddam and Al-Bakr were just using Al-Ansari to test his loyalty and to trap him in a plot. He thought, *I'm afraid that if I say yes to this plan, it will turn out to be a trick and Bakr and Saddam will come after me.* So what he decided to do was to prove his loyalty by going to Saddam and saying, "Ibrahim al-Ansari came to me secretly, and he asked me to help him stage a counter coup against you, but I didn't want to do that." This came as a complete surprise to Saddam. He had not been plotting with Al-Ansari, but because of his own fear and suspicion, Hardan al-Tikriti made the biggest mistake of his life. And, ultimately, it would cost him his own.

At that point, Ansari's plot was uncovered and Saddam fired him as chief of staff. But they didn't like Hardan al-Tikriti any better. Whenever there was a cabinet meeting, Hardan and Saddam would often get into big arguments. Even though he was a party man, Hardan was not like them—he was not as venal or corrupt as they were—so first they retired him from the army and brought up Gen. Shanshal, who was weak and pliable, to be chief of staff of the army.

Next they sent Hardan into exile in London, then they made him ambassador to Sweden and were well rid of him for a while. But Hardan didn't like being out of the picture, so he went to Kuwait where he tried to stir up a coup against Al-Bakr and Saddam. When Saddam found out that he was there, he called the Iraqi ambassador to Kuwait and told him to find Hardan and shoot him, and that's exactly what happened.

The Nuclear Threat

No sooner had the 1968 coup ended than Saddam began thinking about how he could get rid of the next group and increase his own power. Abdurazzaq al-Nayif, Sadun Ghaidan, and Ibrahim al-Daud were still there, but on July 30, 1968, Saddam went to the office of Prime Minister Al-Nayif with a gun and told him he was taking over. He said, "Either I will kill you now or you're finished. Choose the place you want to travel to."

Al-Nayif looked at Saddam with sadness and surprise in his eyes, and he said, "Saddam, why are you doing this?" But Saddam only said, "Don't talk much. It's over." Saddam's people were already calling Al Muthana Airport where they kept a large Russian-made plane called the Ukraina, which was an Antonov-12, and they told them to prepare to take the prime minister wherever he wanted to go. He chose London.

On that day, Ahmed Hassan al-Bakr became the president, prime minister, and minister of defense, and Saddam Hussein was his deputy. Just imagine how quickly it all happened: on the seventeenth of July, 1968, they carried out a successful coup. Less than two weeks later, on the thirtieth of July, Saddam walked into the office of Prime Minister Abdurazzaq al-Nayif, pointed a gun at his head, and told him he was finished. Saddam's henchmen drove Al-Nayif to the airport and put him on the plane to London, where, not long afterward, he was assassinated in the streets by his own military attaché—at the order of Saddam.

Saddam knew exactly what he was doing. He wasn't satisfied to be merely the deputy to Al-Bakr; however, he still needed time to put his plans together. So he took his time and let Al-Bakr remain in charge for a while. Al-Bakr served as general secretary of the Baath Party and Saddam was his deputy, but Saddam was actually in charge of everything. After a while he told the president that he needed to have military rank in order to manage the affairs of government, so they made him a four-star general and even gave him the red ribbon of a Staff College graduate, which was a shock to many who had earned that ribbon legitimately.

But it didn't stop there. Saddam also insisted that, even though his title was deputy to the president, he was to be equal to the president and he would sign all official documents. If you wanted to congratulate the president, you didn't just congratulate Al-Bakr; you had to say congratulations to President Al-Bakr and his distinguished deputy, Saddam Hussein. So it was two-for-one—that's what many people called it. Two presidents for one, and it lasted from 1968 until 1979 when Saddam finally told Al-Bakr that if he wanted to live he would have to leave. Of course, Al-Bakr knew Saddam well enough by this time, so he left immediately.

After Al-Bakr was gone, the practice of two-for-one suddenly ended. Saddam made himself president and prime minister and only chose weak deputies to work for him. His purpose was to grow bigger and bigger while everyone else grew smaller and smaller. Before long he had made himself the absolute dictator of Iraq, and no one dared to resist him because they knew he was a ruthless killer. And this is how Saddam grew very large while the entire nation continued to shrink.

Worst of all, he drained the wealth of the country for his palaces, his personal pleasures, and his own power. He expanded the military to 6,400 tanks, 40 regiments of artillery, more than 1,000 combat aircraft, and sophisticated weapons for all the branches of the military, in addition to his sixty-eight luxurious palaces around the country. He made sure that all the revenue from the oil fields flowed to him, and he didn't hesitate to use the nation's wealth to build more and more rockets equipped with chemical weapons.

Saddam was also attempting to build sophisticated nuclear weapons, and while this was a more difficult task for him because of the intense scrutiny from Europe, America, and the United Nations, he did manage to bring in many nuclear scientists. I believe he would have been successful in manufacturing and mounting nuclear warheads on Iraqi missiles if he had not been deterred, first by the Gulf War, and finally by Operation Iraqi Freedom.

No Moral Limits

Saddam's ambition was so enormous he always believed that he could bluff his way through and do whatever he wanted to do. When he bought SCUD missiles, he was only permitted to buy SCUDs with a range of 220 miles. But this made him very angry because he wanted SCUDs with a range of 440 miles. So he created his own organization, called Military Industries, and he brought in the top scientists and engineers—not only from Iraq, but from Europe and many places in the Middle East—to help him create an arsenal of weapons with which he could conquer the entire region.

The task was to develop new weapons and to modify existing weapons to make them either more powerful or with greater range. For example, if we had an aircraft with a range of only 250 miles, then he would insist on giving them a range of 500 miles. If we had SCUDs that would only go 200 miles, he would say, "That won't even reach Israel! Make it bigger!" And then he would do two things: first, he would have the engineers double the size of the fuel tanks so the rocket could go 500 miles, and, second, he had them build launch facilities on the western border of Iraq, which put them 300 miles closer to the target. At that point he had all the range he needed and he could use those missiles anywhere he liked.

The secret to all of this was money, and Saddam used money to buy, steal, and bribe his way to greater and greater power. If he needed scientists with a certain type of expertise, he would buy them. Whether they were in America or France or Germany, that was no problem. He had millions of dollars to work with, and he found that even the best scientists and technicians had their price. And that wasn't all, of course. If his unscrupulous and dissolute son, Uday, wanted to have a big party with a beautiful woman, he would bring her to Iraq and give her a coupon for a million barrels of oil. If she wasn't beautiful enough, then she would bring two or three others with her who were very beautiful. Like their father, Uday and Qusay used the wealth of the country as if it were all their own. It was as if Iraq was their personal playground. They were the owners, and the Iraqi people were their servants.

There were many times when people tried to kill Saddam, but he was cunning, and he was always surrounded by several layers of security. One was the party. Another was the military, and especially his own palace guards, the Republican Brigades. He had a special unit of bodyguards, very much like the praetorian guards in Roman times. Their only duty was to protect this man. Most of them were Tikritis from Saddam's own city, and they were absolutely corrupt.

Abd Hamoud, who was Saddam's chief bodyguard, was not a regular officer. He was a warrant officer. One of the Tikritis, a lawyer named Fares, fired Abd Hamoud from his job because he was so bad at it. So Abd Hamoud went to the palace and begged Saddam for a place. A short time after that, they made him a lieutenant in the guards, and from there they promoted him to three-star general in charge of the Republican Brigades and much more. In that position he had the right to decide who could see Saddam and who could not, and he would often block ministers, politicians, military officers, or foreign officials whenever he liked. And this man, like his master, recognized no moral limits.

The Baath Underground

What you had to know in Iraq in those days was that the Baath Party was everywhere and you never knew who might turn out to be a party operative. A friend once told me that while he was in medical college in Baghdad, there was one particular janitor who always seemed to be in the way. My friend tried to avoid him, but the rude and troublesome janitor was always there. One day when this medical student was in the sixth and final year of his studies, the janitor stopped him in the hallway and said, "Son, I don't like the way you look at me." The young man said, "Why do you say that? I'm very busy. I'm a student." And the janitor said, "Yes, but you had better remember that it's not the dean who will see that you graduate. I'm the party man. If I say you graduate, you graduate. If I say you fail, you fail."

Suddenly my friend realized that this man was the senior member of the Baath Party at the college, and this janitor was superior to the dean and the entire faculty. Just imagine such a system. When I heard this, I knew that something of the sort could happen but I never imagined that it had gotten to the point that a janitor would have the authority to decide the future of medical students and their professors.

Suddenly the student understood that in Iraq it was the janitor who had the power of life and death over his future medical career. And this is a perfect illustration of the system in Iraq at that time. Even in the military, it was often a warrant officer or an enlisted man who would have the authority to say who was promoted and who was passed over, even among our highest-ranking officers. In the Baath Party, it didn't matter what rank you held or how capable you were. All that mattered was that you proved your loyalty to the party.

As an air vice marshal and a general officer, I often thought about the human aspects of my job. A general may be very senior, and he may have spent his entire life gaining leadership experience and knowledge of his profession, but he is still a soldier. He may be above his men in rank and authority, but he is never above them in human terms. There's a fine line between the duty to command men in combat—knowing in some cases that you may be sending them to their deaths—and the duty to respect those soldiers, sailors, and airmen as human beings at all times. I'm sure that every commander worth his rank has had such thoughts at one time or another.

But then to risk that important relationship by empowering some unskilled laborer, giving them authority to make critical decisions about careers and assignments, is sheer madness. An army is not a political organization. It is an instrument of the political and diplomatic arms of government, equipped to protect and defend the interests of the nation. But in Saddam's Iraq, it was the other way around. In time the army became completely politicized and, I would also have to say, useless.

Furthermore, Saddam created what he called the Popular Army. He wanted the entire nation to be militarized. Even women and children were supposed to learn how to fight and how to carry out Saddam's orders. Just imagine the perversity of that—a nation of 27 million people who were being transformed into a military and political organization, solely to satisfy the power lust and greed of the president.

This is not how it works in civilized nations. The best way to protect a nation from attack by foreign aggressors is to have a sophisticated political and diplomatic apparatus with officers who are very good at defusing tense situations before they become volatile. Then, knowing that they have a well-trained and well-equipped military when all else fails, the ministers, ambassadors, and the chief executive of the nation are able to negotiate in good faith and with confidence. The worst kind of government, however, is one that is all military and all violence, constantly forcing its will on the people and on its neighbors through intimidation. I'm sad to say this was exactly the kind of government we had under Saddam.

In Iraq, there was no foreign service as you know it in America and the free world. There was only the Mukhabbarat, which was the civil intelligence service. It was like the CIA and the FBI combined, with the authority not only to gather information on citizens but also to detain and punish citizens if they were suspected of disloyalty or treason. This meant that there was no one in our foreign service, internal or external (meaning in Iraq or in our foreign embassies around the world) who was not a complete Mukhabbarat. This is why Saddam was able to order the Iraqi ambassador to Kuwait to assassinate Hardan al-Tikriti: because the ambassador was, first and foremost, a spy and an agent of the Mukhabbarat.

Because of these policies, Saddam created what had to be the worst foreign service in the entire world, because none of our ambassadors were foreign service officers; they were all spies. Of course, every embassy has intelligence officers working in it; but the embassy should not be run by spies. In some cases the person legally responsible for foreign intelligence will be the military attaché. He's a diplomat, but basically he's a spy with the title of military attaché. And in any event, he works for the ambassador, who is never a military or political figure but usually a distinguished citizen chosen as an ambassador of goodwill and a spokesman for his country. At least, that's how it's supposed to be.

Border Troubles

There are two things I can say about Saddam Hussein, because I knew the man. First, he was an artist in understanding the nature of power and how to exploit other people to accomplish his purposes. He knew how to manipulate them, pitting one against the other, and how to create an atmosphere of chaos in which he was the only source of resolution and order. And second, he was a genius at doing evil. He was cunning and brutal, and he had enormous skill in doing the most wicked things you can imagine.

Sometimes he would give power to the Baath Party by allowing them to have special favors or privileges. At other times he would take power away from them and give it to the military. Then when it was convenient, he would give power to the people themselves, always playing one against the other. If he ever thought the army was getting to be too powerful, he would arouse the people and the party against the military. But if he felt the party was becoming too powerful, he would stir up the army and the nation against the party. By this kind of manipulation, he was able to make sure that he alone would hold the power of government.

From 1968 to 1979, Saddam was, technically at least, the deputy to Ahmed Hassan al-Bakr. In fact, he made himself the co-president and Al-Bakr could do nothing without him. If Al-Bakr signed any kind of executive order, you can be sure there would be a paragraph saying that it was being done through the wise administration of the esteemed deputy prime minister, Saddam Hussein.

When Saddam came to power on his own in 1979, by overthrowing Al-Bakr, he was insuring that he would be able to wield unlimited power without interference. At about the same time, however, the nation of Iran was undergoing a major revolution in which the monarch, Muhammad Reza Shah Pahlavi, was toppled and sent into exile. The two revolutions, in Iran and Iraq, really have nothing to do with each other except the coincidence of timing.

However, Saddam was frightened that the unrest in Iran, which was being fomented by the radical cleric, Ayatollah Ruhollah Khomeini, from his base in Paris, might spill over into his country. As in Iraq, the majority population in Iran is Shia, and Saddam was concerned that a Shia rebellion in Iran could lead to rebellion in Iraq as well.

When I was in a position to advise the president on military matters, I would always tell him, "Don't fight Iran. It's not worth it." But I think there was always something in the back of his mind, and he was worried that if the Islamic fanaticism in Iran came to Iraq, it would be very bad for him. In fact, tapes of violent sermons by radical clerics were coming in from Iran by the hundreds, and these were being circulated among the Shia population in the south. They were calling for an Islamic revolution throughout the region. So Saddam decided that he would do whatever it took to stamp out that kind of thinking, and I believe that's one reason why there was so much brutal repression of the Shia during his thirty years in office.

By 1980, the Islamic Dahwa (which was the political arm of the Islamist movement) was making trouble for Saddam, and he could see that sooner or later they would try to force him out of power and take over the government. When he came to that conclusion, Saddam knew that if he didn't take dramatic action against them he could lose everything. That's when he shocked the nation and the entire Arab world by ordering the assassination of the Grand Ayatollah Muhammad Baqir Al-Sadr, along with his sister, Amina, who was known as a civil rights activist and defender of women's rights.

They were killed on April 8, 1980, and this was a tremendous shock to the people. But Saddam had made his point, and the people knew exactly what it meant: no one, not even a grand ayatollah, could stand in the way of this man. Saddam would not allow anything or anyone to cross him or to threaten his power.

The ayatollah was a Shia, and the Shia people in the south of Iraq understood that the assassinations were a message to them from Saddam. Some of the Shia leaders wanted to come against him, and they made an effort to join forces with the Shiites in Iran. But when Saddam got news of this, he decided to attack first and ask questions later, and I believe that's how the Iran-Iraq War actually began.

CHAPTER 3

BETRAYAL AND REVENGE

In 1978 I began preparing for promotion to general, and in 1980 I was finally given my first star. Before that we had a Staff College for training senior officers, but we didn't have the War College or the National Defense College. The Staff College teaches officers from the rank of major how to handle routine staff duties and how to perform as an officer in a division. There are many brigades, divisions, corps, and other components in an army, as well as civilians in high-level leadership roles. To prepare leaders at this level there must be a war college and a national defense college to train officers in the scope and complexity of all these units.

I taught all three military colleges for ten years, yet there was only one man with the rank of general who was not allowed to attend the National Defense College or receive the degrees: General Georges Sada. And the reason was because I was not a member of the Baath Party. They said my knowledge was good enough and I was even qualified enough to give the lectures; but I was never allowed to attend the National Defense College myself. So I taught the officers who did attend.

Students attending the National Defense College (NDC) had already earned the equivalent of a master's degree in the Staff College, and at the end of their program at the NDC they would receive the equivalent of a doctorate in military science. Consequently, the policy was that, because of the high level of the students, instructors ought to be the highest level officers in each service. In other words, to learn about the structures, tactics, and strategies of the air force, the instructor ought to be the commanding general of the air force.

But the session titled "The Lecture of the Air Chief" was never given by the air chief, because it would have been too embarrassing for him. Students at that level ask questions, and the lecturer must be capable of answering them. He must be able to give an assessment of the day-to-day air threat in each sector of operations as well as the state of military readiness. And if the instructor gives his students that information, they may well ask him how to deal with the threat, and the instructor had better know the answers.

But our air chiefs were so afraid they wouldn't be able to answer the questions that they never gave the lectures. Instead, they said, "Let Georges do it." And of course I did it, for three air chiefs: Muhammed Jassam, Hamid Shaiban, and Muzahim Hassan al-Tikriti, who is now in prison. Frankly, I loved doing it and the students loved my lectures. They called for me to give the lectures because I always motivated them.

Teaching at this level is an art. You have to keep the students engaged, but you also have to know how to challenge them and get them to participate in the discussion. In the War College and the National Defense College, it's not just the teacher who gives rewards to the students, but the students give rewards to the teachers. At the end of each course, the students fill out evaluations for the teacher, who is called the Director of Staff (DS). So I taught the air studies for all the services, air force, navy, and army—as well as civilians in ministry-level positions, and not only for Iraqis but for students from all the Arab countries. They would come to study in Iraq because our standards were very high, and they were well recognized by the Americans and the British as well. In fact, our Staff College was originally organized by the British in 1929.

Knowing the Enemy

Once in 1990, it came time for Gen. Muzahim to teach these subjects, and he knew he was supposed to do it. But copies of the program for the War College are sent around to all the high-ranking officials, from the president and minister of defense on down. They can see who's scheduled to give the lectures on a particular topic, and then they can decide whether or not they want to come and hear what's being said.

It wouldn't be a big surprise to come to class one day and find Saddam or the chief of staff or the deputy of the president, Izzat Ibrahim al-Douri, or the minister of defense sitting there. They might see a topic that interested them, such as "The Air Threat to Iraq," being taught by Gen. Georges Sada, for example, and they would come. I was never embarrassed to see one of these people sitting there. In fact, I was glad to have them there, because I wanted to see what kinds of questions they would ask. But the air chief, on the other hand, was terrified of that possibility. He thought, *What if Saddam comes and finds out how much I don't know!* So he would always say, "Georges, you go ahead and give the class," and I was glad to do it.

On this occasion I was giving a lecture about aircraft carriers, and I soon realized that these people didn't have any idea what an aircraft carrier could do. But Saddam Hussein had made it known that, by any means, he wanted our army to be able to sink at least one aircraft carrier. But I told them, "Don't even think about it. You don't know what you're talking about." I said that planning and executing a successful attack on an American carrier was beyond the capabilities of the Iraqi Air Force.

There are some secrets that aren't really secrets. This is especially true for countries like America and Russia, because even if you know they have certain equipment at a certain location, there's nothing you can do about it. The Americans weren't afraid that the Iraqi Air Force might find out that one of their carriers was stationed at a certain place in the Gulf. Iraq isn't Russia. The Russians have nuclear warheads and missiles that might be able to hit such a target, but we would never be so foolish as to attempt such a thing.

But on one occasion I was teaching this class and Izzat al-Douri, the deputy prime minister, was there and I could see his eyes were wide open when I started describing the capabilities of an American carrier. I was explaining how many decks there were, how many stories it stood above the water, and how many elevators were on-board, and then I described how many aircraft are kept below decks and how they're brought up to the flight line. And I went into some detail about the weaponry and how the fighters are catapulted into flight and caught by high-tension cables on landing, and all the time I was talking about these things I could see that Al-Douri was absolutely captivated.

When I called for questions, one of the officers asked me, "What will it take to hit one of these ships?" And I said it would be very difficult. They're well defended, they have excellent over-the-horizon targeting radar and satellite links on board as well as support from several kinds of support aircraft. I explained that any aircraft or ship, above or below the surface, that comes within three hundred miles of the carrier would be challenged to identify itself as friend or foe. If they fail to identify, immediate action would be taken against them. If it's in the air, they'll send up one or more F-14 Tomcat fighters. The Tomcat's radar can scan twenty-four targets simultaneously over a range of 150 miles. They climb quickly and can engage six enemy aircraft or other aerial targets simultaneously with their Phoenix rockets.

In addition, each carrier is escorted by a complete battle group that includes destroyers, frigates, and other ships capable of engaging submarines or anything else below the surface, as well as a helicopter group. And all these ships have air defense systems, cruise missiles, long-range guns, and a staggering arsenal of weapons. Saddam wanted desperately to hit one of these carriers, and our people were eager to know how this could be done, but I made clear that this was beyond our capabilities. Even if we could hit it with an Exocet missile, which was our most capable weapon, the carrier would be able to turn its heavily armored shoulder in the direction of the attack and, more than likely, the missile would have little or no impact.

An Officer and a Gentleman

A few days after I had given this lecture, Saddam sent for me but I didn't know why he wanted to see me. When a man like Saddam sends for you, your first reaction is to wonder, *What have I done? Did I say something wrong?* No reason was given why Saddam would want to see me, but I went to the palace and told the guards that I'd been called for a meeting with the president. So they told me to go on in to the office of Saddam's personal secretary, Hamid Yousif Hamadi.

When I got there, Hamid said, "Oh, hello, Georges. Just have a seat and the president will be with you shortly." When he said that, I knew I didn't have much to worry about. There was no urgency or fear in his voice. When I sat down the secretary said, "It will be a few minutes until the minister of defense arrives, and then you can both go in." Whatever Saddam wanted to talk about, I knew now that it would involve both me and Adnan Khairallah, who was both a cousin and a brother-in-law of Saddam—Saddam had married his sister, Sajida.

And I think it's only fair to say that this man was a real officer and not simply someone to whom Saddam had given high rank. He was an officer and a gentleman, a graduate of the military academy, and a capable leader. He earned the rank of colonel on his own and after that Saddam promoted him from colonel to four-star general. That's a big jump, to be sure. But, even so, it was obvious to everyone who knew him that Adnan Khairallah had an important role to play in Iraq, and that he would eventually become the minister of defense.

He was a good leader and he had all the right connections. Not only because his sister was married to Saddam, but Khairallah's wife was the daughter of Ahmed Hassan al-Bakr, who was the president of Iraq before Saddam.

It's true he was intimately connected with Saddam and I don't doubt that he knew about many of the things that Saddam and his evil sons were doing. But so you can appreciate the kind of respect the people of Iraq had for him, I can tell you that of all the statues of Saddam and other Iraqi leaders that were erected in my country, the only one left standing today is the statue of Gen. Adnan Khairallah because the people still admire him. And there are other things named for him as well, such as the Martyr's Hospital in Baghdad.

A good example of this man's character was something that happened shortly before the end of the Iran-Iraq War when Gen. Khairallah made arrangements to take me with him to England to try out the new Anglo-French Jaguar supersonic ground attack fighter to see whether or not this was an airplane we might want to buy. We'd been authorized to purchase 120 aircraft with the latest high-tech weaponry, and I was selected as the pilot to fly these planes and determine which one was best for our systems.

I've never told this story until now, but after I flew the Jaguar our British hosts said they were very pleased with the way I handled the aircraft. Subsequently the British minister of defense told us he had arranged a special dinner for Gen. Khairallah and me. All through the meal that evening, the officers kept talking about the way I'd flown the Jaguar, and Gen. Khairallah was obviously very pleased to hear that kind of praise for one of his pilots.

The next day he said to me, "Georges, you did a fine job yesterday. I'm very glad you came with me on this trip, and I want to give you a nice gift as my way of saying thank you. The English defense minister was very impressed with your skill and the way you handled the plane. So as my gift to you, I'd like to buy you a nice London suit." I said, "Thank you, sir. I have many nice suits, but I would be honored to receive such a gift from you."

It was flattering to be honored in that way, so I gladly accepted his offer. A little while later I received an elegant and very expensive Savile Row suit, tailored for me, and I still have it in my closet today. It has the broad shoulders and huge lapels that were popular at the time, so I can't actually wear it anymore, but I must say, it's still a beautiful suit.

The importance of this episode wasn't the suit or the trip, but the trust that developed between us. The success of our trip to England helped create a strong bond of friendship between Gen. Khairallah and me. Later, when he became minister of defense in the summer of 1977, I was one of the first ones he called to tell about his new position, and he told me I was welcome to come to his office anytime. And our friendship was such that he trusted me enough to share some confidential information that would eventually have very serious implications for him.

Secret Information

One day in 1984, Gen. Khairallah called and asked for me to meet with him privately. When I arrived, he said, "Georges, I want to discuss something with you, and I don't want a word of it to get back to Saddam." I said, "I understand. And believe me, sir, if you tell me it's strictly between us, it will remain a secret." He thanked me and shook my hand; then he asked me a question that took me by surprise. He said, "Georges, do you remember the way we attacked

Iran?" I said, "Yes, sir. I remember." He said, "You remember that we were told that Iran had shut down their air space and that was a sign that they were preparing to attack us?" Again, I said, "Yes, sir. I remember that too."

He said, "Georges, was that true?" I said, "No, sir. Of course not. I said at the time that merely closing your air space doesn't necessarily mean that you're planning an attack. There are many reasons why this could happen." I mentioned a few of those reasons, and then I told him, "Sir, there's another reason why I know this is the case. As you know, we captured many Iranian pilots during the war, and in the interrogations I specifically asked them, 'Why did your country close your air space?'

"What those pilots told me," I said, "was that a group of officers in the Iranian Air Force had rebelled against the Khomeini regime, and when the plot was discovered, many of them were killed. But some of the rebels tried to make a run for it, and they were taking any plane they could get their hands on and flying away with them. To put a stop to that, Khomeini decided that he had to close the Iranian air space and order the military to shoot down any plane attempting to enter or exit from Iran without permission."

This meant that all air traffic had to be grounded, I told him, both military and civilian. But because of Saddam's paranoia, I suppose, this was translated in Iraq as an act of war—as the first sign that the Iranian military was preparing to attack us. This all happened on September 17, 1980, and five days later we were ordered to launch the first strike on Iran.

That's what I told Gen. Khairallah during our meeting. After I explained what I found out, he said, "Georges, I want you to prepare a report for me, and you're free to use any military resources you need. I want to know for sure whether the Iranians were trying to attack us or not. Can you do that?" I told him I would be glad to do it. So he said, "How will you do it?"

I said, "It won't be hard to do, sir. I'll make a questionnaire and ask as many of the Iranian pilots we captured as I can, and from their answers I'll know whether or not they were prepared to make an assault on Iraq." So that's what I did, and when I had all those forms compiled and analyzed, it was clear that none of the Iranian pilots was prepared to fly against Iraq. There had been no training, no mission plan, no armament of the Iranian fighters with combat weaponry, and no alerts had been issued from the air command center that would have suggested that war was imminent.

When I presented this information to Gen. Khairallah, it was obvious that he was troubled by the news. He just looked at me and said, "Georges, why did our air force commander believe we were going to be attacked? And why did he order that we carry out the first strikes?" I told him I didn't know the answer to that, but perhaps Saddam had pressed him to give a negative report in order to legitimize his decision to attack Iran.

Obviously, Saddam felt threatened by Ayatollah Khomeini and the Shiite regime in Tehran. If Khomeini continued his verbal assaults on Iraq's secular government, he might have been able to persuade the large Shia population in the south of Iraq to join a revolution against Saddam, and he wasn't going to let that happen. So a preemptive strike against Iran was, for him at least, the obvious solution.

When Gen. Khairallah realized it was Iraq, in fact, who had started the war, he was deeply distressed. I don't know, but he may even have gone to talk to his cousin, Saddam, about this, and if so, I'm sure he expressed his disappointment that Iraq had done such a thing. As I said earlier, Adnan Khairallah had the temperament, the character, and the moral authority of a leader, and this is probably why Saddam decided he had to get rid of this man before he, too, threatened his power. The Iraqi people loved him, and Khairallah was the only man who might actually have been able to take Saddam's place. But, unfortunately, that would never happen.

Confidential Sources

I continued to wait for Khairallah outside Saddam's office for a few more minutes, and when he finally arrived, the secretary went in and told Saddam that the minister of defense and I were there, ready to see him. But Saddam told him, "Send in Gen. Khairallah and tell Gen. Sada to wait."

As I sat there I wondered how long I'd have to wait, but after no more than ten minutes the secretary's telephone rang. It was Saddam telling him to send me in. So I went in and saluted the president. As I started to sit down I noticed that there were several chairs, some close and some far away from the president's desk, so I walked toward one near the back. But immediately Saddam said, "No, no. Georges, you come up here." And he pointed to a chair very close to his desk, between himself and Gen. Khairallah. So I walked up to that chair and took a seat.

As I sat down, Gen. Khairallah spoke directly to me, and he said, "Georges, the president is going to ask you several questions. I want you to answer these questions as the Georges we all know and trust." Suddenly, I was worried about what would come next. The meeting was beginning to sound more like an interrogation than a conversation about military matters. I was afraid that Saddam was going to ask about the trip to London or something like that. Maybe he wanted to know if Khairallah had shared some classified information about the Iran-Iraq War or something else of a more personal nature.

But Khairallah went further and said, "Georges, even if the president asks you about Adnan Khairallah, I want you to answer him honestly, as I know you will." This really puzzled me. I couldn't imagine what sort of questions Saddam was going to ask. But I remembered my conversation with Gen. Khairallah when he asked me to do the research to find out if we had attacked Iran without provocation. At that time he had sworn me to secrecy.

This was especially troubling because, on one hand, he was telling me to be honest with the president, but he had previously made me swear never to tell anyone, especially Saddam, what I found out. So I decided that if this was what Saddam was going to ask me, then I would have to say I didn't know anything about it. For all I knew, it could have been a trap. But I had given Gen. Khairallah my word as a fighter pilot, so even if they killed me, I wouldn't go back on my word of honor.

But thank God he didn't ask me that. In fact, his first question struck me as rather odd. He said, "Why is Gen. Khairallah calling you Georges, and I call you Gyorgyes?" Saddam was saying my name the Assyrian way, so I smiled and said, "Sir, they're both the same name. It's a fairly common name among the Assyrian people, as you know—I was named for St. George." Then I explained, "When Gen. Khairallah calls me Georges, he's simply using the European name which is just a more affectionate way of addressing me."

Saddam said, "Well, if Georges is a more affectionate way, then I will also call you Georges." I smiled and thanked him, and I thought, *Thank God he's in a good mood today. Maybe he won't hang me after all!*

Sniffing Out Rebels

Then Saddam said, "Georges, do you have any idea why I've sent for you?" I said, "No, sir, no idea at all." He said, "But didn't you meet with the minister of defense before you came in?" I said, "No, sir. I only saw Gen. Khairallah in the outer office briefly when he arrived a few minutes ago. We greeted each other, and the minister asked me how I was doing. That's all."

Then Saddam asked me the question, and finally I understood what he was looking for. At that time there were people in the city of Mosul, in the north, who were becoming more and more power-ful, and Saddam was becoming concerned that maybe they were too powerful. During the Iran-Iraq War, a large number of officers in the military command staff were from Mosul, and almost all of them were Sunni Muslims.

On top of that, the army chief of staff, the intelligence chief, the chief of air force intelligence, six of the eight top air force command-ers, and most of the corps, division, brigade, and unit commanders in the Iraqi Army were all Sunnis from the same area around Mosul. In Arabic, these people are called *Muslawis*. But most Iraqi Assyrians live in this area as well, especially in the mountains to the north of Mosul. It's the area where my family comes from. But apparently, in his all-consuming paranoia, Saddam had begun to wonder about this, and he realized that the Muslawis could easily form a coalition to challenge his power.

Saddam would, of course, do anything to hold on to power, so he wanted to find out if any of these people might pose a threat. Suddenly I realized that my visit to his office, along with Gen. Khairallah, was part of his personal fact-finding mission. Saddam said to me, "Georges, I want you to tell me how all these Sunnis from Mosul came to hold all the top positions in the military."

"Sir," I said, "that's an easy answer. We all know the Shia have no chance of becoming senior leaders and commanders in the military of Iraq. Since we're always fighting with Iran, which is under the control of the Shia in that country, it's only natural that the majority of our leaders would come from the well-trained Sunni population in Mosul and the north—and this also happens to be where our best military schools are located."

It crossed my mind that several years earlier the army had been looking for a new base commander in Basra, which is in the south. They decided the logical choice would either be me, an Assyrian Christian from Mosul, or another officer who was a Sunni from Mosul. The chief of staff said they would trust either of us more than they would trust any of the Shia officers who lived in that area. They knew we would remain loyal to the military and not simply be puppets of the political and religious groups in the south.

But Saddam lifted his head slightly and sniffed the air, and he asked me, "Didn't you smell something in this collection of officers and commanders in the army and air force? Did you smell that these Muslawis might have a plan to start a rebellion against us?"

"No, sir," I said very seriously. "I've never heard of anything like that at all."

That was the substance of our conversation that day. Fortunately, he didn't ask me about the loyalty or the love life of Adnan Khairallah. And he didn't ask about my research on the war. So the general's strong words to me about keeping our conversation a secret were never put to the test.

But what did happen was that shortly after the end of the Iran-Iraq War, Saddam ordered a large number of his top commanders, all of them from Mosul and the north, to be hanged. And when those executions were actually carried out, there were two pilots among them: Gen. Salem, the deputy air force commander and Gen. Hassan, who was director of operations for the air force. These were both good and honest men, even though I didn't agree with them on many things. But, once again, Saddam thought nothing of killing innocent men if it served his purposes.

When it came to protecting his own power, Saddam was ruthless. If he thought there was the slightest chance that someone might be conspiring against him, it didn't matter whether he was Sunni or Shia, he would finish him off without batting an eye. Part of this, of course, was because Saddam was not religious. He was from a Sunni tribe, but Saddam's only religion was Saddam, and his personal glory was the only higher power he recognized. Toward the end of his regime, when he was trying to convince the Iraqi people that he was a good Muslim, Saddam had photographers come in and take photographs of him kneeling on his prayer rug, praying toward Mecca. But everyone knew it was all an act. He couldn't have cared less about Islam. Religion, like everything else, was merely a tool he could use whenever it suited his purposes.

Saddam's Demons

If you pursue this line of thought, you soon realize that Saddam was no more loyal to the Baath Party than he was to Islam. He was no more loyal to the army than he was to the party or his religion. He never actually served in the army. When he became president, he declared himself a five-star general—to make himself equal to Gen. Eisenhower, who was the highest-ranking allied commander in World War II.

Whenever Saddam wanted to confer an honor on one of his hand-picked favorites, he would give them a high rank in the military or any other title he could think of. He did this most conspicuously, perhaps, for a man named Izzat Al-Douri, when he raised him to the rank of four-star general. To understand the significance of that, you should know that before being appointed a four-star general, Izzat was the ice seller in the village of Dour, which is just across the river from Tikrit where Saddam was born.

At Saddam's whim, Izzat was put in charge of several divisions of Iraqi soldiers. At last report, Izzat the ice seller was very ill, suffering from leukemia. Some have suggested that he may have been a leader of the insurgency in Iraq, helping to plan attacks on Americans and to destabilize the new government. In reality, he's not smart enough to lead anyone in battle. But he was incredibly loyal to Saddam who had trusted him enough to put him in such a lofty position.

During our meeting, I did my best to assure Saddam that nothing was happening. There was no plot and no plotters. There was no rebellion in the military at that time, but apparently I wasn't able to convince him. The truth is, if there had been a plot or some sort of secret plan to overthrow Saddam, the plotters would never have told me. As a Christian, I was an outsider, and I also had a reputation for telling the truth. That's why Saddam had called me in the first place, because both he and Gen. Khairallah knew I was an honest man. But, to the best of my knowledge, there was no plot at that time.

This was simply another example of the personality of Saddam. He was paranoid and he wouldn't think twice about cutting off heads if he felt that a certain person was against him. This was especially true if the person he suspected was a high-ranking officer or a cabinet minister who might pose a legitimate challenge to his authority. And Saddam had thousands of ways of killing his enemies.

One of the most tragic examples of this was a story I know well because it affected me very deeply. There was a brilliant medical officer named Dr. Raji al-Tikriti, and we became very good friends. He was a specialist in spinal injuries and he advised the air force on the design of ejection seats in our fighters and other things of that nature. He earned his degree in neurosurgery in England, so he was not only a highly skilled physician, but he eventually became commanding general of the medical branch of the Iraqi Army.

All through my military career, I was a fighter pilot. I flew and tested all the supersonic aircraft in the air force. But flying aircraft of this type is stressful on the body, so you need to be strong, and you need to be very well conditioned physically. But one time when I was doing a lot of high-G flying, I found that I was having discomfort and cramping in my back, so I went to see Dr. Raji and I asked if he could help me find out what was going on.

He, of course, agreed, and after the examination he told me that I have an unusual torso. From my shoulders to my waist, I have the build of a man who ought to be three or four inches taller than I am. My legs and my upper body, he said, were disproportionate, which is a common characteristic of people who live in the mountains of Iraq. As an Assyrian, I was raised in that part of the country, in the mountains, so this made perfect sense to me.

When I fly an aircraft, the first thing I have to do is to adjust the seat and put it all the way down. If I don't do that, my helmet will hit the canopy. There are people taller than I am who put the seat higher, but my proportions are unusual. So this was my problem. Anyone with an extended spine like mine has to endure more stress when the aircraft is experiencing heavy gravitational pressures, which we call G-force. Dr. Raji diagnosed my problem, and gave me a combination of medication and instructions on how to reduce the stress on my spine, and after that I never had any more problems.

The Mind of a Sadist

I really respected and admired Dr. Raji. Like me, he was not a member of the Baath Party, which meant that there was a limit to how far he could advance in his career. But despite the limitations, he managed to become commander of the medical corps. Then one day he was sitting with a group of doctors, and he apparently made some disparaging remark about Saddam. He said, "Who is Saddam Hussein? He grew up in the streets of Tikrit. He's uneducated, and he only became president because he'll stop at nothing."

Unfortunately, in Saddam's Iraq it was unwise to speak so openly, and someone who had been sitting nearby that day let it be known what Dr. Raji had said. A few weeks later, Dr. Raji was traveling in Jordan on some sort of military business, and he happened to be sitting with the ambassador to Jordan, Nouri Al-Weis, who was also a Tikriti. They were at the Iraqi Embassy in Amman when a call came from the palace in Baghdad. When the ambassador took the call, he was surprised to be speaking with Saddam himself. They spoke informally for a few minutes, and then Saddam said, "I understand that Dr. Raji al-Tikriti is in Jordan. Have you seen him?"

The ambassador said, "Why, yes, sir. He's sitting here with me now." So Saddam said, "Nouri, whatever you do, don't let him leave. I want you to give him your car and send him to me as soon as possible. I need to see him urgently." Nouri was surprised by that, but as soon as he hung up he said, "Raji, you have to go back to Baghdad right away. The president needs to see you urgently."

So Raji told him, "Yes, of course. I'll get my bags and return immediately." And that's what he did. He didn't think anything about it. If there was an emergency involving someone at the palace, he would be glad to go there and help. Perhaps he thought it was something simpler than that. But, in any event, the ambassador drove Dr. Raji straight back to Baghdad in his own car that night.

When he got to the palace, Saddam didn't greet him, and he soon discovered there was no medical emergency. Instead, he was taken to a large room in the basement where the president's elite guards had their headquarters. He was surrounded by perhaps fifty or sixty of the biggest, most muscular guards in the army, and each of them was in their uniform which included large, heavy boots.

Off to one side, Saddam was just sitting in a chair with his legs crossed. He took out a big Havana cigar and lit it, and he said to the soldiers, "Okay, do it." At that, one of the soldiers reached out and knocked Dr. Raji to the ground. The others immediately moved in and started stomping him with their hob-nail boots, pounding, jumping, kicking, and crushing him to death right there on that floor. And while this was going on, Saddam just sat there, smoking his cigar.

When the soldiers finished the grisly business, a guard opened the door of a kennel and unleashed a pack of dogs that had been starved for days. Those dogs consumed that poor man's body completely and licked up his blood from the floor. He was a medical doctor, a general, a Tikriti from Saddam's own city, and a Muslim, but Saddam ordered that horrendous act of brutality and murder simply because Dr. Raji had dared to utter some unkind words about him.

That was the real Saddam Hussein. And you have to wonder what kind of human being this could be. But he also had two sons, Uday and Qusay, and they were worse than Saddam, a hundred times over. It was one of those sons, Qusay, the younger of the two, who came to me on January 24, 1991, and told me that the coalition pilots we had captured during the Gulf War and now held as POWs were to be executed. When I tell you that story in another chapter, I hope you'll understand the kind of brutality and violence we lived with under Saddam.

Settling Old Scores

The Russian-made bomber nicknamed "Blinder" is a supersonic aircraft made to carry heavy nuclear weapons. When it was given to Iraq, it was only equipped for conventional weapons, but it was a large aircraft with long-range capabilities, and Saddam knew that one day it would be very useful to him.

In the spring of 1980, a group called Al Dawah for Islam, made up mostly of Shias with links to Iran, tried to assassinate Tariq Aziz when he came to speak at the Al-Mustansiriya University in Baghdad. The grenade attack killed one young woman named Ferial and wounded several others, but Tariq Aziz escaped with only minor injuries. When he heard about this, Saddam was very angry because he realized that this was the same group that tried to assassinate the minister of culture and information, Latif Nsayif Jasim, the year before.

His first response was to send the Republican Guard to round up the supporters of Al Dawah in Iraq, and he had thousands of them deported to Iran. Later that year, Saddam ordered the executions of the Ayatollah Muhammad Baqir Al-Sadr and his sister, Amina, who had Al Dawah connections as well. When the war started between Iraq and Iran, he decided this was the right time to make an even bigger statement. So he called the air chief and told him he wanted a good pilot to take the TU-22, which carried up to nine tons of bombs, and destroy the University of Tehran, in the capital of Iran, on a day when all the students would be in class.

Do you know how he explained it? In traditional Arab culture, the father of the bride will demand a dowry from the family of the groom. This is called the *mahar* in Arabic, and it can be paid in gold, currency, livestock, or whatever is most appropriate. So Saddam said, "The mahar of Ferial must be very high!" The Iranians had tried to kill his deputy, he said, and somebody would have to pay. And that's why he decided to target university students. The perversity of such a criminal mind is impossible to understand.

When I saw what actually happened, I was sure it was an act of God. They set the date, loaded the bomb bays with nine tons of ordnance, and the pilot took off to carry out his mission. I knew that pilot. He was a lieutenant colonel and a former fighter pilot who had converted to the TU-22 because they needed highly skilled people to fly this model. But as he was flying toward Iran, the plane suddenly developed what's called "longitudinal vibration," meaning that it began shaking so badly it couldn't be flown. The stabilizers were useless, so the procedure then was to put the plane on autopilot, because this would often correct an anomaly of that sort.

But after only a few minutes he realized the autopilot had no effect on the vibration and the plane was shaking uncontrollably. He thought about ejecting, which was the only option he had left, but he also knew that if he escaped alive he would have to answer to Saddam. And he knew that would be very bad news. Not least because the pilot, the navigator, and the bombardier were all Shias, and since they were going to bomb a Shia city in Iran, they knew that Saddam would accuse them of treason. But it was too late to worry about that, and at the last minute they ejected.

A Comedy of Errors

What happened next is one for the record books. When the three men ejected, the canopies that had covered them were released and fell away. And as soon as that happened, the plane suddenly became stable and continued to fly for more than an hour with no one on board. Someone called me from air headquarters and said, "Georges, come quickly!" I said, "Why? What's happening?" And they told me, "One of our TU-22s is flying without pilots, and it's loaded with bombs headed for Tehran."

I raced immediately to the operations center, and for the next hour we tracked that plane. It flew east toward Tehran, and then it must have run into strong winds from the mountains because it turned and circled back and flew straight over Baghdad. It didn't fall on Baghdad, thank God, but it kept going and was headed toward Ramadi. So I told the air chief, "Sir, you've got to call Saddam and tell him what's happening." When I said that, he looked at me like I'd lost my mind.

His eyes were as big as saucers, and he said, "Georges, no! I can't do that!"

I told him, "Look, you don't know where this plane is going to fall, and just imagine what Saddam will do to you if you don't call and tell him about it before something happens." They understood that, so they called the palace and, predictably, Saddam was livid. He said, "What!? The airplane is flying without pilots?" They said, "Yes, sir, but we called General Sada and he has everything under control." So Saddam said, "Is he there now?" They said, "Yes, sir," and they quickly handed the phone to me.

I took it and spoke to Saddam, and he asked me, "Georges, what are you doing about this?" I said, "Sir, there's only one thing to do in this case, and I've scrambled two of our best pilots. Each one is carrying four guided missiles and I've told them to shoot down the TU-22 as soon as they can, but to make sure it's over an unpopulated area if possible." Well, he was glad to hear that, so I went back to the radio room to check on the fighter pilots, but they told me the target was now flying at more than twenty-two thousand feet and there was a lightning storm in the area, and they couldn't get in position to lock on with their weapons and shoot the plane down.

It would have been funny if the situation wasn't so serious, but eventually the problem solved itself, because the TU-22 crashed in a totally uninhabited part of the western desert. Since the bombs in the bomb bay had never been armed, there was no risk of an explosion, but everything was lost. And when the salvage crews got there, they found nothing but junk and twisted metal. It was a total loss, but it was an object lesson I hoped Saddam would never forget.

Unfortunately, it wasn't entirely over because I got a call a couple of days later saying that the pilots who had ejected were in custody and there was a court of inquiry under way, and, again, it was clear they were intent on hanging all three of them. I said, "A court of inquiry? How can that be? I'm the director of flight safety and I handle all the investigations. These things have to go through me, and only if I believe there's evidence of some sort of criminal intent can there be a court of inquiry!"

So I took the telephone and called the president, and I said, "Sir, I'm sorry, but there's something wrong with this investigation. There must not be a court of inquiry until the safety director has determined that this was not a mechanical problem. If I find that it wasn't a problem with the aircraft, or that there was a deliberate attempt to disobey orders, then we will turn it over to the court of inquiry."

Saddam said, "Okay, Georges. You're right. Finish your investigation and let me know what you find out." So I said, "Thank you, sir," and I hung up the phone and told them to stop the court of inquiry immediately. So I went to work and, once again, I found that there was a Russian officer at the headquarters. He was an expert in the airframe of the TU-22, so I asked to have him included on my team.

When we went through the process, we found that longitudinal vibration was one of the known structural flaws in the TU-22, and it had been reported on many occasions by other pilots. We were able to refer to the specific page and paragraph of the flight manual which said that pilots who confronted this problem were to first try the autopilot, and if that wasn't effective, then they were to eject, just as our pilots had done. I had the authority to make the final decisions in cases like this, and I'd been given permission to speak directly to the president, using a special telephone number, whenever there was a crash of this nature. I concluded that the pilots were innocent so I said they should be released.

I wrote a quick report and sent it to the president, and he agreed and told the security officers to let the pilots go free. But, once again, all three were released from the service and retired. Later they came and thanked me for saving their lives, and I told them I only did what duty required. But, I'm sad to say, there were really very few people in the military in those days who would have gone to Saddam in time of war merely to save a life.

Looking Backward

Any way you measure it, the Iran-Iraq War was a disaster. It lasted for eight miserable years and everybody suffered. For all the destruction and loss of life, no one gained a thing. But after it was over, our two countries participated in months and months of complex negotiations about captured territory, prisoners of war, reparations for property and equipment that was destroyed, and many other things, including the agreement to share the Shatt-al-Arab waterway between Iraq and Iran. That was one of the issues that had provoked the dispute in the first place. But there were no winners in that war: only losers.

At one point I thought they would put me in prison because I dared to ask the questions no one else seemed willing to ask. I said, "Okay, we fought for eight years with the Iranians, and after it was over we decided to negotiate. And through the negotiations, each side was able to resolve hundreds of issues that were of concern to them. Wouldn't it have been much better to have done the negotiation on the front end of the war instead of on the back end? It would have been so much easier and we would have kept all those Iraqis and Iranians alive." No one dared to speak the truth in that way, of course, but they knew I was right. More than a million lives could have been spared, all our lives would have been better, the economy would have been much better, and everyone would have been happier.

But of course there was one big problem for us in Iraq, and that was Saddam Hussein. The problem was that Saddam didn't want peace, and he didn't care how many people were killed in his rage for absolute power. Yet, even here, I would say that if the people of Iraq had stopped to think about what was happening, using what I call "prehap" planning instead of waiting until it was a "mishap," we would never have let a man like Saddam become the ruler of the country. Germany had their Hitler; Russia had their Stalin; and we had our Saddam. But how much better if we could have stopped these men before they unleashed their terrible destructive appetites on the world.

Some people, I suppose, understood the risks of Saddam's little adventure in Iran. On September 22, 1980, shortly after the war started, a cartoon was published in the *London Times*; it was a caricature of Saddam kicking the Ayatollah Khomeini in the rear. The joke was that Saddam was trying to pull his boot out of Khomeini's backside but it was stuck there. Despite the rather graphic nature of the cartoon, the point was well made. Saddam might be able to start a war with Iran, but it wasn't going to be so easy to end it. Before it was over, that turned out to be a very prophetic image.

I remember some Saddam loyalists in Iraq mocking that drawing when they first saw it. They said, "The English don't know what they're talking about. We'll be out of there in fourteen days!" But eight years later we were still fighting in Iran, and the toll was horrendous. Hundreds of thousands were killed and maimed. Estimates of casualties are hard to pin down, but most analysts say there were a million killed and wounded in that war, and government sources put the Iranian dead at a half million and Iraqi dead at between 200,000 to 300,000. In the end, it was only Saddam's decision to invade Kuwait that made him agree to a quick settlement and a negotiated peace that turned out to be very, very unprofitable for Iraq.

On the day the war ended, August 8, 1988, I happened to be driving to the Al-Sanjar Army Base northwest of Mosul where my son was training to go to war as an army doctor. Saddam had said, "What good is a doctor or an engineer to us if Iraq is destroyed?" So he ordered that all our medical students and physicians should be trained as soldiers. My son was an outstanding student and a good soldier, and I used to go up there to visit him every weekend to see how he was doing. During the summer, they were on bivouac, living and working outdoors, so I would take him cakes, cookies, and other food cooked for him by his mother and sister. As I was driving to the camp that day, I heard the news on the radio that the war was over.

I knew that negotiations were still going on, but I was happy for my son, that he wouldn't have to go to war. But I was also happy for everybody else. So many pilots, officers, and soldiers were lost in that war. But the statistics don't account for the suffering that we endured because of that war. And, for that matter, the official numbers in the government reports don't account for the thousands slaughtered by Saddam and buried in mass graves. There's no way of knowing how many more died in that way.

So I was very happy to know that my son wouldn't have to go to war, and he could get on with his medical studies. Living conditions in Iraq had deteriorated terribly during the war, and our currency was nearly worthless. But the day the war ended, the value of the dinar started to rise again and our standard of living also improved dramatically. One Iraqi dinar used to be equal to just over three U.S. dollars. During the war it collapsed to nearly nothing, so to be able to use our money once again was wonderful.

The oil wells were still pumping, thank God, and we had plenty of it, so after the war the European and other Western ships began coming back to our ports. The Kuwaitis agreed to loan the government $10 billion to help us rebuild our country, and both the Russians and the French started selling us weapons—as many as we wanted. Within a matter of months our pantries and our arsenals were replenished and there was euphoria in the air.

CHAPTER 4

A NEW BEGINNING

I was involuntarily retired in 1986 at the top of my career, when I was just forty-six years of age. I was one of the only high-ranking officers in the Iraqi military who was not a member of the Baath Party. After the revolution in 1963, they came and asked me to join the party but I said no. I didn't want to be part of the Baathi organization. I never joined any party or took seriously any other type of allegiance because I believed that, as a professional soldier, my duty was to the air force which had trained and commissioned me, and not to any political group.

There's an old saying: "The army belongs to the king," which means that the military belongs to the nation and should not be engaged in politics. But when the Baath Party came into power in 1968, the first thing they did was to politicize the army, air force, and coastal forces of Iraq. The goal was to make sure that everyone, from the newest recruit to the most senior officer, was a member of the party, loyal to the rulers of the nation.

There's a saying in Arabic: "The Arab nation is one motherland with an eternal message." What does that really mean? The explanation given by Michel Aflaq, who was the founder of the Baath Socialist Party, was that "the body of the nation is Arab and the soul of the nation is Islam." So whenever the Baathis would call me, asking me to join the party, I would ask them, "How do you expect me to join a party in which the body is Arab and the soul is Islam, when I'm neither Arab nor Muslim? I'm an Assyrian Christian, so clearly I don't belong in such a party."

But they would just say, "Come on, Georges. You're a very good pilot, you're rising very fast in rank and responsibility. Why don't you join?" But I said no. My people are the original inhabitants of this land. For more than twenty centuries, long before the Arabs came here, the Assyrians ruled this land. My ancestors were the rulers of Nineveh and Babylon. I'm the genuine Iraqi. It wasn't until the Arab conquest of AD 634 that there were Arabs in this place, so why would I claim to be something I'm not?

A Royal Performance

Iraq's army and security forces have been in the hands of Sunni officers and commanders ever since the modern military was established in 1921. And particularly since the uprising by the Kurdish nationalist leader Mustafa Barzani in the mid-1940s, few Kurds have been accepted into the military academies. It has always been difficult for Kurds to achieve high rank in the military. The Kurdish people have their own militia groups, of course, but like the majority Shia population, they were never more than a small fraction of our military forces.

The Baath Party tried to downplay the differences between the various religious and ethnic groups, but everyone in Iraq knew there were differences. In the first place, these groups never liked each other, and some of them had been at war for centuries. There were also distinctions between Muslims and Christians, and there were many times when being a Christian, or just having a Christian name, could be a handicap. This came home to me on one occasion when I was asked to fly a special aerobatics demonstration.

This happened in 1968 when the Emir of Bahrain, Sheikh Issa Ibn Salman al-Khalifa, the father of the present king, came for an official state visit to Iraq. My base commander called me and said they needed someone to put on a demonstration of low-level aerobatics for the emir. At that time I was very advanced in the MiG-21 and the only Iraqi pilot who would do low-level aerobatics with that high-performance aircraft.

So they chose me as the pilot, but when they introduced me to the emir they didn't say my name, Captain Georges Sada. Instead, they took me to meet the emir and they told him, "This is Captain Laith." Obviously, I was surprised by that: why did they say Laith instead of my real name? So I took a few steps away from the emir and said to the officer who introduced me, "Why did you say my name is Laith?

You know that's not my name!" Well, everyone could see that I was unhappy about this. The prime minister, the air force commander, and many other dignitaries were there, and they wanted to know why I was arguing with this man.

The officer said to me sheepishly, "You know, Georges. You have a Christian name, and the emir may be offended if we send a Christian to fly the demonstration for him." Well, that was a big mistake for many reasons. For one, there were hundreds of British officers in Bahrain at the time, and many of them, no doubt, were named George. It's a fairly common English name. In any event, the emir couldn't care less whether the pilot had an Islamic name or a Christian name. So I said to that officer, "Okay, if that's what you want, then you can go and find a pilot with a name you like better. I will not fly."

He looked at me in shock and said, "What do you mean? You have to fly. It's all planned. You can't disappoint the emir and the prime minister, who is here as well." So I said, "If I can't use my own name, then I won't fly."

When the prime minister saw that we were arguing about something, he called out, "Why is that captain shouting so much?" So the wing commander went over to him and said, "Sir, the captain is a very good pilot, but he's upset now because they didn't use his proper name when he was introduced." Now, I should also point out that the prime minister knew me very well because many years earlier he had been an assistant to my father-in-law, who was the regimental commander of the Iraqi cavalry.

He said, "What do you mean they didn't use his proper name?" And the officer told him, "They introduced him as Captain Laith instead of saying he is Captain Sada."

Lion of the Air Force

The prime minister was angry when he heard that. "Why did you do this? Why did you call him Captain Laith if his name is Captain Sada? You said he is a very good pilot, and the best man to do the aerobatics. So why wouldn't you want to tell the emir and the prince his real name? You should be ashamed. Go and solve this problem."

The wing commander came over to me and said, "Georges, the prime minister is with you, and he's very angry about what happened. God only knows what he will do to the base commander and the air chief for this insult."

So I said, "Okay, then, I'll do it." I said a silent prayer because I knew that I was going to be doing some very dangerous low-level flying, and then I went up, and the show I put on for the dignitaries was really outstanding. Everything went beautifully and I could feel it. The MiG-21 handled perfectly, and it simply couldn't have gone any better. So when I landed the plane, there was a tremendous round of applause and the air controller came on the radio and told me to park the aircraft and come straight to the reviewing stand, because the emir and the prime minister wanted to shake my hand.

I thought, *Oh, my! Something has happened.* There was a big change between not mentioning my name and then suddenly being called over to receive their congratulations. But when I walked up to the platform, the air chief said to the emir, "Sir, when we brought this pilot to meet you earlier, we didn't mention his name, we just called him Captain Laith." You see, in Arabic the word *laith* means lion, so they told the emir and the prime minister they had called me Laith because, "He is 'The Lion of the Air Force,' and our finest pilot."

Needless to say, I did a double-take when they said that. To my knowledge, no one had ever called me the lion of the air force before, but I liked it. I was only twenty-eight years old at the time and I knew that an introduction like that could only help my standing as a fighter pilot. So, when I thought about it for a moment, I was glad they had done it that way.

When they explained everything, the emir took my hand and said, "Son, you are a lion of the air force and an eagle of the Arabs. When you come to Bahrain, I don't want you to go to the hotels. I want you to come to the palace and you will be my guest." And then he said, "Before coming here today, I selected some gifts to give to the people here, but now that I've seen you fly, I realize these presents aren't up to your standard. So when I return to my country, I will choose something you will like much better." And he asked me, "You are married, aren't you?" And I told him, yes, I was married. So he said, "I owe you two presents, then: one for yourself and one for your wife." I said, "Thank you, sir. You are very kind. God bless you."

A few weeks after that meeting, I did receive a package from Bahrain. Unfortunately, I discovered it had been opened by someone else. Inside the box there was a beautiful Omega gold watch, but it wasn't the one from the emir. A senior officer told me later that the actual presents sent to my wife and me by the emir had been stolen by someone in the air force.

The one the emir had sent for me had four diamond insets at three, six, nine, and twelve o'clock. It must have been enormously expensive. And there was a beautiful necklace of pearls from the Gulf of Bahrain for my wife. But I never saw either of them. Instead, the base commander ordered a new gold Omega for me, but nothing for my wife. I have no idea what happened to the emir's gifts, but nevertheless it was an unforgettable experience.

Facts and Factions

One reason I mention this story is because we were always told that there was no difference in Iraq between Sunni, Shia, Kurds, and Christians. We were all the same, they said, but that wasn't entirely true. There may have been less persecution in Iraq than some countries, but the differences were always apparent. It's true that from time to time someone from one of the minority groups could rise to a position of influence. Tariq Aziz is a good example. He was from a Chaldean Catholic family in the city of Mosul. He had a Christian name but he had to change it to improve his chances of success.

But even so, there were occasionally problems for him too. I recall one time when his son, Ziad, was thrown into prison for some reason and Tariq Aziz was anxious to get him out. He was the deputy prime minister, so he should have had easy access to the president. But for whatever reason, Abd Hamoud, who was Saddam's chief bodyguard, wouldn't let him in to see the president. He was denied access for at least six months, but one day Tariq Aziz was called to a high level meeting at the palace. He was seated close to Saddam, so he slipped him a note.

It said, "Sir, my son Ziad has been in prison for more than six months. If you please, I need to speak to you about this." When Saddam read the note, he said, "What does this mean? Why haven't you come to me before now?" And Tariq Aziz told him, "Abd Hamoud, your bodyguard, wouldn't let me come to see you."

When he heard that, Saddam turned to Hamoud and said, "Hamoud, by this time tomorrow I want Ziad to be having lunch with his father." So that was it, and the next day Ziad was released from prison. It was true that Ziad had been involved in illegal activities involving foreign currency and money changing, or something of that sort. But because Tariq Aziz was a Christian, he wasn't allowed to intercede for his son, and it was only because Saddam intervened that Ziad was finally set free. The point is that when people say there was no difference between Muslims and Christians in Iraq, you should know that this wasn't always the case.

Even among the Sunnis there were factions, and if they were not loyal to Saddam, there could be a stiff price to pay. And this was true for the people from his hometown, Tikrit, as well. If they were not absolutely loyal to the president, they would be punished. On many occasions I have seen high-ranking officers, including general officers from Tikrit, who were punished or killed because they had spoken a few words out loud that someone interpreted to be against Saddam and his regime. Such things were not at all uncommon.

Defensive Measures

But there was another incident I should mention that casts some of these religious and ethnic distinctions in a slightly different light. I flew many combat missions during the Iran-Iraq War, using both offensive and defensive tactics. On one of them my orders were to take a flight of four MiG-21s to an area near Al Kut, on the eastern side of Iraq, halfway between Baghdad and Basra and very close to the border with Iran. We had received intelligence that a group of fighters from Iran was being sent to attack our base in that region.

We were patrolling that area, keeping an eye out for Iranian aircraft, when a call came in from our radar station. They shouted, "General, come back to Baghdad as quick as you can. We're about to be attacked by Phantoms." They already had the aircraft on the radar, and it was obvious they were going to hit our refineries on the east side of Baghdad. We still had plenty of fuel but it was a long way back there, so I ordered the others in my flight to put on the afterburners so we could catch those planes before they could do any damage.

I thought this was going to be a good fight, but I also knew that the F-4 Phantoms don't usually engage in air-to-air combat. They're not made for that, so when they're engaged by another fighter, they normally drop their ordnance wherever they are and make a run for it at low level. That plane flies beautifully at low level, and a good pilot can fly for more than six-hundred miles at less than fifty feet off the ground. And because that's well below radar level, there's no way for infrared rockets to lock on and shoot them down.

By the time we got to Baghdad, the sun was going down and I saw a huge column of black smoke rising in the east. I thought, *Oh, no, we're too late. He has already destroyed the refinery.* But as I got closer, I could see the refinery, and it was untouched. But beyond that there was an electrical generating plant that was fueled by oil stored in several large tanks. This was what the Iranian pilot had hit. He had made a big mistake. Hitting those tanks may have created a lot of smoke and flames, but the power plant was untouched, and replacing the oil tanks would be no problem at all.

But once I realized what had happened, I looked to the east and could just see that pilot trying to make his escape. So I checked my gauges and the fuel level was very low. Still, I only needed to complete one turn and I could go after him and I would have been able to lock on with no problem at all. But before I could turn around, I got a call from the command center: "Sir," they said, "you can return to base. Our ground unit just got the Phantom; we hit him with a SAM-3 missile, and he's on the ground."

I said, "God bless you! I'm landing." So I checked in quickly with the other pilots in my flight and we returned to base. Just as we were landing, I saw the helicopter coming in with the captured Iranian pilot. Then, as I was beginning to taxi to the shelter, the tower called again and said, "Sir, Gen. Khairallah called and gave orders that he wants you to talk to the Iranian pilot, and no one else is to speak to him until you've interviewed him."

I said, "Okay. Keep him in the station commander's office until I get there."

The Face of All Islam

When I exited the aircraft, there was a car waiting for me. They drove me straight to the commander's office, and that's where I found the pilot. He was just a boy, a young captain, and he was trembling, obviously scared to death. So I said, "Okay, boy, relax." I spoke to him in English because I knew that, as a pilot, he would speak English. Actually, this is common when an Iraqi speaks to an Iranian. The Iraqis speak Arabic and Iranians speak Farsi (or Persian), so we can't understand each other very well unless we speak English or French or some other common language.

"Nobody's going to hurt you now," I said. "But I'll tell you something. If I had caught you up there, I would have shot you down in a heartbeat. No doubt about that. But you're here now and you're a prisoner of war. Fifteen minutes ago I could have killed you without blinking an eye. But I have nothing against you personally. You're a pilot, and you can be sure you will be treated fairly, according to the Geneva Convention."

At that time we had some nice peaches that had been imported from Europe, so I took one of them and handed it to the boy and I said, "Go ahead, son. Relax. Here, have a peach." But he wouldn't take it. So I brought him a cup of the traditional Iraqi tea, but he didn't want to drink it. Maybe he thought it was poisoned, or maybe he was just following orders not to accept hospitality from his captors. In any event, I said, "Okay, I'll drink your tea and you drink mine."

When I asked him where he was from and where he learned to fly, he told me he had gone to the Air Academy in Iran, and then he went to Lackland Air Force Base in Texas where he learned to be a fighter pilot. Well, this was a surprise, since I had also done part of my training at Lackland. So we had something in common. We talked for a while and he eventually believed that we weren't going to torture him, so he relaxed.

I told him, "Young man, you are now a guest in the land of Ali ibn Abi Talib." The Shia sect of Islam is the dominant sect in Iran, and they say that Ali, who was the cousin and successor of Mohammed, had died in Iraq. So I wanted this pilot to know that he was in a safe country. He was not in danger and his life had been spared. After a few moments he looked up at me and said, "Sir, can I say something?" And I said, "Yes, of course. Anything you like." He said, "Sir, when I look at you, I see the whole of Islam in your face." I had to smile at that. Because I had been nice to him, this young pilot thought he could see all of Islam in my face.

Well, Col. Al-Hakim, who was close to Saddam, was the commander of that base and he didn't miss the irony of that boy's words. So he said in Arabic, "You stupid jerk! You're so stupid that you've decided you see the whole face of Islam in the only guy in this room who isn't a Muslim!" We all had a good laugh at that, but since I outranked Col. Hakim, and since he was a former student of mine, I said, "Okay, Hakim, will you please shut up?! This boy isn't talking about Christians and Muslims. He just feels that he sees the spirit of Islam in the way I've been treating him!"

So Hakim said, "Okay, I'm taking him downstairs right now to the intelligence officers. Do you know what I'm going to tell him? I'm going to say, 'Okay, kid, until now you've been in the hands of Islam. But now I'm going to put you into the hands of the Christians, and just wait till you see how they treat you!"

What he meant, of course, was that the intelligence officers were going to beat him to get more information out of him, and that would teach him what Christians would do to a good Muslim boy. So again we all laughed, and I said, "Shut up, Hakim! Don't tell him that!"

The Last Line of Defense

The truth is, when I was responsible for interrogating prisoners— both in that war and in the Gulf War years later—I wasn't the least concerned whether the pilots were Christians or Muslims or anything else. I only wanted to do my job, to find out any information that might help our side achieve its objectives, but in the process to treat the prisoners fairly. I was cautious to follow the Geneva Convention, and, more importantly, the even more basic laws of human decency.

But not everyone appreciated this, and some of the officers in my unit in Baghdad at the beginning of the first Gulf War apparently wrote a report saying that I was treating some of the coalition prisoners better than others because they were Christians. They said it reached the point that it was just a big joke. But that was not true.

The reason for the report was something that happened after we captured the American pilot, Lieutenant Jeffrey Zaun, on the first day of the war. Zaun was very young. He was a nice boy but very outspoken—and much too much so for a POW. But he noticed from my uniform that I was both a general and a pilot, so he asked me about that. He said, "Are you a general?" and I said, "Yes, that's right."

After that, he asked, "Are you a pilot?" Again, I said yes. Then he said, "Sir, may I ask you what kind of aircraft you fly?" At that point I laughed and said, "Look, Lieutenant, you're a prisoner of war, and you're in no position to be asking me about my rank or what kind of aircraft I fly!"

That was it. But that was the basis of the negative report they wrote against me. They thought I was joking with the pilots, which was not what I was doing. I believed that if I could get the prisoners to relax, they would be much more willing to speak freely to me when I began asking them important questions about military matters.

An Inevitable Conclusion

The air force and military commanders never stopped asking me to join the Baath Party, but every now and then someone would tell me it was going to hurt my career if I didn't agree to join. And then in 1986 I found out what they meant. I was called to a meeting with the chief of the intelligence service, the head of the Baath Party in the military, and two other pilots who were also general officers and friends of mine. They said, "Georges, this time we're not asking you to join the party, but we want to know why you won't join."

I said, "Okay, I'll tell you again. But do you want me to tell you the truth or do you just want me to tell you what you want to hear?" They said, "By all means, tell the truth." I said, "I've told you this before, but let me simplify. You say the body of the party is Arab and the spirit is Islam, and I don't fit either qualification. I'm not Arab; I'm Assyrian. I'm not a Muslim; I'm a Christian. That's it. I'm not trying to fool anyone, and I'm not lying. This is the real reason I can't join the party."

They understood what I was saying, and they knew that I was right. I was the second-highest ranking officer in the Iraqi Air Force at that time, and they were deciding who was going to be promoted to become the next commanding general. What they were telling me was that, since I had repeatedly refused to join the party, there was no way I was going to be chosen for that job. And furthermore, this also meant that the only place for me to go, since I could rise no higher, was retirement.

So this is what they said, "Georges, you can go no higher in the air force, so you may as well retire now and save everybody a lot of trouble."

"Okay, if that's what you want," I said. "You know I'm a young general, only forty-six, and you've told me many times that I'm the best pilot in the air force. There's no airplane I can't fly. There's still a lot I can do, but if you say I must retire, then that's what I will do."

They were embarrassed and said, "Look, we're not angry with you, Georges. You've been a faithful soldier and you've served in every war and every struggle since 1963. You have an excellent record of service, but surely you realized that you were going to be retired early."

I said, "Yes, I've thought about that, and it's okay. I've had a wonderful career, gone to the Air Academy, and learned to fly the best and fastest fighter jets in the world. So I'm satisfied."

And it's true, I'd had a wonderful career—aside from the obvious problems of being in a country troubled by one coup after another and ending up with a tyrant like Saddam Hussein as my commander in chief! But in what other career could I have traveled for advanced training in Russia, America, England, Italy, and France, and gone on assignment to so many other places? I've known kings and princes, and I've had a part in making history. I've been recognized and respected as a pilot, and even achieved the rank of general by age forty.

How could I complain? This is how the military works: you work hard, you earn rank, you serve your country faithfully, and then you retire. I wasn't surprised or terribly disappointed, but at least I understood why they were asking me to retire. I still didn't believe that the military should be involved in politics, but I accepted the decision and went back to my unit. One month later I received my final orders saying I was officially released from active duty and retired with my full military pension.

A Gentleman Farmer

At that time, officers were able to retire with their full salary. So whatever I was earning on my last day of service would be the amount I would receive in retirement. The only thing that really changed was that I didn't have to go to the post exchange (PX) to do my shopping anymore. Active duty generals have to go to the PX themselves if they want to buy something, but once they retire the PX comes to them. A van comes to the house and the general or his wife can buy almost anything they need—food, clothing, magazines, sporting goods, or most anything else—without leaving home. It was a convenient perk in retirement.

I told myself I wasn't losing anything. I hadn't joined the air force to steal from the people or enrich myself. I wasn't interested in gaining political power or being appointed to some high public office; I was there to serve. If they didn't want my service, then I would retire. So I took retirement, and frankly, I was excited because I already knew what I was going to do.

For the past couple of years I'd been reading about scientific farming methods. The idea of using modern technology and production techniques to maximize the yield of a harvest was fascinating. It was a wonderful cooperation between nature and science: only God can make the crops grow, but if we understand how the process works, we can participate in that process in a very creative way, and that was something I wanted very much to try.

Whenever I'd been around farming as a young man, I thought it was very interesting. The idea of preparing the land, planting the crops, feeding and watering them, and then bringing in the harvest in the fall was something that captured my imagination. But of course I also knew that in many places in my country the land is poor and there isn't always enough rain; so it's important to have a plan for fertilization and irrigation, and this really interested me.

As I was getting ready to begin my new life outside the military, I wrote to my sister who lives in Chicago, and I asked her to send me some literature on certain types of crops that would do well in our part of the world. And I especially wanted information on how to grow them scientifically. I also wrote to my brother who is a chief engineer in Kuwait. He also loves agriculture and is very well informed about modern farming methods, so I asked him to send me the best books he could find, and he sent me four large volumes.

I spent the next few months reading things like: *How to Grow American Corn*; *How to Grow Sunflowers*; *How to Grow Summer Wheat*; and even *How to Grow Barley and Malt*. So I had everything I needed. It was all there—step-by-step instructions, almost like a baker's recipe. As soon as my retirement was official, I went down to the government offices and applied for a farm. I needed a good piece of land to begin such a project. Because the government of Iraq was socialized, the government owned all the land and people like me had to apply for the kind of property they wanted. But sure enough, they gave me a large farm of more than 10,000 acres near the town of Aziziya, about sixty-five miles south of Baghdad on the Tigris River, which was just what I was hoping for.

Fortunately, that farm had once been a government farm and had been developed with concrete irrigation canals connected directly to the Tigris River. It had metal storage sheds, fertilizer tanks, and everything I'd need to begin my project. So I hired some farm workers from Egypt to come and help me with the work, and I ordered seeds and fertilizer and everything else I thought we would need. Frankly, it was a lot of fun getting organized and planning the work and then going out to the fields in the spring and planting the first season's crops.

I can honestly say that within the first year, I became an expert in scientific farming. I read those books cover to cover. I devoured those and others, and I learned that the best crops for the soil and climate in that part of the world were the things I wanted to grow—sunflowers, corn, wheat, and barley. Those crops thrive in warm, dry climates. So that's what I did. I had sunflowers, nine types of American corn, summer wheat, and a type of barley commonly used for making beer. And these turned out to be the perfect crops. We have a lot of sunshine in Iraq and not much rain, but I had a first-class irrigation system and large open fields for planting. So everything worked out very well.

Tending to Business

All that first year I worked the crops. I prepared the soil and planted the seeds, and it was exciting when the first sprouts began to appear. I used the best organic materials and natural insect repellents, and I made sure there was plenty of water at the right time of day. Then, when the time came for our first harvest, I suddenly realized that we were going to have to prepare in a big way. It was going to be a huge harvest, bigger than I had ever imagined, so I had two new tractors shipped in by Volvo. I got two new pickup trucks and three beautiful Class forage harvesters from Germany. Everything came from Europe, and it was magnificent. They were all brand-new machines, and they were just what I needed to bring in the crops.

All that equipment and machinery was very expensive, as you can imagine. And even with the farm subsidy from the government, I had to spend a lot of my own money. Most large farms in my country were supported by the government, but I had to pay a large portion of the costs from my own funds. But then, when we brought in that first harvest, I realized I had discovered the secret of wealth. I made arrangements to sell the crops, and on the day my first big check arrived, I said, "So this is how you get to be a millionaire!"

We worked very hard, from morning to night most days, all by modern scientific methods. When I started the farm, I learned that the typical corn crop from an Iraqi farm produced about 250 kilos per acre. The first crop from my farm was 1,250 kilos per acre—five times the normal yield. That's because I did it the right way. I tested the soil and used chemicals to enrich the soil before we planted.

The first time I did it, the other farmers all laughed at me. They said, "Look at this crazy Christian! He's throwing chemicals in the ground."

Other farmers would plant the seeds, then when the crops began to sprout, they would add chemicals to the soil. But the books my brother and sister had sent me said I should enrich the soil first and then plant the seeds. If the seeds had plenty of food and water at the beginning, they would grow very well. When they reached a certain height, I was to give them a second feeding, and they would grow much stronger and bigger that way and produce a much larger harvest. So that's what I did. And I had the finest crop in the country.

Each mature head of corn had exactly 1,460 grains. They were huge, and each stalk produced two large heads. Just imagine what kind of production we were getting. For the sunflower crop, I had planted American hybrid seeds, and each seed produced one stalk with one enormous flower, nine inches across. From every one hundred kilograms of sunflowers we extracted thirty-seven kilograms of oil, compared to the typical sunflower crop which produced only about twelve kilograms of oil per one hundred kilograms of seeds.

So that's how I made my living for the next four years. I was a gentleman farmer, and I really loved it. I didn't need to follow the headlines anymore. I wasn't watching the political situation as much as I had done as a military officer, but I was aware of what was happening in the world, and I knew that we were on the verge of yet another war. Saddam was moving the army and air force to the south; clearly he was up to something dangerous and stupid. But this was none of my concern. It was peripheral to my interests now. Summer would soon be over, and I was preparing for the largest harvest of my new career.

Even though I was officially retired, I soon discovered that no one is ever completely retired from the service of Saddam. Everyone in Iraq was on a short leash, including me, and I was called upon to provide service or advice on several occasions, even during my years as a farmer.

A New Direction

After the liberation of Iraq in 2003, I was asked to meet with U.S. military and State Department officials, and I told them about many of the problems with the Iraqi military under Saddam. I also told them about some of the incidents and missions I had been part of as an aviator, and I believe that's why they asked me to be part of a multinational team to help plan the new ministry of defense in Iraq.

They invited me for a series of discussions in Baghdad, and at one of them a senior officer said to me, "Georges, everybody talks about you around here—Sunnis, Shia, Kurds. Everyone seems to know you, and I'm glad to know that they trust you. So we'd like you to work with us and help us design the new Iraqi military." Of course, I was delighted to be asked to help with such a mission. Not only because of my experience in the air force and the Staff College, but I understood the source of the problems in Iraq. I also knew many men who had served with distinction whom I could now recommend for positions in the new government.

One of the men I recommended was a very good pilot by the name of Col. Allaā Attayeh who was nearly hanged by Saddam. I first became acquainted with this man in 1989 when Saddam sent me to find out what had happened in two separate crashes, the second of which involved Col. Attayeh. The first was an accident involving Saddam's nephew, Fadhil Dham, who was a student pilot at the Air Academy. He had been flying an L-39 Alpatros, a very advanced Czech-Russian trainer, when something went wrong and the plane crashed with two pilots on board.

When Saddam got news of this, he was very upset because he assumed that the accident was probably another attack on his family. So he had everyone involved with the flight arrested, including the technicians, ground crew, mechanics, and even the instructors at the Air Academy. They were all put in prison until Saddam could find out what happened. So when he sent the intelligence officers to the crash site, Saddam told them, "Don't let anybody touch anything. I want General Sada to go there and find out what happened."

I had been out of uniform for more than three years at that time, so someone told him, "Sir, you know that Georges is retired now."

Saddam said, "Of course I know he's retired, but I want him."

His people started running everywhere looking for me. They went to my house, my brother's house, my farm, and everywhere else they could think of. When they finally found me, they said, "Georges, Georges! You must come quickly. Saddam wants you!" They were so excited they'd found me—now Saddam wouldn't be angry at them. So I went to Baghdad to meet the president, and when I arrived at his office, he said, "Georges, I know you're very good at reading the black box and that's why I sent for you. As you know, my nephew Fadhil was in a very serious crash. I want you to find out if this was an accident or if somebody was trying to kill him."

I flew straight from that meeting to the site of the crash and examined the wreckage. We retrieved the black box from the wreck and I took it with me back to air force headquarters where I could examine the data in some detail. It was soon apparent that this was not a case of attempted murder or sabotage. Instead, there was a combination of several different things that had gone wrong during the flight.

First, there had been a mechanical failure and an explosion in the combustion chamber at high altitude. But there was another problem. This aircraft was the instructor model with two seats, and according to the flight manual, the instructor, who sits slightly elevated in the back seat, is supposed to eject first if there's an unpreventable emergency. If the pilot in the front seat were to eject first, the rockets could burn and possibly kill the person in the back.

But because the pilot was Saddam's nephew, the instructor in the back seat was afraid to eject first. If he ejected safely and the student failed to eject and went down with the plane, Saddam would kill him. According to the data recorder, the instructor repeatedly asked his student to eject, but he wouldn't or couldn't do it. So they attempted a crash landing in the desert, and when they hit the ground the plane skidded a long way, then flipped over and caught fire.

Pilot Error

What I found was that Fadhil pulled the ejection lever when the plane first began to skid. This propelled him upward, but to such a low level that his chute was not able to open fully before his body slammed into the ground. When he fell, the force of impact was so great that it shattered every major bone in his body. The instructor was trapped in the plane, but rescuers managed to get there quickly enough to cut him loose. Fadhil was rushed to the hospital in terrible shape. He was given forty-seven pints of blood, but to no avail, and he died a short time later.

No one had the courage to call Saddam and tell him his nephew had died. None of the government officials, military officers, or hospital personnel wanted to be the one to call and give him the bad news, so they insisted that I do it. I didn't mind making the call; I already had Saddam's private phone number with me, and I didn't need to go through anyone to speak to him. There was a standing policy in Iraq that if an aircraft went down and the pilot was killed, I was to call Saddam directly and tell him what happened. So I made the call.

Saddam was eager to hear the news. He took the phone immediately and said, "Yes, Georges, tell me, what did you find out?" But I had to say, "Sir, I'm very sorry. I offer my condolences to you, but your nephew is dead. The doctors at the hospital did their best to save him, and they even gave him forty-seven pints of blood. But it was too late. He died a few minutes ago."

Saddam was furious and exploded when I told him that. "What?" he yelled. "How could they do that? Don't they know this boy was the nephew of the president?" I said, "Yes, sir. Everyone knows this, and I'm very sorry. But if you like, I will come and explain everything to you." But he began yelling even louder, "I don't want you to come here. Make me a flash report, and send it to me immediately!" So that's what I did. I made a report and gave him all the information I had found, broken down into twelve separate points. He must have understood, because I never heard any more about it, and the technicians and instructors were allowed to leave the prison and go back to work.

The second incident that Saddam wanted me to investigate happened on the morning of July 2, 1989. The situation this time was that Saddam had told the air force commander he wanted a group of our pilots to stage a mock attack on his family home in Al Oja, which is the village near Tikrit where he was born. He had apparently received intelligence saying that the Israelis were planning to hit that house while he was there, and a squadron of thirty of their best fighters would be making a low-level attack, coming in from the west.

To help our guys find out how to counter such an assault, Saddam had ordered the local base commander to send up a squadron of Iraqi fighters to fly over the house at low level from the same direction. That way, he said, they would be able to check out the effectiveness of our air defenses and make sure he wasn't hit.

The commander sent a group of nine Sukhoi fighters, and Saddam was there at the time so he could observe everything. The weather was not very good that day, but the pilots moved into formation and the jets came in low and fast from the west. But just as they began making their approach, the engine on one of the Su-25s suddenly cut out and shut down, at which point the pilot had no other choice but to eject at the last minute.

The plane crashed, but fortunately it didn't hit Saddam's house. It came close enough, however, that Saddam was convinced the pilot was trying to kill him. So he had the officer arrested immediately, along with his air crew and ground personnel. And it was certain that he was going to be hanged if there was even the slightest hint that the pilot was trying to kill the president. But, before giving the execution order, Saddam once again sent men to find me so I could carry out the investigation, examine the wreckage, and tell him what really happened.

Following the Leads

After the crash, that pilot was in very serious trouble—it was clear that they were already prepared to hang him. As soon as they told me his name, Col. Attayeh, I knew who he was. His father had been a member of the Communist Party and his brother was in the Al Dahwa Party, and both of them paid a heavy price for their dissident status. The father was hanged and the brother was currently serving a life sentence in prison. But I also knew that Attayeh was a trustworthy officer and a good pilot, because he had been one of my students at the Operational Conversion Unit (OCU). He had always earned very high marks, so I was eager to find out what went wrong.

When I arrived at the base to begin my investigation, I took a seat in the waiting room. After a few minutes, a general I'd never seen before came down the hall. I was officially retired, so I wasn't in uniform. In fact, I was wearing a T-shirt and slacks. Apparently this general, who had been assigned to assist me in the investigation, was expecting someone in a military uniform, and he came over and said, "Excuse me, but can you tell me if General Sada is here?"

So I said, "Yes, I can tell you if he's here. Who are you?" He told me his name, and I said, "I'm General Sada." He was obviously surprised, but he sat down and, without being asked, began telling me all about the pilot's family background and his suspicions about the act of sedition he had committed. In effect, he had already decided the case. He had made himself judge and jury; my former student was going to be found guilty without further investigation.

I just looked at him and said, "What's your branch of service, General?" He told me he was an infantry officer. So I said, "Are you a pilot?" He said no. So I said, "Do you know anything about the mechanical configuration, airframe integration, or avionics of the Sukhoi aircraft?" He said, "Oh, no, sir. I know nothing about it." He was obviously surprised by the question. "Well, then," I continued, more forcefully this time, "surely you must be an engineer, to know so much about this accident already." He answered nervously, "No, sir. I'm an intelligence officer, not an engineer."

At that, I stood up and said, "Okay, here's what I want you to do. I want you to go to your commander, or whoever is in charge of intelligence around here, and I want you to tell him that General Sada doesn't want you." He said, "What? What do you mean?" I said, "Go and tell your commanding officer that I don't need an infantry officer who knows nothing about aircraft for my investigation. Tell him to send me a pilot, or an engineer, or a specialist who understands the mechanics of a jet engine. And tell him I said you won't do."

Mechanical Problems

The man was humiliated, but he left and went to report to his boss. In the meantime, one of the sergeants who worked in that office told me that a group of Russian officials were working there that day, and they were sitting over in the cafeteria at the moment. So I walked down to the cafeteria and I saw a group of men, obviously Russians, sitting at one of the tables. I went over and spoke to them in Russian. I introduced myself, and they were delighted that I knew their language.

I told them about the crash and the pending fate of my former student, and I asked if they could help me sort out some mechanical questions and make some sense of what had happened that day. They assured me they knew all about the avionics, hydraulics, power configuration, and other mechanical features of that aircraft, and they would be delighted to help. They said that if I had any questions, they would be glad to help me find out exactly what went wrong and why the Sukhoi's engine had failed.

This was just what I'd been hoping for. So with the assurance that I would have access to expert opinion, I walked down to the room where they were holding the pilot, and an intelligence officer let me in. When I entered the room, the pilot was visibly shaken and in tears. He began blubbering to me, "Sir, there's nobody who can save my life except God and you! You know I've done nothing, sir, you've got to believe me!"

I knew what he was feeling, but his crying was inappropriate, so I chided him. "Okay, stop that and listen to me. You're a fighter pilot, an officer of high rank, and I don't want to see you behaving in this way. Do you hear me?" He said, "Yes, sir. I understand." He may have understood me, but his demeanor didn't change very much, and the tears continued to flow. So I said, "Tell me exactly what happened. What was your position in the formation?"

He said, "Sir, I was in position, and we had just made our turn and were going in for the flyover, and as soon as I leveled out the engines just shut down." I said, "Okay, but that aircraft has two engines. You're telling me that both engines shut down at the same time?" And he said, "Yes, sir, both of them. It just went dead." So I said,

"What was your fuel level?" He told me the gauges indicated that there was plenty of fuel and each drop tank had at least 1,100 liters.

Well, that caught my ear because there's no way there should have been so much fuel in the tanks at that point. The Su-25 is designed to use the fuel in the drop tanks first, and when that's gone the system switches over to the main tanks on-board the aircraft. So I asked him to tell me again what the gauges had said, and he repeated everything exactly as he'd said it the first time.

So I said, "Okay. Don't worry. It sounds like there was some sort of mechanical failure and your drop tanks didn't function properly. That explains why the gauges were so high. Instead of taking fuel from the outside tanks, the engine had already switched over to the internal supply, and when you ran out, the engines just shut down."

I asked him, "If the drop tanks don't work on that aircraft, what kind of signal would you expect to get in the cockpit?" He told me that there are three small green lights down by his leg, and if the fuel tanks don't work they blink four times and then stop. So I asked him, "Did you see them blinking?" He said, "No, I didn't." So I said, "Okay. What was your position in the flight?" He told me, "I was number five, sir, flying very close to the ground, below and behind the leader."

An Obvious Conclusion

At that point I understood what had happened. The planes were coming in from the west with the sun straight ahead of them, which meant that the cockpit panel would have been in the shadows. It was ten o'clock in the morning, but the sun had been behind the clouds most of the morning, as it was when they began the maneuver. In addition, because he was in the number five slot, close to the ground and looking up at his leader, the pilot never saw the green lights blinking down by his leg.

So I called the intelligence officer and told him, "Okay, take this man from the room and let him sit in the pilot's room." He said, "Sir, I can't do that. The order to put him there came down from the main intelligence headquarters." So I said, "Okay, I want you to listen to me. I am in charge of the investigation of this case and the only man above me is the president. Unless you want to explain to the president why you're not obeying my orders, you had better take this man to the pilot's room right now!"

He got the message, and they moved the prisoner down to the pilot's day room. His spirits were much better by that time, but I still had to take a helicopter and go out to the crash site to see what was there. I needed to speak to the Arabs who lived in the village nearby to find out what they had seen. The villagers are always afraid of these official investigations and they don't want to get involved, so I had to talk to them for a while and reassure them that everything would be okay. I told them that I was sent by the president and if any of them had lost anything in the crash, I would make sure they were compensated.

Suddenly everyone became very vocal. They all had something to report, and one of them told me, "When this airplane hit the ground, a sea of gas and oil came out and went all over our cattle, and now they're dying." As I began looking around to see if he was telling the truth, the man yelled to his son to bring the cows for me to see, and I could see that they had been covered by jet fuel. They had tried washing it off, but already a few of the cows had died, and they showed me the carcasses.

Now I knew my theory was correct. I said a silent prayer, *Thank you, Jesus!* and then I compensated the farmers for their animals. Of course, they saw this as a chance to make some money, so one man said he had lost twelve cows. I looked him in the eye and said, "Yes, twelve cows?" He said, "Well, you know. If you pay me for six, that will be okay." I knew it was two, but I paid him for six. I was glad to have this information confirmed.

I went back to the air headquarters to put together my report, and I wrote a letter to go to Saddam. I told him what I had found out, and I said, "Sir, I know this man, and he's a good pilot and a good officer. If someone tells you about his father and his brother, that's all true, but it has nothing to do with what happened here." I told him it was a mechanical failure which had happened before on these types of aircraft, and the fault was in the design.

"If anyone was to blame," I said, "it was the Russian engineers who had used three small green lights instead of a beeper or a horn or some other audible and more visible warning that tells the pilot the fuel system isn't working. Furthermore," I continued, "if you permit me to go to Gen. Amir Rashid in the military industrial division, I will ask them to come up with a modification that will solve this problem." We had about fifty of those planes and there was no reason to risk losing any more of them.

Shortly after receiving my report, Saddam wrote to the commanders to congratulate me on my findings. He agreed to release the pilot and other personnel who were being held by the intelligence service, and he told the air force commander to observe my recommendations and to have a new warning system installed in the Sukhois so that this kind of accident would never happen again. And then, much to my surprise, he also had a special present sent to me: ten thousand dollars and a gold watch.

Saddam was glad to know that he wasn't the target of his own pilots, but he nevertheless ordered the commander at that base to relieve the pilot of his duties. He didn't want him in the air force anymore, so the young man was retired. But, given the options, which were death by hanging or retirement, I'm sure he felt this was a more than satisfactory solution. Later, when I was asked to help form the new Iraqi Ministry of Defense in 2003, I proposed that this man be brought in as deputy to the air force commander. So Col. Attayeh was promoted to the rank of general, and he even served for a time as deputy commander of the air force.

There were many short-term assignments of this sort during my four years of retirement, but by 1990 I could see the storm clouds rising on the horizon. By all rights, I shouldn't have been surprised by the next call I received from Saddam. What he had in store for me this time, however, would bring an end to my farming career and would turn out to be one of the biggest challenges of my life.

PART II

CHAPTER 5

A SUDDEN CHANGE OF PLANS

On August 2, 1990, when I received an urgent phone call from the air force headquarters in Baghdad, I was told that Saddam had just ordered the army to invade Kuwait. They said that Gen. Georges Sada was the first officer Saddam had recalled to active duty. I was also told I was going to see the president, and that I would likely be called as an adviser for the air force.

What was I to do? The law in Iraq said that if you were recalled to active duty and you didn't go, you would be hanged. No questions asked. So I went. I went to the headquarters of the air force and met with Gen. Muzahim Hassan al-Tikriti, who had been a student of mine at one time. I was his flight instructor and squadron commander, and I gave him his first solo in the MiG-21 in 1971. At that time I had been his commanding officer, but now he was chief of the air force—in part because he also happened to be a cousin of Saddam Hussein.

When I reported for duty, Gen. Muzahim said there were three things he wanted me to do. First, I was to find out the capabilities of the coalition air forces—that is, America, Britain, and any others who would be coming against Iraq. Second, he wanted to know the destructive capability and accuracy of the cruise missiles used by the United States Navy. And, third, he wanted to know the combined capability of the five American aircraft carriers that were being deployed in the Red Sea and the Persian Gulf, which we refer to in Iraq as the Arabian Gulf.

Of all the assignments Muzahim could have given me, I was fortunate he had given me this one. I had taught all of this for ten years in all three military colleges—the Staff College, War College, and National Defense College—where I served as director of staff. Part of my responsibility in those days was to teach these very things, so

I already had some of the material and I knew I could easily get the rest.

The only thing I asked for from military intelligence was a current assessment of the number and distribution of American and coalition aircraft in the region. They told me which squadrons were in Oman and how many fighters they could deploy, how many were in Saudi Arabia, and so on, and they gave me an estimate of how many of each type of aircraft were in the region—Tornadoes, Harriers, Black Hawks, Jaguars, F16s, and so on. It eventually turned out to be about 2,700 combat aircraft, fully armed and ready for action.

My task then was to do the analysis and report on how much damage these aircraft could inflict. It wasn't a difficult assignment: this had been my daily bread for so many years. If all those aircraft were sent up, I could report on their exact capabilities, and I could do the same sort of assessment for the cruise missiles that, more than likely, would be launched either from the four carriers in the Persian Gulf or the *USS Saratoga* anchored in the Red Sea. In addition to missiles, some carriers could send up seventy or eighty aircraft, so that's the kind of analysis I was asked to do.

In addition to statistical data I had several videos that described all these weapons in detail and showed their destructive potential. The sad part was that I was given this assignment on August 2, 1990, after Iraqi tanks, helicopters, and aircraft had already crossed the border into Kuwait. Nevertheless, I began preparing the report, confident that I would be ready to make the presentation whenever I was called on to do so.

A Dangerous Scheme

Meanwhile, tensions continued to mount in the international community concerning the invasion and likely repercussions, and all sorts of resolutions were being passed by the United Nations. It seemed clear also that America and Britain were preparing to lead an offensive to drive the Iraqi Army out of Kuwait. In November 1990 I made a frightening discovery: Saddam had ordered the air force to begin planning for a major aerial assault against Israel. If the Americans were going to attack and force him to give up Kuwait, he said, then our pilots would be ready to attack Israel as soon as the first rockets hit, and they would extract a heavy price. They would attack in two massive, back-to-back assaults, with three types of chemical weapons: the nerve gas Tabun, as well as Sarin 1 and Sarin 2.

The mission was to deploy ninety-eight of our best fighter aircraft—Russian Sukhois, French Mirages, and the MiGs—fueled and equipped to penetrate the Israeli borders through Jordan and Syria, but without telling either of those countries that we were coming. Clearly this would be an unauthorized invasion of Syrian and Jordanian air space, with payloads of deadly toxins. I was shocked that such an order could have been given; but I knew that if this mission ever took place, crossing restricted air space would be the least of our worries.

A few days after I first learned about the plans, I got a call from the palace. They told me that Saddam was asking for me personally, and he wanted to see me in his office right away. So, again, I went to meet with the president, and I was surprised to see that the entire general staff was already assembled in the conference room when I arrived.

Saddam had checked me out many times, and I think he respected me. I know why he trusted me: he couldn't trust most of his generals to tell him the truth because of their fear of him and their allegiance to a religious or political agenda. Either they would say whatever Saddam wanted to hear, or they would say what was politically advantageous to their own people. So he would often say to me, "At least Georges will tell me the truth." And even Saddam occasionally needed to hear the truth.

I didn't know why he had called me that day, but I knew it was going to be something very important. Several of the officers in the room were of higher rank than I was, but it was prearranged for me to sit right in front of Saddam. By right, my place should have been on the second row, but he had instructed his aides to put me on the first row, so that's where I sat.

When everyone was seated, Saddam made a few remarks and then he looked at me and said, "Georges, do you know why you're here?" I said, "No, sir, but it's a great pleasure to be here." He said, "I've decided that the air force will attack Israel." Suddenly I knew what this was all about. Although I had no idea where the conversation would end up, it was clear that Saddam was looking for justification for a decision he had already made.

So I asked, "Attack Israel, sir?" and he said, "Yes, that's right." He gave me a moment to reflect on that, and then he began asking me all sorts of questions.

The first question he asked was surprising. He said, "Georges, who's stronger, Israel or Iraq?" I knew what he wanted me to say, but I had to be realistic. After all, the reason Saddam had called for me was because he knew I would answer him honestly and correctly. So I paused for a moment and said, "Sir, what you're talking about is the difference between men who are blind and men who can see."

He looked at me quizzically and said, "What do you mean, Georges?" I said, "Sir, there are two groups, one which is blind and one which can see, and they're preparing for battle." "Yes," he said, "and which is which? Which ones are blind and which ones can see?" "Unfortunately, sir," I told him, "we're the blind ones, and the Israelis are the ones who can see." With that, Saddam erupted. "Why!?"

Believe me, I knew I was on shaky ground. Many good men had died for words less offensive than the ones I'd just spoken. Saddam had personally shot and killed high-ranking officers on the spot, and he had ordered men to be executed for thoughts or actions he only imagined. So before I answered the question, I decided to make one more defensive maneuver, and I said, "Sir, if I speak the truth to you now, will you, according to the custom of the Arabs, give me permission to speak freely, with immunity?" In other words, I was saying, Will you promise not to shoot the messenger?

Saddam's eyes were threatening, but he knew what I meant. What I was asking for was a centuries-old tradition among the desert Arabs, an oath sworn by tribal leaders to allow a messenger to speak freely without fear of being killed. As he folded his arms across his chest, Saddam said, "Yes, I give you immunity." Then, more forcefully, he said, "Now tell me what you mean!" I had no choice but to answer him. I knew full well that he had given immunity to others in the same circumstances and they were hanged, but I was honor-bound to tell the truth. So I breathed a silent prayer, *Lord, give me the courage to speak,* and I spoke.

Answering to Saddam

From beginning to end, my answer took one hour and forty-one minutes. When I served as air vice marshal in the air force, I studied all these things in detail, so I had extensive knowledge of the military capabilities of the forces in our region, as well as those in Europe and North America. So I was able to cover those topics in detail. But the minute I finished, Saddam erupted once again in anger. Fortunately, this time the anger wasn't directed at me but at the others who had not told him the truth about these things.

Most of these men were eager to assure Saddam that two plus two is nine, because they knew that's what he wanted to hear. But, thank God, Saddam listened to me, and that was a miracle in itself. He never listened to anyone. He had his own ideas, and he never wanted to be confronted by the facts if they would prevent him from doing whatever he had already decided to do.

As an example of how far he would go, on one occasion Saddam sent me on a mission to England, the purpose of which was to persuade the English and American people to change their minds about him. He didn't want to change himself in any way; he wanted to change England and America. Saddam was the kind of man who believed he could do whatever he wanted. After all, in Iraq Saddam could create generals and commanders and government officials with the wave of his hand, and he was sure he could command the English and Americans to believe he was a good and generous leader, and that they would actually do it.

On another occasion, I was speaking to Saddam about the strength of our military and I remarked casually that America was the only remaining superpower. He immediately interrupted me and said, "Georges, don't ever say that again. I never want to hear you say that."

And that's how it went. If the facts didn't please Saddam, he would just shut them out. It wasn't only military matters; it was the same with the economy, with government statistics, or with numbers of any kind. He would deny realities so obvious they were common knowledge, often by saying that these things were just matters of mind over matter, or that they were spiritual facts. Of course, he was anything but a spiritual man. But Saddam lived each day in a fictional world of his own making.

At one moment he would pretend he was the most ardent Muslim in Iraq, and he would have photographs taken of himself praying, kneeling on his prayer rug, or wearing the *ihram*, which is a pilgrim's robe. In reality he was far from being a good Muslim or anything else. He used and abused his power, and he wouldn't think twice about doing something forbidden by Islam if it pleased him. And his sons were immeasurably worse than he was.

This is why it was so hard to speak to Saddam, to tell him important information. If you spoke openly and honestly to him about any subject, you never knew what the consequences might be. Scores of men had died for simply speaking the truth.

Discouraging Words

When I told Saddam that attacking Israel would be like the blind attacking the sighted, we were surrounded by all of the members of the general staff, and Gen. Amir Rashid Ubaidi, who was deputy air force commander for technology and engineering, leaned over to his colleague and whispered, "Georges is going to be killed, now, right on the spot. His head will be separated from his body." I didn't hear the remark, but they told me later what he'd said.

Gen. Amir, incidentally, was a true genius. He had been number one in his class at the University of London, where he earned his Ph.D. in engineering. After the Gulf War, he was taken into custody by the Americans and imprisoned in Iraq. He had been in charge of the "superweapons" program but claimed that Iraq never had chemical weapons or WMDs of any kind, and of course that wasn't true and he, of all people, knew it.

In any event, I told Saddam that the reason I had used that expression is because Israeli aircraft have very advanced radar with the capability to see more than 125 miles in any direction. On the other hand, 75 percent of Iraqi aircraft were Russian-made, and the range of the radar on our fighters was only about fifteen miles. This meant that the Israeli fighters could see our aircraft at least 110 miles before we would even know they were there. And that's not even the worst part. Their laser-guided missiles could lock on our fighters while they were still sixty-five miles away, and we'd have no idea that enemy fighters were anywhere around. Then the Israeli pilots could fire their rockets at a range of at least fifty miles and our pilots would never even know what hit them.

At that point I asked Saddam, "Sir, don't you agree that this is a fight between men who are blind and men who can see?" Saddam just sat there for several seconds, looking straight ahead. Then he turned sharply to his left where Gen. Amir was sitting and he yelled very loudly, "Amir, what is Georges saying?" In other words, Saddam was asking his weapons expert: Why haven't you told me this before now? This is your area, and I hold you personally responsible for telling me these things.

I didn't change my expression but continued to look at Saddam. But then I realized, *Oh, no! Gen. Amir is not that brave. I'm afraid he will not tell Saddam the truth, and he'll try to put the blame on me or someone else.* So I turned quickly and looked Amir straight in the eye, and he could see that I was very serious. After the meeting he came to me and said, "I knew, Georges, when you turned to look at me that way that you were sending a message." And that's exactly what I was doing. Without saying a word I was telling him to speak the truth because we were both speaking directly to Saddam Hussein. If he disagreed with me or tried to lie his way out of it, I would have defended myself in the strongest terms, and Gen. Amir knew exactly what I meant.

Well, God was with me that day because Gen. Amir said to Saddam, "Sir, what Brother Georges is saying about the difference between the Israeli aircraft with sophisticated American and European technology, and our Russian-made aircraft with Russian technology, which is not so sophisticated, is right." And then he began explaining it to him in very detailed engineering terms, telling Saddam everything about the technology of the different fighter aircraft. Amir knew that Saddam didn't care in the least about any of those details: he was just covering his own backside. But what it came down to was that he told him, Brother Georges has told you the truth about our fighters, and we're no match for the Israelis.

When he finished, Saddam just sat there, silently, staring straight ahead. For more than a minute you could have heard a pin drop in that room. And, believe me, a minute of silence in the presence of Saddam Hussein could seem like eternity. There were at least ninety people in the room, all generals and high-ranking commanders, and there wasn't a peep out of them.

War Games

It was obvious that Saddam was angry, and it struck me that he may be thinking that I was painting a negative picture because I'm a Christian. On more than one occasion my Muslim colleagues had said that Christians are weak, and maybe Saddam was thinking that I was afraid of going to war. Whenever another officer would say something like that, I usually pointed out that there have been a few good generals I could name—such as Gen. Montgomery, George Washington, Douglas MacArthur, and even Erwin Rommel, the Desert Fox—who were all Christians, and most people would say they were pretty good fighters.

Nevertheless, Saddam's expression hadn't changed for a long time, so I said, "Sir, what I've just told you is all true. But that doesn't mean we will not fight. A good military man will fight whenever he receives orders from his commander. If you still want us to fight, then I assure you we will fight, and who knows what will happen? As a good officer, I can only give you my best advice and prepare the commander for the decision he will make. My job is to tell you the truth, to the best of my ability, and then wait for your decision. And, sir, that's what I've done."

At the end of the meeting, the only thing I could be sure of was that Saddam had listened to me, and he knew that to the best of my ability I had told him the truth. I had no idea what decision he would make, but at least he had heard me and he understood what I'd said. Then in mid-December 1990, less than a month from the deadline that had been set by the United Nations for Saddam to pull his forces out of Kuwait, I was told that the president was ready to announce his decision.

On December 17, we received the message we'd been expecting. Saddam's message was worded very deliberately, almost poetically in Arabic, to give the impression of a decree of great solemnity and importance. It said, *"Uwafiq Tunafath Ala Barakatalah,"* which means roughly, "I agree to the attack, and we shall attack with the blessings of Allah." It was as if Nebuchadnezzar had spoken. But what he was saying was that we were being ordered to proceed with a massive chemical-weapons assault on Israel, in two waves, one through Jordan and the other through Syria.

Obviously Saddam had thought long and hard about this invasion which, if we actually carried it out, would be the most scandalous act of his entire regime. No doubt there would be some in the Arab world who would praise Saddam for accomplishing what no other Arab nation had ever done. After all, Syria, Egypt, Jordan, Saudi Arabia, and Iraq had all failed and suffered humiliating defeats in the past by trying to overpower the Israelis. But to attack in such a fashion, with ninety-eight fighters and forbidden weapons, would bring forth an outcry from the civilized world that would no doubt be deafening.

If even 10 percent of our aircraft made it into Israel and were shot down with chemical weapons on board, there would be tremendous loss of life. Thousands of Israelis would die in the first strike, and as the effect of the chemicals was dispersed, many thousands more would die. For Saddam, this was enough. This would be a victory for him, and he wasn't worried at all about the consequences.

He believed he would be hailed as a hero in the Arab world. After the Gulf War he bragged about firing SCUDs into the heart of Israel. He would say, "Iraq fired thirty-nine missiles into Israel. Who else has achieved such a great feat? Who will make it forty?" This is the way he thought. Even if we lost the war, the fact that he had fired thirty-nine missiles into that hated nation was all the victory he needed. He used to say, "We don't need the Arabs to help us. Just give me a piece of land on the border of Israel and I'll show you what the Iraqis can do."

But even though I knew what was in his mind, I felt compelled to call the palace and arrange to speak to Saddam one more time. This time I was on my own, but when I was given a chance to speak to him, I said, "Sir, I have seen the orders to launch the attack on Israel, and we all know what this means. But there's something else I need to tell you, and I want to be sure that someone has done it. The Israelis have very advanced early-warning systems, and they have the ability to destroy any aircraft coming from the east before they ever cross the borders.

"It's possible," I told him, "that some of our planes may slip through the web if they can exploit holes in the radar and come through in sufficient numbers. So even if you send aircraft with chemical weapons, it is possible that a few of them will actually get through. But I assure you, sir, that most of them will not. They will be destroyed, not over Israel but over Jordan and Syria. And if that happens, the whole world will say that you didn't attack Israel, but that you attacked your own Arab people in those countries."

Saddam was listening but he didn't speak, so I said, "Sir, you're the commander, but you should know that most of our aircraft will not make it to Israel. It's possible that maybe ten of them will penetrate the borders. If that happens, there will be chaos, and it's certain the Israelis will retaliate with nuclear weapons. They have them, and if we strike in this fashion, you can be certain they will not hesitate to use them against us."

Defying Common Sense

I knew that what I was saying was true because I had seen the plans. The Israelis had Pershing missiles they'd acquired from the Americans, and they had been modified to carry nuclear warheads. Those missiles were already targeted on Mosul, Baghdad, and Basra, the three largest cities in Iraq. But logic also said that if Israel was attacked by chemical weapons, they would be within their rights to retaliate in any way they liked, even if it was with nuclear weapons.

I knew that Israel's military planners had already targeted three of our cities, but who could say it might not be six or eight cities? It was certainly true that the Israelis had plans for fighting all the Arab countries, and they were prepared to fight them one at a time or all at once, if need be. Their technology was (and still is) very advanced.

Militarily, this only made sense, because whenever there was a fight between Israel and any one Arab country, the other Arab countries would all come as well. This was what happened during the Arab-Israeli War of 1973. Iraq wasn't asked to be part of the alliance with Egypt and Syria, but Saddam wanted to go in anyway. So he sent our troops and aircraft without any agreement or authority to do so. The Israelis know this is what happens, and they're prepared to fight not just one Arab country, but all of them if they must.

I told all these things to Saddam, but he wouldn't be dissuaded. He was determined that Iraq was going to attack Israel, regardless of the consequences. And just to make sure there was no turning back, he made another dramatic pronouncement. He called all the military commanders together once again and told them, "We will attack, so you must be ready. But I'm afraid that our enemies may find someone who looks like me and sounds like me, and they will put him on television and radio, and he will tell you not to attack. But I want you to listen to me: If this happens, do not believe them. Even if something happens to me, you must not stop. You must attack, and you must carry out all the plans I've given you, because this is a holy task and it must be done."

When that order went out to the commanders in the field, they were stunned. They were afraid of what would happen next. But the very next day the commander of the squadron of Mirage fighters our pilots would be using in the attack came to me with tears in his eyes, and he said, "Sir, our pilots will not be able to do this. There's no way to fly this mission because the loads we've been asked to carry are much too heavy. The pilots won't be able to keep the planes in formation. They'll be flying at full power the whole flight with nothing in reserve." He looked at me pitifully and said, "Please, sir, can't you do something? At least let us practice flying under these conditions."

Understand that this was several days after December 17 when Saddam had first given the order to attack, and less than a month until the deadline of January 15, 1991, set by the United Nations, which was also the day I fully expected the coalition led by the Americans to attack Iraq. So there we were: less than a month from a coalition assault. The air force commanders had been ordered to get ready for a massive assault on Israel with chemical weapons, and they hadn't even trained the pilots on how to fly under those conditions. So I went to see the air force commander, Gen. Muzahim, my former student, to tell him what was happening. I told him what I'd learned from the wing commanders and he was shocked. He said, "Georges, are you sure about this?" And I said, "Yes, sir, I'm sure. But why don't you call the squadron commander and have him come here and tell you himself?"

He did that, and when the commander came in, Gen. Muzahim asked him, "Is this true what Georges has told me? Your pilots haven't trained for the attack carrying the special weapons?" The commander told him it was just as I had said, and he added, "Sir, how can our pilots carry all this heavy ordnance if they haven't been shown what they're supposed to do? And how can anyone expect them to make this attack, drop their payload, and then return to base if they can't even refuel in flight?"

Saddam's Edict

Here was something else that no one had considered. With such heavy loads, the fighters would expend all their fuel very quickly. Even if they were able to reach the targets with their onboard supply of fuel, they could never return; so somehow they would have to refuel in flight. But how do you do that on such a risky combat mission? They couldn't use tankers, because tanker refueling takes place at very high altitudes which would clearly be seen by defensive radar, and the advantage of surprise would be lost. The only answer was that they would have to refuel by using other fighters, such as the Mirages that, instead of carrying weapons, could be reconfigured to carry jet fuel and apparatus for refueling the attack planes air-to-air. It was an unusual approach, but it could be done.

This was another critical part of the mission for which the pilots had never trained, and unless they could successfully refuel before crossing into Israeli air space, it would be nothing short of a suicide mission. They could never return to base, so we would lose the pilots and the planes. And as brutal as Saddam was in his dealings with the military, even he was not willing to risk losing all his fighter pilots in that way. Remember, he was preparing to send two flights, fully loaded, with a total of ninety-eight combat aircraft, gambling that at least ten of them would make it into Israel!

Somehow I managed to get the commander's attention, and he instructed his officers to begin training their pilots immediately to fly the mission under those conditions. By this time, it was already the twentieth of December, just a few weeks from the U.N. deadline, and our pilots began training for a mission they knew they would have to carry out, regardless of the cost. Saddam's order had made it clear that there was no other option.

Everyone in the army and air force had been on edge for weeks because of what they feared was coming. There could be no turning back. "Even if someone comes on the television who looks just like me," Saddam had said, "don't believe him. You must attack."

We know now that coalition forces were aware that Saddam might try to attack Saudi Arabia. I learned later, several weeks after the war, that it had even been reported on CNN and other networks at the time that Saddam was sending tank divisions toward the Saudi borders, apparently planning to attack in that area. Most people, however, had no idea what he was planning to do in Israel, and the story of that mission would not be revealed until now.

What the world did see, however, was Saddam's attempt to fire SCUD missiles at Tel Aviv, Haifa, and other Israeli targets within range. The Americans had come in and set up Patriot missile batteries all over the area, so on television in the U.S. and Europe, many people were able to watch those very dramatic events as they were actually happening. The Patriots were not terribly accurate, we now realize, but they were accurate enough to stop many of Saddam's SCUDs, and just knowing that they were there seemed to calm the worst fears of people in Israel and the West. If they had known what all was on Saddam's mind, I don't think they would have felt quite so secure.

In fact, when they were planning the attack on Israel in the early part of December 1990, none of the operations officers in Baghdad were talking about using SCUD missiles at all. The events that took place when I gave my briefing in the operations room on January 12, 1991, just three days before the U.N. deadline and five days before the attack, were very important, and I want to talk about that. But first, let me say something about the attacks on Israel.

The plan signed by Saddam had the words across the top in his own handwriting, saying, "I agree to the attack, and we shall attack with the blessings of Allah." The idea of hitting two countries simultaneously was remarkable enough, particularly when one of them (Israel) was considered an enemy country, and the other (Saudi Arabia) was not only not an enemy country, it was an Arab country on our southern border with which Iraq was supposed to have close ties. Furthermore, Saudi Arabia was an Islamic country, the place where Mecca is located, a sacred site to all Muslims. Yet, Saddam had the arrogance to write those words on the order, and attacks on both countries were part of his plan.

Saddam actually believed that God would bless him for attacking Israel with chemical weapons. And at the same time, he believed he would have the blessing of Allah when he attacked Saudi Arabia! It's hard to imagine that kind of evil—to do such a thing, believing that God would bless his plan. I wish I'd kept a copy of that document to print here in these pages. Unfortunately, I don't have it, but this is how he thought.

When he was preparing the attack against Israel, Saddam would say, "If the Americans attack us in January, then we will hit Israel very hard." The key word for anyone who followed the negotiations in those days was the word *if*, because it was the consensus among all our commanders that America (meaning, of course, the coalition forces) would not attack. During the Clinton administration, America never retaliated when their ships or bases or citizens were attacked. Instead, they would send Secretary of State Madeleine Albright to complain loudly and rattle her papers. But the military did nothing.

No commander in the Middle East could ever respect such a response, particularly when the provocation was so strong. So our commanders were all saying, "You see? The Americans are weak. They're afraid to fight, and they will never attack us."

Everyone believed this, but when I spoke to them, I said, "Look, the American and coalition forces that are here now standing by in the Gulf and the Red Sea are very expensive to maintain, and this build-up will cost the Americans billions of dollars. There's no way they're going to spend so much money for nothing. How would they explain to the American people that they've spent billions sending the army, air force, navy, and marines to the Middle East just to sit on their hands and do nothing? The news media would tear them to pieces. So, please, don't tell me they won't attack."

Meaningless Boasts

By the middle of January 1991, things were incredibly hectic. Our army was in Kuwait, stealing everything in sight, and the news wasn't good. The world had condemned Saddam and the invasion of Kuwait. The people were nervous about all this, and the military was in denial. When the minister of military affairs, Gen. Shanshal, called a meeting of the general staff for January 12, three days before the United Nations' deadline to leave Kuwait, I thought that finally we'd be able to get to the bottom of what was happening.

I took my seat next to the air force commander and looked to see who else was there. The minister of defense, the air force commander, the intelligence officers, the chiefs of staff and their deputies, as well as Gen. Shanshal who had been chief of staff for many years, were all present. Everybody, in fact, except Saddam himself. Gen. Shanshal had been named minister of military affairs in 1990, and everybody respected him and listened to him. He was a wise man and had been first in his class in the Staff College. So I was glad to see him there.

His only problem was that he was afraid of Saddam and he would always do whatever Saddam wanted him to do. Like Tariq Aziz, the deputy prime minister, Gen. Shanshal had knowledge and ability, but he was incapable of acting on his own without first checking with Saddam. And if Saddam asked for information that was unfavorable to his schemes, Gen. Shanshal would say whatever Saddam wanted to hear. He wasn't brave in that way, but Saddam loved him because he never said no.

When the presentations began, a spokesman for Gen. Muzahim, the air force commander, went first, and then each officer spoke in turn. But I must say, they were the worst presentations I'd ever heard. If it weren't so serious it would have been comical. They had no idea what they were talking about. The spokesman said, "No coalition aircraft will be able to penetrate Iraqi air space." In fact, he said, "Not even a house fly can enter our air space without being intercepted by our fighters." It was all I could do to keep from laughing. But then he went on to say, "We have the best radar, the best fighters, the best rockets, and we will obliterate any aircraft that tries to cross our border." And it just went on like that, with examples of what would happen if fourteen, twenty, or thirty aircraft came at us from different directions and how we would respond. They were thinking like Saddam. It was pure fantasy, and not a word of it was true.

Once they got through the presentations, Gen. Shanshal raised his hand and said, "General, may I ask a question?" Gen. Muzahim said, "Yes, sir. Please ask anything," and Shanshal said, "Do you mean that our army and navy can move at will without any concern for possible attack from the air?" That was a great question and I was eager to hear the answer. Muzahim's spokesman said very firmly, "Yes, sir, that's correct. You can conduct operations without the slightest concern for any threats from the air."

I couldn't believe my ears. What an incredibly stupid thing to say! But the real surprise was that Gen. Shanshal didn't immediately say, "Shut up and sit down!" He didn't say a word, and I simply couldn't hold back any longer. I had to speak, so I said to the air force commander, "Gen. Muzahim, will you please stop this nonsense?"

He looked at me and said, "Now, Georges, don't interfere. And don't say anything else." But I couldn't just sit there, so I said, "With all due respect, you know this is wrong!" I'm afraid I was a bit loud, but it was such a ridiculous presentation I couldn't restrain my emotions. So I said, "Look, I'm only an adviser and you all know that. Officially, I don't have authority to challenge what you're saying. But

I must tell you that I don't agree with any of your assessments. Gen. Muzahim, you are the air force commander and you're responsible for the effectiveness of the air force and the air defense command. You are responsible for the lives of our soldiers and the safety of our country. And, sir, you must be reasonable."

At that point, Gen. Muzahim leaned over to me and whispered, "Georges, why are you being so difficult? I have to say this. You know I do. And besides, what are you worried about? There's not going to be an attack." Finally, I understood what was going on. Once again, these men were proceeding on the assumption that Ambassador Glaspie had assured Saddam that the Americans would not interfere and we were free to do as we pleased. So all the bravado and boasting were meaningless—done purely for show.

Tactical Errors

Nevertheless, I realized that giving an unrealistic presentation was dangerous, because the army officers in the room needed to know what sort of air support the ground forces would have, and what sort of defenses they would need in the event of an American assault. So I said, "I know what you're saying, Muzahim. You can boast all you like to Saddam, but you cannot give a presentation like this to the officers of the military."

At that point Gen. Shanshal looked over at us and saw that Gen. Muzahim and I were talking seriously about something, but he didn't say anything. Then, after a moment, I looked at him and raised my hand. Gen. Shanshal nodded at me and said, "Yes, Georges. Do you have something to say?" I said, "Yes, sir. I have many things to say."

He said, "Is it going to be substantially different from the presentation we've just heard from the air force?" At that point I knew Shanshal understood that everything Muzahim's spokesman had said was ridiculous. So I said, "Yes, sir, it's 180 degrees different."

Gen. Shanshal said, "Yes, okay, Georges. Please go ahead." So I stood up and walked to the front of the room. As I looked at each of the men seated around the table, I said, "I want to give you this presentation because I was ordered to do an analysis to find out the answers to three questions. First, what is the capability of the enemy air force? Second, what is the destructive capability and accuracy of their cruise missiles? And third, what is the operational capability of the five aircraft carriers stationed in the Persian Gulf and the Red Sea? And I want you to know that the information I will share with you now has been provided to me by Gen. Sabir, who, as you all know, is commander of the intelligence service of the military."

I realized that if I were to give these officers my assessment based only on my own knowledge, they wouldn't believe it and they wouldn't trust me. But if I let them know that everything I'd discovered was based on information I'd been given by our intelligence officers, then they would know it wasn't just my opinion but the official assessment of our best military analysts.

When I began, I decided I would use the same examples that Gen. Muzahim had used. The first was fourteen aircraft coming from the west to target Iraq. According to the air force's presentation, all fourteen would be destroyed. How? He said 25 percent would be shot down in air-to-air combat, 25 percent would be shot down by surface-to-air missiles, 25 percent would be destroyed by anti-aircraft defenses, and only two would make it into Iraqi air space, and they wouldn't be able to acquire targets because of the flack and anti-aircraft fire in the air. So the result was no damage done.

My analysis was somewhat different. I said, "Of the fourteen aircraft in the example we've just heard, I can assure you that all fourteen will be able to penetrate our borders and carry out their strikes successfully. Why? Because these fighters will not be the first to come across. They will only come after the missiles have taken out the key targets. In addition, these aircraft will have support from AWACS Sentries overhead, giving them a detailed map of exactly what's happening on the ground and in the air around them, so they can maneuver and avoid hot spots.

"Many of them," I continued, "will be carrying HARM missiles. These weapons are designed to target radar. Which means that as soon as they detect a radar signal from any direction, they can follow the pulse of the radar to the point of origin and destroy the tracking station. And even if the technicians were to switch the radar off, the coordinates of the installation will already have been stored in the missile's computerized memory, and it will continue to its target and destroy it.

"Furthermore," I continued, "when these fourteen aircraft have destroyed our tracking radar, the Iraqi fighters will be unable to scramble because, for all practical purposes, they will be blind. They will have no way of seeing the enemy aircraft they're expected to engage until it's too late.

"Any Iraqi fighter that engages in air-to-air combat under those circumstances," I said, "will be a sitting duck for coalition pilots. They won't have a chance. You should also know that the American Tomcat fighters have a forward-scanning radar with a range of more than 150 miles, while our best scanning radar can see no more than 15 miles ahead. And the Tomcat has the capability of scanning twenty-four targets at a time, and then firing on six targets simultaneously with pinpoint accuracy. If the coalition aircraft go up," I told them, "they will penetrate our borders. And if they penetrate our borders, you can be sure they will hit their targets."

A War of Words

When I paused for questions, I could see that nobody liked what I'd said. One of them, who was chief of staff of the army, growled at me, "Georges, are you trying to frighten us?" I said, "No, sir. I'm not trying to frighten you. I'm telling you the truth according to the best of my knowledge." He hadn't expected anyone to answer him back; these men were accustomed to intimidating people with their outbursts. But I was certain we were going to be attacked, and it would have been immoral not to warn them. So I persisted.

Since there were no more questions, I decided to talk about a topic that had often been mentioned by Saddam. He had said many times that, more than anything, he wanted to destroy an American aircraft carrier. He didn't have any idea how difficult that would be, but Saddam was never dissuaded by facts. The chances of our getting anywhere within striking distance of a U.S. carrier were non-existent. Unfortunately, some of our commanders thought of an aircraft carrier the way they thought of a fishing boat. They had no idea that a carrier is, in fact, a floating city—a heavily armed and dangerous floating city.

But when I explained what a carrier can do, its size, the armaments of the warships that accompany it, and all the weapons she could carry, most of these men were amazed. I told them, "If you want to attack an aircraft carrier, you'll have to send at least ninety-seven fighter jets against it, knowing that ninety-six of them will be destroyed before they get close." I had said the same thing to Saddam in a previous briefing—that we could lose as many as ninety-six fighters for the slight chance that one might get through—and he was ready to do it anyway, even at the cost of so many lives. That was how much he cared about his men.

As I continued, I told the generals that when a carrier's radar detects an enemy aircraft coming from a certain direction, the captain can initiate an automatic weapons release program that will detect incoming rockets and destroy them in flight, from sea level up to three thousand feet above the surface. By contrast, our best rocket, the Exocet missile, was not very large, and even if one of them were to hit the armored shoulder of an American carrier, it would have about as much effect as a house fly scratching the shoulder of an elephant.

This made Gen. Hussein al-Rashid, who was a relative of Saddam, very angry. He scowled at me and said, "Okay, Georges. What's the solution? What are we going to do?" I said, "The solution is very simple. We sent the army into Kuwait with a piece of paper and we can bring them back out with a piece of paper. President Bush said that if we withdraw our forces before January 15, nothing will happen." And then I added, "Unless we're prepared to go to war with America, we should order our forces to withdraw immediately."

The minute I said that, it was like a bomb had gone off in the room. Somebody yelled at me, "Georges, you've said that one time, but if you ever say it again your head will be separated from your body!" I said, "For God's sake, let my head be separated from my body, but at least let my nation live! If we insist on staying in Kuwait, believe me, this country will be destroyed." Everybody heard what I said, and to this day they remember it. Many of the men in the room that day are dead now, and many more are incarcerated, awaiting their trials. But in their prison cells, I'm sure they hear my words echoing in their minds again and again, because I was speaking the truth, and they all knew it.

Nevertheless, someone said, "Okay, Georges. We hear you, but we want you to stop now." So I stopped. Gen. Muzahim looked at me and said, "Georges, I don't know why you always have to speak this way. Your words are so harsh; can't you speak words that are a little softer?" I said, "No, sir. I cannot speak softer. It's the other way around. As much as we're able, we ought to explain our situation to the people of Iraq, because I'm not making these things up. Everything I've told you is the truth, and you know it. This is precisely what's going to happen if we don't withdraw our soldiers now."

I could see that he wanted to end the conversation, but I added, "General, you have an army of a million men, and they're all deployed in the south, either in Kuwait, Basra, or other places. And these are the boys who are going to take the brunt of it when the Americans come. As generals, the least we can do is tell them the truth." But Gen. Muzahim wasn't listening anymore. In his head, much like Saddam, he was convinced the attack would never come.

Selective Amnesia

Before going to that meeting, I had prayed silently, *God, please help me to speak plainly and tell the truth. I will tell them everything, and then I will gladly accept whatever happens to me.* The thought of lying to our troops, lying to our pilots, and lying to the nation was more than I could stand. It was as if all our commanders had selective amnesia. If nobody was willing to stand up and speak the truth, then there was no hope for us. I'm convinced God heard that prayer, and he gave me the courage to say it. On my own, I'm not that brave. It's not easy to swim against the current when everyone else is pretending that everything is going to be okay.

I'd been brought back out of retirement and put back in uniform on the grounds that I was to observe and advise the general staff on everything, but I was told I would have no command authority. I was not a member of the party like everyone else in the room. So how was I chosen to speak about things no one else dared to address? I don't know that anything like it had ever happened in Iraq before that day. But as I stood there in that room, I realized that I'd been given a very special privilege, and I was determined to fulfill my duty with honor.

There's a saying in Arabic, "Don't be a mute Satan." It means, if you have important information that may help someone in a difficult situation, say something. Don't be a devil and keep silent when you can say something to help. And you know, if I'd failed to warn them about the risks to our military, they would certainly remember after the invasion, and then they could come to me and say, "Georges, why didn't you tell us what you knew?" They didn't like what I had to say that day, but they could never accuse me of keeping my mouth shut when I knew that all our armed forces would be at risk.

I'm convinced it was Jesus who gave me the courage to say what I had to say. And today everyone knows that when the time came to speak, only one man told them the truth, because the invasion did come and everything happened just as I'd said it would. But there were two big problems with their way of thinking. First, Saddam had spread the idea that we didn't have to worry because nobody was going to attack us. But it was also because, as I've said repeatedly, when Saddam wanted two plus two to be nine, then they would gladly say it was nine.

I didn't do that, and I didn't stop with my assessment of the air war. I also told them about the aircraft carriers, the cruise missiles, the long-range artillery, and all the other weapons that the Americans could use against us. And in the middle of this, Gen. Al-Rashid interrupted me again and said, "Georges, don't you think that you're exaggerating the capabilities of the Americans and the accuracy of their weapons?"

The question made me angry and I didn't have any respect for this man. He was younger than I was and he'd been given higher rank simply because he was a relative of Saddam. So when I answered him, I didn't call him "sir." I just said, "No, I'm not exaggerating. What

I've told you is exactly correct. This is the capability of the weapons, and believe me, the coalition forces know how to use them." I knew what was going to happen just three days from that day, so there was no need to be polite. But I said to everyone in the room, "If you have any other questions, I will be happy to answer them." But there were no more questions.

Before we left the room, I told them one more thing. I said, "I want you to know that everything I've told you is from the intelligence given to me by my brother, Gen. Sabir, the head of military intelligence." Gen. Sabir was sitting there quietly, so I looked over at him, but he didn't say a word. He knew that what I had said was correct.

Removing the Impediment

There was to be another meeting on January 14, one day before the deadline set by the United Nations, and this time it was to be in Saddam's operations room. He had sent orders that all the field commanders were to be there, and we were supposed to do our presentations for him. This would be the last presentation before the action deadline.

But as I was preparing my remarks the night before, I received a phone call from the air force headquarters, and they said President Saddam had chosen me for a special mission. I was to fly to Mosul on the morning of the fourteenth to make a presentation to the Jordanian pilots who had joined the joint fighter squadron. They were being called back to their bases and were preparing to leave Iraq that day to return home to Amman.

About a year earlier, Jordan and Iraq had reached an agreement to create a series of national squadrons—meaning, basically, that they were to be defenders of the "Arab nations." The plan was for each squadron to be made up of ten Iraqi pilots and ten Jordanians. The aircraft would be Iraqi, but the pilots would come from both countries. At that time we had two of these squadrons, but on the evening of the thirteenth, King Hussein ordered a C-130 Hercules transport to be sent from Jordan to pick up his pilots and bring them home the next day. For me, this was one more indication that something big was about to happen.

King Hussein had always maintained close ties with the West, and he knew what was coming. He didn't want his young pilots to be in harm's way, and that's why he ordered them to return home immediately. This only made my suspicions of an imminent attack that much more certain. The king obviously knew something that Saddam didn't know, or didn't want to believe. In the meantime, I was told, Saddam had decided that he wanted me to go and meet the pilots before they departed. I was to thank them for their service in Iraq, and then to present each one with a handsome new pistol—a special gift from President Saddam. When they called me from the command center, they said that Saddam had told them, "I need one good, high-ranking officer to go and represent me."

They said I would be taken in Saddam's personal airplane, which was a nine-passenger JetStar with all the most luxurious amenities. Saddam's Republican Flight Command maintained four aircraft that were used solely by the president. But at Saddam's order, they sent a car to drive me to the airfield. When I got to Saddam's four-engine plane sitting on the tarmac, they said, "Gen. Sada, you are the obvious one to take these pistols and make the presentations to the pilots." And they loaded on-board the boxes containing all those weapons, in the passenger section.

I was glad to take the twenty pistols and present them to the Jordanian pilots, but I was disappointed that I wouldn't be there for the big presentation to Saddam. I was anxious to do my presentation because I had put together three large files covering the issues I'd been researching for several months. But it was obvious that the army and air force commanders didn't want me to be there because they knew I would tell Saddam the truth. I'd have to say that two plus two is four, and that's the last thing they wanted him to hear.

So I made the trip to Mosul and I took with me one of my former students, Staff Colonel Riadh Abdul Majid al-Tikriti, who happened to be from Tikrit. In fact, he was a relative of Saddam, but I told him that I didn't want to go to Mosul alone and it would be good if he would accompany me. He would have a chance to meet the pilots when I made the official presentations before they boarded their aircraft and headed back to Amman. So that's what we did.

We flew there, met the pilots, and had a nice dinner. The base commander had arranged a big farewell dinner for the Jordanians, and that's where I made the presentations. I thanked them on behalf of the president for the year they'd spent with us in the new national squadron program. Then, afterward, they boarded their C-130 and left.

A Return to Reality

When I got back to Baghdad, I went straight to the operations room at headquarters. As soon as I walked in, several of the young officers pulled me aside and said, "Gen. Sada, the meeting with Saddam was much worse than the one you attended on the twelfth. They lied to him even more than before, and no one dared say a word."

They had even told Saddam that our technicians had modified a large number of surface-to-surface rockets to make them capable of surface-to-air strikes on the American AWACS and B-117 Stealth aircraft. Of course, this was absolutely absurd. There were no weapons in our arsenal that could come close to either one of those high-altitude aircraft. But this was the time when Saddam went on national TV and told the people, "No Iraqi needs to be afraid of 'Stealth' airplanes. We have the weapons to destroy them."

I asked the officers, "Who did that?" and they told me it was Gen. Yaseen. So I went to see that man and I asked him, "General Yaseen, can you please explain to me how you plan to destroy the AWACS Sentry aircraft and B-117 Stealth bombers capable of flying at more than thirty thousand feet with your modified surface-to-air rockets?"

Of course, he couldn't answer me, and he didn't try. This was a lie concocted for the benefit of Saddam. So instead of answering, he said, "Georges, why are you always so negative? They all loved my presentation, and President Saddam was very happy with the things I told him." I just shook my head and left the room. This was the mentality of the people whom Saddam had surrounded himself with.

I was certain it was only a matter of time until we would be hit by rockets and missiles, as well as many other weapons the coalition aircraft could throw at us. I was sure of it. But the fifteenth came and went, and nothing happened. I must say, I was more than a little bit surprised. The next day it appeared that I had been wrong, and by that time everybody in the air force was laughing at me. Some of the officers who had been at the briefings where I had spoken so force-fully began making fun of me: "Georges, you told us we'd be hit by the Americans, didn't you? Where are the bombs, General?"

Some of the officers started calling me General Catalog, because I had all the facts and figures, like a catalog, and they knew I didn't like to go into any operation without a wide assortment of substantial and reliable intelligence data. Of course, I was embarrassed that I had spoken so confidently about the impending attack by the Americans when, in fact, nothing happened. I was beginning to look foolish to everyone, and I was feeling very bad about it.

I went around to all the officers on the general staff and apologized for my mistake. I said, "Gentlemen, I'm sorry. I looked at all the evidence and analyzed the intelligence data that was given to me by Gen. Sabir, and I was certain we would be hit. It looks like I was wrong, and I'm sorry if I upset you." I made a particular point of going to see Gen. Muzahim, the air force commander, and I said, "Sir, I'm sorry. I was wrong and you were right. But I hope you know that I truly believed we were going to be hit. All the factors I examined told me we were going to be hit."

I told him, "The foreign press, intelligence data, everything pointed to the same conclusion. But, frankly, I must say I'm glad I was wrong about that. At least the country is safe." And then I added, "But please, tell the young officers to stop making fun of me. It's not wise for these men to make fun of a general, especially since I was doing my best and offering you the best information I could give you about the threat of an invasion." General Muzahim shook my hand and gave me a pat on the shoulder, and he agreed to tell the young men to leave me alone.

Mixed Messages

I was 100 percent certain there would be an attack, and that was the message I was trying to convey. Unfortunately, most of my colleagues had decided that Saddam had worked a deal with the Americans under the table. They said that American forces had come to the Gulf to make a show of force, to show the world they didn't like what we did in Kuwait. But, in fact, there was an agreement between Saddam and the American ambassador. Everybody knew that Saddam would be free to do whatever he liked, and the Americans would never intervene.

Those who recall the meeting between Saddam and Ambassador April Glaspie will remember what happened. It was televised to the entire world by satellite. And in Iraq, everybody knew what Glaspie had said. She told Saddam, "We have no opinion on your Arab versus Arab conflicts, such as your dispute with Kuwait. Secretary Baker has directed me to emphasize the instruction, first given to Iraq in the 1990s, that the Kuwait issue is not associated with America." It couldn't have been clearer. An American ambassador had told an Iraqi dictator that he could do whatever he liked, and what he liked at that moment was transforming Kuwait into the nineteenth province of Iraq.

The day the film of that meeting appeared on Iraqi television, copies were made and sent to every commander in the field. And when they saw it, they understood the message, and they were enthusiastic to get busy and carry out the president's orders. There were some commanders who thought that Glaspie had been sent by President Bush to trick us. In other words, the Americans had already decided they were going to attack Iraq, so they were telling Saddam to go ahead and do whatever he was going to do so they could turn the coalition forces loose on us. Honestly, I didn't know what to think of that, but I saw what Ambassador Glaspie had said, and I was certain she wasn't warning Saddam that he had to stop immediately and get out of Kuwait.

On the day I reported for duty, after being reinstated as an adviser to the general staff, I was prepared to do whatever I could to serve my country in a time of great difficulty and stress. But I didn't need to be in the military to know what was about to happen. I understood that if we didn't leave Kuwait right away, we were going to be hit by the Americans. I was sure of it, and I was telling everybody who would listen those first few days that the only way to avoid war with the West was to stop where we were, get out of Kuwait, and bring our forces home.

I was worried what would happen to my country and my people if Saddam didn't listen to reason, but he wasn't worried in the least. Saddam wasn't concerned about the consequences to Iraq if this adventure failed. He had said that if anything ever happened to him, or if he were no longer president, then why should he care what happened to Iraq? I had heard him say it many times: "If anybody ever comes to take this country from me, I will not give it to them the way it is now. I'll give it to them completely destroyed!" He had even said it on national television, and every Iraqi knew it.

There was no point in trying to reason with such a man. And it seemed no one in Iraq was willing to try.

CHAPTER 6

THE CONSEQUENCES OF WAR

The years between the Iran-Iraq War and the first Gulf War were two of the sweetest I can ever remember. The fighting had ended in the north and the invasion of Kuwait had not yet begun. We were so glad to be done with fighting, but then in 1990 things started escalating all over again. Saddam was saying that Kuwait was stealing our oil, drilling slanted wells into our underground reservoirs. No one in Iraq cared about that; surely there was enough for everyone. But then Saddam started saying, "Of course, Kuwait actually belongs to us. It's not a separate country but the nineteenth province of Iraq."

That may have been true a hundred years earlier, before the British partitioned the land. Centuries before that, all the Arab lands in the Middle East belonged to the Assyrians, but you can't throw out history and diplomacy just because you covet your neighbor's territory. History changes things, and there's no going back. But Saddam was only looking for an excuse to start another war, and Kuwait, which was one of the richest countries in the world, had become the object of his affections.

Part of Saddam's argument was that Kuwait had been dumping oil on the world market in such large quantities that it was forcing down the price of Iraqi oil. At that time Iraq was shipping 3.5 million barrels a day, but the price had dropped so much that Saddam estimated he had lost at least $10 billion. He said it was the Kuwaiti's fault and they would have to pay Iraq the difference.

The debate escalated to the point that each of the countries involved determined that they would have to send representatives to meet in Saudi Arabia for a conference to air their differences and come to a fair settlement. Saddam decided to send his deputy, Izzat al-Douri. Prince Abdullah would be the representative of the Saudi monarch, King Fahd, and Sheikh Saad would represent his own country, Kuwait. The story of the encounter in Riyadh is striking, to say the least, and the account which follows is what happened as it was related later to me.

The meeting was set for July 31 and August 1 of 1990. But before Izzat al-Douri left for Riyadh, Saddam spoke to him privately and told him, "Look, Izzat, whatever you do, I don't want you to accept their offer. No matter what happens, make sure that you find a way to refuse any settlement Sheik Saad offers you."

So Izzat al-Douri went to Riyadh with that message firmly planted in his mind, and as soon as the conversation began the first words out of his mouth were, "Sheik Saad, I demand that you pay my government $10 billion in cash." It was a strange way to begin a discussion, but that's how it began. There was much discussion and debate, and Al-Douri was asked to explain his demand. But eventually Sheik Saad told him, "Okay, Mr. Al-Douri. I agree to your demand, but we will not pay you $10 billion. We will pay only $9 billion."

The Deal Breaker

That was certainly a lot of money, even for Kuwait. But the reason Sheik Saad refused to pay the full amount had nothing to do with the size of the demand. It had to do with saving face—or the Arab tradition of *sukrah*, which means that the bargainer was not defeated in the negotiation because he was able to strike a better deal.

However, Al-Douri refused his offer, because this was exactly what he wanted to happen. He shoved his chair back noisily from the table and said, "Okay, Sheik Saad. If you will not pay the full $10 billion, then I suppose we have your answer. I hope you know that this conversation is now finished and I'm leaving."

Prince Abdullah, who was the Saudi crown prince at that time, succeeded his half-brother as king in 2005, and he had been watching everything very closely. When he realized that Izzat al-Douri was going to leave without resolving the matter, he said, "Stop, stop! Please, gentlemen, sit down. If you will give me a moment, I want to speak to His Majesty, the king," and he made a telephone call to the palace to tell King Fahd what was happening.

He said, "Majesty, the two parties are agreed that Kuwait should pay Iraq $10 billion. But Sheik Saad will not pay so much. He will pay only $9 billion. What shall we do?" Without a moment's hesitation, the king said, "Tell the Iraqi that I will pay the $1 billion, and tell him I will call Saddam Hussein myself this very minute. And I will tell him that an airplane will be on its way to Baghdad within the hour with $1 billion in cash."

There was the money that Al-Douri had demanded, nine billion from Kuwait and one billion from Saudi Arabia. Everyone knew this was nothing but extortion by Saddam Hussein, but they didn't want to give the tyrant any more excuses to cause trouble. Sheik Saad was content, and to seal their agreement he suggested that they all join hands and drink a toast—a glass of juice or tea or whatever was available—to celebrate their success.

But as they were walking the thirty feet from the meeting room to the table where glasses and beverages had been arranged, Sheik Saad said, "Well, Mr. Al-Douri, I think we are both satisfied now, and it's finished. But I hope you won't come back to me six months from now and complain about the borders between our two countries as you've done so many times in the past. We are agreed now, and everything is settled between us."

He should have known better than to bring up this old dispute, but no doubt those words were just what Al-Douri had been hoping for. He was terrified that he would have to go back to Baghdad and tell Saddam he had accepted the sheik's offer—especially since Saddam had sent his cousin, the notorious "Chemical Ali," as a member of the delegation, to observe and report on everything that happened. Izzat al-Douri may have gotten the $10 billion, but Saddam was going to eat him alive. First, Saddam would humiliate him; he would say, "Look, you ice seller! Didn't I tell you to find a way not to agree with those people? And you've disobeyed my orders! Do you know what I do to people who disobey my orders?" But now that conversation would never happen, because Sheik Saad had given Izzat al-Douri the perfect pretext.

So he said, "Oh, no, Sheik Saad. Please don't speak to me about borders! That's another matter altogether. That has nothing to do with this! And you know very well that we must settle the border problem before there will ever be peace between us."

Sheik Saad stopped dead in his tracks. He couldn't believe that Al-Douri was doing this after he and King Fahd had agreed to pay Iraq such a handsome settlement. So he said, "Mr. Al-Douri, what are you saying? We've just given you $10 billion to settle this matter, and you still want to argue about borders?"

Al-Douri shook his head and yelled back at him, "Okay, Sheik Saad, forget about it! I see what you are doing now." He made himself appear to be very angry, but on the inside he was laughing, knowing that he would now be able to go back and tell Saddam that he had accomplished everything just as he'd been instructed to do. So Izzat al-Douri quickly gathered the members of his delegation and said, "Gentlemen, this meeting is over now, and I'm leaving." And that was it.

The meeting finished late in the evening and Izzat al-Douri arrived back in Baghdad sometime after one o'clock on the morning of August 2, 1990. As soon as he stepped down from the plane, the first thing he did was call Saddam at the palace and tell him, "Sir, everything is fine. We didn't agree."

Saddam was delighted, and he said, "Izzat, as always, you are the faithful one. This is very good news, indeed!" Then Saddam put down one telephone and picked up another that was connected to the operations center at the Iraqi base south of Basra, where his field commander, Gen. Hussein al-Majid, was waiting. When Gen. Hussein picked up the phone, Saddam told him, "Hussein, let the boys get in." That's all he said, and with those reprehensible words, the invasion of Kuwait began.

A Pretext for War

Hussein Kamel Hassan al-Majid was Saddam's son-in-law, married to his oldest daughter Raghad. Saddam had made him minister of defense, minister of industry, and a half dozen others, including the minister of oil. When he hung up from speaking to the president, Hussein al-Majid reached for the telephone and called the commander of his helicopter squadron. He barked into the phone,

"General, how many helicopters did I tell you to have ready?" The commander answered, "One hundred helicopters, sir." Hussein said, "Are they ready?" And the answer came back, "Yes, sir. They're ready." Then Hussein told him, "Let them fly."

The commander did have his helicopters and pilots ready, mechanically at least. But he hadn't anticipated that they would have to fly at night. So in response to Hussein al-Majid's order to let them fly, he said, "But, sir, not all our pilots are trained for night flying."

Hussein's anger flashed suddenly, and he yelled back, "What do you mean they're not trained to fly at night? What's the difference between night and day? I can drive my Mercedes in the nighttime as well as I can in the daytime. So why can't you fly a helicopter at night?" This is how ignorant this untrained military commander was of operational logistics. He had never held rank higher than a corporal in the army. But because he was Saddam's son-in-law, he was suddenly a general in charge of an invasion, and he didn't know the difference between driving a car and flying a helicopter at night.

Unfortunately, that wasn't all he didn't know. He also didn't know the way to Kuwait. He hadn't seen the maps and didn't know which way the pilots were supposed to go. The Iraqi pilots had not been briefed on obstacles they would encounter or when to fly low level and when to go higher and gain altitude. Because they had no idea what was ahead of them, and because they had little or no experience with night flying, we lost forty-seven helicopters and four attack fighters that night.

Why did we lose them? Because pilots without proper training, briefing, or equipment crossed the border at low level and flew straight into the high tension wires that ran parallel to the Kuwaiti border. Each helicopter was carrying between sixteen and twenty-four commandos, and all of them were lost.

Another group of helicopters was lost while attempting to locate and destroy the Kuwaiti radio and television station. In each helicopter they had a local guide to show them the way to the station, but these Arabs who knew the way on the ground in daylight had absolutely no idea what they were looking at from a helicopter at night. So they kept circling, looking right, left, up, and down, flying from one place to the next, trying to find the station. Then, as dawn approached, Kuwaiti machine gunners were able to pick them off one by one.

At least 50 percent of the Iraqi aircraft sent into Kuwait were lost in the first hours of the assault because of the stupidity of our commanders. And the situation on the ground was just as bad. Whenever a modern army prepares for battle, there are supposed to be operational orders—called "ops orders" in military shorthand—that provide details on the route and methods of attack, the types of weapons and equipment to be used, the number of men to be deployed in each area, and clear descriptions of the objectives. And most good plans will also have a Plan B, or an alternate objective, in case the offensive runs into unexpected obstacles or resistance.

But our ops orders went like this: "Hussein, let the boys get in." That was it. First, Iraqi jets came and attacked the two airfields so that the Kuwaiti jets couldn't take off. This was followed by a ground assault led by the Republican Guard. There were four columns of tanks, trucks, and armored personnel carriers (APCs) all jammed up together—thousands of military vehicles—going into Kuwait. The main road was so full of cars, trucks, and tanks that it soon became a huge traffic jam.

But not all the Kuwaiti pilots were stopped by the bombing. One of them, Staff Colonel Mohammed Mubarak Sultan Mubarak, managed to get one fully armed A-4 Skyhawk off the airfield and onto a service road. By some miracle, he was able to take off and avoid the automatic weapons fire coming at him. Once he was airborne, he immediately attacked all four columns of Iraqi vehicles with anti-tank rockets and machine guns, and before it was over he had destroyed thirty-eight tanks with their carriers, dozens of cars, trucks, and APCs, and killed hundreds of soldiers.

After that, the Kuwaiti flew to Dharan and remained there until the beginning of the air war, on January 17, 1991. Not long after that he was shot down and taken prisoner, and that's when I met him. When Saddam found out about his actions, he insisted that Col. Mubarak was a war criminal and demanded that he be killed, but I couldn't help but admire the courage and skill of this brave and resourceful pilot. Even though I was an officer in the Iraqi Air Force, I was impressed by the tenacity of any pilot who refused to be stopped by a damaged runway. After the war, he was released and he returned to his country. From there he went on to serve on the staff of the American commander, Gen. John Abizaid, in Qatar.

Punish, Pillage, and Destroy

When the Iraqi forces entered Kuwait, they didn't just go in, take over the palace, and declare a military victory. Because of the hatred that had been stirred up by Saddam, the soldiers went in as thieves, looters, robbers, and rapists, and they did their best to destroy the whole country. They stole everything they could get their hands on from government buildings, shops, stores, and especially private homes. They took currency, gold, jewels, furniture, clothing, automobiles, personal items, and everything that wasn't nailed down.

Furthermore, Saddam had issued an order to the ministers of all departments of the government saying that each of them was to go and confiscate everything they could carry from the Kuwaiti ministry in their area—including everything that was nailed down. In other words, the Iraqi minister of education was to take everything from the Kuwaiti ministry of education—furniture, files, computers, books, financial records, everything. Doctors and dentists did the same, taking operating tables, dentist chairs, hospital beds, and even the bed pans. And they took boxes of Korans from the Islamic Ministry to give to the citizens of Baghdad.

How are such things possible? Because Saddam was so full of hatred, jealousy, and the lust for revenge against a nation that had only helped him—giving him money, access to a deep-water port, and so much more. Saddam set out from the first to make the Iraqi soldiers hate the Kuwaitis, and he had even told them that Kuwaiti soldiers were saying they could buy the favors of any Iraqi woman for five dinars. He said this because he knew such insults would incite the men to greater acts of violence.

It was not a clean war. It was not a war to reclaim territory or to settle an old dispute. It was a war to punish, pillage, and destroy—all to satisfy Saddam's evil desires. I wasn't called back to active duty until after the invasion had begun, so I wasn't aware of any of this at the time. But when I began to review action reports and human intelligence about what had actually happened during the rape of Kuwait, I felt angry, and I also felt guilty for my country. There's no question our army made mistakes—strategically, tactically, and every other way you can think of. But, worst of all, they were not performing like the professional soldiers they once had been.

And the stupidest thing of all from a military standpoint was that Saddam and his commanders concentrated the entire Iraqi Army, the entire reserve, and the entire popular army on the Kuwaiti border, on the farthest southern border of the country more than 350 miles from the capital. By doing that, he left the entire nation undefended. So I asked, "What happens if somebody decides to attack us from Syria or Jordan?" And the answers I got were disturbing.

Within forty-eight hours we were no longer fighting only in Kuwait; we were fighting the entire world. And it was escalating rapidly. The United Nations immediately condemned what Saddam had done, and the world's only superpower, America, condemned the invasion as well. Great Britain and other European countries were threatening that if our army didn't leave Kuwait immediately, there would be war on a much bigger scale. If any of them had decided to send troops at that time, all of Iraq would have been entirely undefended.

Saddam was not a stupid man. As I've said many times, he was a genius at doing evil. But how do you explain such a strategic blunder, concentrating all of our manpower and material in one place at one time? The only answer that makes any sense is that Saddam was convinced that Ambassador April Glaspie had given him carte blanche to invade Kuwait and do whatever he pleased. If your aim was to punish, pillage, and destroy a nation, and you believed there was no one to stop you, then there was no need to keep even one soldier in reserve.

Everyone I spoke to, every commander and every soldier in the field, was convinced they had nothing to worry about. They said, "Georges, please don't worry! It's all prepared. Nobody will come and ask for Kuwait, and nobody will attack Iraq." And this was their belief right up to January 17, 1991, when the American attack began. No one had ever considered withdrawing even a small part of our army to defend the rest of the country. And that was perhaps the biggest blunder of all.

A Rude Awakening

When I made my presentation to the generals on January 12, as I described earlier, I had told them the capabilities of American warships, aircraft carriers, and related weapons. They asked me, "So, Georges, what's the solution?" and I told them, "Get out of Kuwait. That's the only solution." But they didn't listen. So when I arrived at the command center on January 16, which was the day after the United Nations' mandate expired, I was still anticipating an attack of some kind. Consequently, I planned to stay and monitor communications as long as I was needed, and I would try to sleep a few hours here and there on a couch or a cot in one of the offices.

When the air force commander, Gen. Muzahim, saw what I was planning to do, he said, "Georges, I want you to have my apartment." A few years earlier, when he was still a pilot, I had been Muzahim's commanding officer. By the time I came back to active duty, however, he was my superior officer. But he remembered that I was senior to him and treated me with respect. His apartment in the command center was small, but it had a sitting room, a bedroom with a small bed, and a bathroom and shower. It was modest but comfortable, and it was ideal for someone involved in long planning sessions in the operations center.

I thought this gesture, offering me the apartment, was a sign of respect, but I said, "Sir, this is your apartment and you should have it." But Muzahim interrupted me and said, "Georges, no. I would be very happy if you would just use the apartment. You deserve it and, besides, I would be glad if you stayed near the operations center so you can monitor communications and stay on top of what's happening in the field."

I said, "Okay, sir, I understand," and I agreed to sleep there and continue my work in the operations center. After that conversation, I went back to the communications room, and worked there for the rest of the night until well past midnight. I finally rolled into bed at 1:30 on the morning of the seventeenth, without bothering to take off my uniform. I went right to sleep, but at precisely 2:30 I woke up from a sound sleep. I looked at my watch and thought, *I ought to go and check on Col. Bahnam in the communications room and see what's happening down there.*

Col. Bahnam was a good man, and he happened to be a fellow Christian. I thought it would be a good idea to speak to him and find out if anything was showing up on the radar, or on the radio from the bases in the south. So I got up and walked quickly down the corridor to the communications center to find out the news. I didn't anticipate that there would be anything special to report, but, for some reason I just felt I ought to go down there and check it out.

Our radar had been tracking movement around the clock, and there was always a chance the duty officer would know something from Kuwait, from the Gulf, or elsewhere on the Iraqi borders. But at the exact moment I entered the communications room, the earth began shaking under my feet. There was a series of muffled explosions—boom, boom, boom—at least three of them in rapid succession, followed by violent aftershocks, like an earthquake on the surface above us.

I knew what it was: we were being hit. But then, all of a sudden, the very next explosion struck the command center where I was standing. It was such a tremendous explosion it rocked the whole building and knocked out the power instantly. I was knocked off my feet, but when the emergency generators came on, all I could see was sparks flying in every direction. Electrical wires had been ripped out of the walls, and there was fire and smoke shooting in every direction.

I got to my feet and ran back down the hall toward the apartment where I'd been sleeping just moments before. Water was spraying out of the pipes like geysers, and electricity was arcing overhead between the severed power lines. Suddenly the air was full of dust and debris and smoke, and I knew it was time to get out of there while I still could. It was a nightmare, like a scene from hell. We were still able to move around, as we tried to find out the condition of our equipment. But there was total chaos and confusion in the bunker.

Someone told me later that ABC news anchor Peter Jennings was conducting an interview with a correspondent in Baghdad when the rockets hit. Looking out the window of his room at the Al Rashid Hotel, the reporter told Jennings he saw flashes of light coming from the Al Mansour district, and he said, "It's like fireworks on the Fourth of July, multiplied by a hundred!" It must have been an awesome sight, but whatever the viewers were seeing on TV in America from the safety of their homes thousands of miles away, I can assure you, it paled in comparison to what we were seeing inside that bunker in the middle of the attack.

Seventeen Seconds to Eternity

The moment the bombs hit, I knew what was happening, and I also knew I hadn't been wrong after all. I had only been wrong about the date. Ironically, one of the first missiles to strike Baghdad had come close enough to kill me and everyone else in the command center. It was only by the grace of God that I'm alive to tell this story.

When I surveyed the damage, I realized that the first missile had hit right in the middle of that little apartment where I'd been sleeping. To be more precise, it hit my bed. One of the first bombs to fall on Baghdad went right through the place where I'd been lying just seconds earlier. It came through the building, penetrated the concrete reinforcements, and exploded in the very spot where I would have been lying if I hadn't woken up in time.

If I had been in that bed, I would never have known what hit me. Slabs of concrete were thrown around like toys, and one of them was lying on top of the crumpled bed frame. No one could have survived such a hit. But, thank God, I woke up and decided to go to the radio room to see what was going on. I know now that this was no accident: I'm convinced that God woke me up and sent me to safety. That's the only thing that could have saved my life.

Ironically, my first thought when I heard the explosions was, *Aha, I was right after all! The Americans did attack.* But then I immediately thought, *Oh my God! My country is being destroyed.* And the sense of vindication that I felt for the briefest of moments was quickly replaced by concern for my fellow Iraqis who would be killed and whose homes would be destroyed that night.

When I made my way back down the corridor to see where the bomb had exploded, I checked my watch to see how long it took to walk from the apartment to the communications center—I wanted to see how soon after I'd left the room the bombs actually struck. It was precisely seventeen seconds from the bedroom to the radar room where I was standing when the explosion occurred. That's how close I had come to death that night—seventeen seconds.

As I began looking for the others, I said aloud, "Thank you, Jesus, for saving my life." Seconds later I heard someone yelling my name from down the corridor. They were saying, "Where's General Sada? Where's General Sada?" I walked toward the sound and I yelled, "Who's calling me? What do you want?" A young officer came running toward me and said, "Sir, the air chief wants to see you immediately."

I went with him down the hall to where the air force commander was standing, and he was clearly shaken. He said, "Georges, are you all right?" And I said, "Yes, sir. I'm okay." He said, "I heard that the apartment where you were sleeping was hit." And I said, "Yes, sir, that's right. It was destroyed by the bomb." He said, "But you weren't there?" And I said, "That's right. Something told me to go check on Col. Bahnam." He said, "And the apartment was destroyed?" I said, "Yes, sir. Everything. Totally destroyed."

As I spoke those words, we both realized how accurate the intelligence of the American pilots had been. They placed a laser-guided missile precisely in the place where the air force commander should have been sleeping. Later, of course, some of our pilots teased me about that, saying that Gen. Muzahim knew the Americans were going to hit his apartment, and that's why he gave it to me. Well, I don't know if the thought actually entered his mind, but he had been one of the loudest opponents of my report, boasting that we'd never be hit. So maybe there was some truth to that after all.

A Fateful Decision

The accuracy of the strike wasn't lost on anyone. And there was another explosion just as sobering immediately after the first one. At the far end of the bunker, there were two small closets that were each less than one meter square, and this was the place where all the cables for military communications were connected. They went from there to the telephone exchange, which was located in a bunker across the street, below ground. The same strike that destroyed the commander's apartment on one end of the building included two more rockets that hit those two cubicles, immediately knocking out all military communications.

And to make sure there would be no command and control coming from that place, the pilots placed, very precisely, three more bombs on the telephone exchange—one in the bunker below, and two more in the center of the building where the cables and junctions came together. At that point we had to go to our emergency backup systems, and they were old and unreliable. So in reality we had only makeshift communications after the first hour of the war.

As we were standing there in near darkness, Gen. Muzahim put his hand on my shoulder and said, "Thank God you're safe." But then he asked me in all seriousness, "Georges, what will we do now?"

It was all I could do to keep a straight face. "I'm sorry," I said, "there's nothing you can do now. It's too late. Surely you remember that I told you at the meeting on the twelfth that this was going to happen. Well, now it has happened. From this point on, there's nothing we can do. You can only listen to the reports coming in from all our installations around the country, and you'll discover that they're being knocked out, one by one.

"I'm sure," I continued, "that every single one of our command centers, in all five military sectors, will soon be reporting that they've been hit just as hard as we've been hit." It was about 2:33 a.m. at that time, just minutes after the first strike on our command bunker, but I knew that if the Americans had been able to target the communications center with such pinpoint accuracy, then they would know how to hit all the others as well.

Gen. Muzahim looked at me and said, "Okay, then we'll scramble the fighters!" I shook my head and said, "No, sir, don't do that. If you do, you'll lose them, I promise you. Either you'll lose them on the runway or you'll lose them in the air, because there's no radar and no communications for the pilots."

He said, "How do you know that, Georges?" I said, "Because the minute you turn on the radar, the HARM missiles will track down our radar stations and take them out. As soon as their sensors detect a live radar signal, they'll lock on and release the missiles that will destroy it. That's just what they're waiting for." Suddenly, Gen. Muzahim became very angry with me, and he yelled, "Georges, I won't accept that answer! How can you tell me not to do anything when the Americans are attacking us at this very minute? We've got to send up the fighters!"

So I said, "Sir, please listen to me. You're talking about sending up your best pilots, without radar support, in the middle of the night, with no plan of action. How many pilots do you have who are trained for that? In case you've forgotten, it's January, and the weather may be very bad up there. How many pilots do you have who know how to fly under these conditions, without radar, and in bad weather? And most of all, please remember who they'll be flying against. They'll be up against the best pilots, the best planes, the best AWACS Sentry aircraft overhead, and the best rockets. Plus, the Americans have the advantage of being out there already, just waiting for our pilots to show up. If you're smart, General, you won't do it!"

But he shook his head and said, "No. I won't accept that, Georges. We'll scramble our pilots." A few minutes later Gen. Muzahim gave the order to scramble the fighters, and they sent up eighteen of our best fighters. Most of them, I'm sad to say, were destroyed on the runway before they ever took off, and several were shot down as soon as they were in the air. Only one of our pilots, Capt. Zuhair, who was flying a MiG-25, flew a successful mission. Zuhair was the Iraqi pilot who shot down Navy Commander Scott Speicher.

Avoiding a Disaster

Saddam arrived at operations headquarters at 5:00 a.m., and he was fit to be tied. But I was really surprised he showed up so late. The first strike had come at 2:30 in the morning, and all of the general staff went immediately to the operations room to decide how to respond. It was essential that Saddam be there, since he was the one making all the decisions. But he didn't show up until two and a half hours after the bombardment began, by which time hundreds, and perhaps thousands, of key targets had already been hit.

It's possible, of course, that Saddam didn't really understand how quickly and how hard they were going to hit us, so he didn't feel the need to hurry. But, more likely it was because the missiles and rockets were so overwhelming that he didn't want to take the risk of coming across the city by car. By the time he arrived at the operations center, our hands were tied and there wasn't a lot we could do to defend ourselves.

Saddam called all the senior officers together, as he always did whenever he was involved in a critical operation. If you've seen films of those meetings on television, then you've seen the setup: Saddam in the middle with five generals around him. I was seated on his right, and on the left were the commander of the air force, the director of operations, the deputy air force commander for operations, and the training commander.

So there we were. We had been hit by cruise missiles and rockets, and it was obvious that the first strike had been incredibly precise. Even Saddam realized that the level of American intelligence was astonishing. They knocked out our primary radar and radio communications, and in a matter of minutes they managed to destroy some of the most sensitive targets in the country. He couldn't miss the significance of all that. But the first thing he did was to tell the air force commander to call off the attack on Israel. "It's too late now," he said, "and we have many other things to think about."

But then he turned to the air force commander and said, "Gen. Muzahim, tell me how it's possible that we were struck so hard without warnings of any kind. The air raid sirens didn't even go off! How could this happen?" When I looked over at Muzahim, I could see that he didn't know how to answer the question. He looked at me, and I knew he was pleading for me to answer for him. So I motioned to Saddam and said, "Sir, if I may, the sirens didn't sound because we weren't hit by aircraft. The first attacks were all by cruise missiles, and those weapons don't show up on our radar like an aircraft. The main characteristic of those missiles is that they present such a small radar image that it's almost impossible for defensive radar like ours to pick them up in time. In most cases we won't even see them until they hit us."

Saddam looked at Muzahim sternly, as if to say, "Why can't you answer my questions?" Many of our planes sitting on the runways had already been destroyed. If we tried to send up any more, it was very likely they would be destroyed as well. And, of course, that was true. On his way out of the building, Saddam mentioned to me that he had told Gen. Muzahim to call off the attack on Israel. I confirmed this later with Muzahim.

I was saddened by all this because I had done my best and nobody listened. We were attacked from every direction, from north to south. We were hit by F-111 aircraft in the north, by Tomahawk missiles from the Saratoga in the Red Sea, by cruise missiles from the carriers in the Gulf; and we were even hit by the B-117 Stealth bombers from high overhead—it was the first time these virtually invisible bombers had ever been used in actual combat.

I was thinking, *My God, what has happened to our country?* And I was also sad because when Saddam finally came, hours after the war had started, his first question was why the sirens didn't go off when the first bombs hit. That was all he could think about. The attacks were still going on, bombs and missiles were falling all over Baghdad, but Saddam wasn't worried about that. He wanted to know why the sirens hadn't gone off at the beginning.

But, fortunately, he wasn't finished yet. After calling off the attack on Israel, he called the army commanders and changed their orders too. Originally, he had wanted to send twelve armored and mechanized divisions into Saudi Arabia, and their orders were to destroy everything in their path for a distance of at least two-hundred miles.

From the borders of Kuwait to the city of Dharan, the army was instructed to wipe Saudi Arabia's industrial zone off the map. He wanted to destroy that complex of high-tech businesses because King Fahd had supported the American invasion and allowed coalition fighters to use his bases.

Scorched Earth

When you understand what Saddam actually had in mind for our Saudi neighbors, you can't help but see what a madman he was. Saddam was consumed by hatred, and he hated Saudi Arabia even more than he hated the Americans, because the Saudis had helped Kuwait. And in the end they had allowed American fighters to use Saudi bases. So Saddam decided that if he was going to be attacked by America, and possibly defeated, then he wanted to attack Saudi Arabia and do as much damage as possible before he was forced from power.

When he ordered the air force to prepare for the attack on Israel, he ordered an aerial assault on Saudi Arabia at the same time. But this would be different. The attack on Israel was to be carried out by the air force using chemical weapons. The first strike on Saudi Arabia would be carried out by Iraqi aircraft armed with tactical weapons, but it would be followed by a full-scale assault by armored and mechanized infantry. Ground forces were to go in after the air strikes with tanks, armored personnel carriers, and mechanized artillery. And then the air force would make a second strike on the capital, Riyadh—this time with chemical weapons.

The plan was to send twelve divisions of armor and infantry across the border, keeping one division in reserve. They would be going through Kuwait into Saudi Arabia, and he would hold back the reserve forces, safe inside the Iraqi border, to make sure they would be ready to fight when the time came. When he gave the order, they were supposed to go forward in three columns: one column on the highway, one along the coast, and one on the desert side. This was Saddam's strategy.

They were to cross the border at night and destroy the industrial area between Kuwait and Dharan, which is about two-hundred miles to the south. He was also thinking that we would transfer about 120 aircraft to the two airfields in Kuwait, Al-Sabah and Al-Salim, to provide close air support as these columns moved forward. At the same time there was another plan to send bombers on to Riyadh. The city of Riyadh is divided into two halves. On one side are the king, princes, and aristocrats, and on the other are the common people. Saddam said we didn't want to destroy the people, just their rulers, but this attack would be done with chemical weapons.

To be sure the plan to drop chemical weapons would actually work, he even had the air force do a series of test drops at the Al Kut Air Base in Iraq. The test weapons didn't actually contain chemical compounds, but the drop tanks were filled with a material that simulated what would happen. The idea was that in the actual strike on Riyadh an active agent would be added at the last minute, and when the spray was released it would create a toxic cloud that would disperse throughout the city, killing everyone in its path.

This would have been a terrible atrocity if it had happened, but this is what Saddam had in mind for the rulers of Saudi Arabia. Saddam knew there would be a strong reaction to this, but he was unconcerned. After all, he had dropped poison gas on the Kurds in 1983 and 1988 and nothing happened. So he had two Mirage fighters equipped and ready to fly the mission, but both planes were shot down by Saudi fighters at the start of the war before they could carry out their mission.

During the planning stages for the attacks, Saddam had the pilots and support crews brought in to see films showing the layout of Riyadh, where everything was located, both from the air and at ground level. I attended some of those sessions, and they showed films of the massive warehouses used by the Saudis for storage and shipment of parts for military equipment. They had very sophisticated computerized conveyer systems for delivering parts to the right place, and it was very impressive. But Saddam wanted to make sure those warehouses were totally destroyed.

When I learned of the plan, I asked the planners how they were going to carry out such a large operation without the benefit of air cover. I said the air force could provide air support for armor and infantry for about seventy-five miles inside the country but not for the remaining 210 miles to Dharan. The concentration of Saudi and American aircraft at that point would be much too great to go any further. Well, I soon discovered that Saddam couldn't have cared less about that. As far as he was concerned, it was a suicide mission. In fact, two of our Mirage fighters penetrated the Saudi border and were destroyed by Saudi F-15s, but Saddam wasn't the least concerned.

He didn't care if our soldiers or pilots came back alive so long as they destroyed everything in their path on the way to Dharan. And even more diabolical, he wanted Iraq to be destroyed as well. According to his twisted logic, if he was going to be defeated, then he wanted to make sure there would be nothing worth saving after he was gone. And all this was authorized by Saddam on December 17, 1990, on the same sheet of paper on which he wrote in Arabic that we would attack with the blessings of Allah. But, thank God, it never happened, because when we were hit one month later, he realized it was too late, and he cancelled both missions.

A New Assignment

As I had predicted, we weren't hit by aircraft in the first series of strikes. We were hit by missiles. A good plan of attack would be to strike first with precision missiles in the first wave and knock out radar and communications, damage airfields and runways, and disable the power grid. Then, in the second wave, the plan would be to send in F-117 "Nighthawk" Stealth fighters, which are almost invisible to radar, to hit key military targets and take out the command and control structures. And that's precisely what the American commanders did on the morning of January 17, 1991.

After achieving air superiority, coalition pilots were able to fly with almost no restraints, and this was why the air raid sirens never went off until they were switched on manually by our ground personnel. When I explained this to Saddam, he was totally surprised. He said, "You mean we weren't hit by aircraft?" I said, "No, sir. Not at the beginning." He had a pencil and paper and he started jotting some notes. Then he looked at me and said, "Okay, then, why shouldn't we start the artillery barrage now? If we know that aircraft are coming from the south, then we'll put up a barrage on that side of the city and let them run into a wall of steel."

I said, "Sir, that's very dangerous. If you start too early, the batteries may use up all their ammunition before the enemy fighters get there. Furthermore, American fighters have forward-looking radar and AWACS Sentries overhead that can scan more than 150 miles ahead, and when they detect an artillery barrage in a certain sector they'll simply turn and go around it. You can't keep up a barrage forever, and it would be risky to waste our ammunition that way."

This didn't make Saddam happy either, and he was getting angrier by the minute. But as we were having this discussion, the telephone in front of us began ringing. I waited to see what Saddam would do, but obviously he wasn't going to pick up the phone. The air chief should have done it, but Saddam wanted me to answer it. So I picked up the receiver and it was Gen. Ali Hussein, calling from Nasiriyah.

He said, "Who is this?" and I said, "This is Gen. Sada." He gave me a warm greeting. He was one of my former students as well, when I headed the Operational Conversion Unit. Pilots who had been trained in France, England, or America had to make the conversion to Iraqi equipment and tactics, and Ali Hussein had gone through that school. Now he was a general and commander of a base in the south.

After a very brief exchange, Ali Hussein proceeded to tell me what was happening in the southern sector. I listened to his report, then I looked at Saddam; it was obvious he was hoping for good news. So I said, "Sir, this is Gen. Ali Hussein, and he's telling me that our air defense missiles have just shot down a British Tornado in the south. They've captured both pilots and they're ready to be processed as prisoners of war."

Suddenly Saddam's eyes lit up. He was excited to learn that we were able to bring down an enemy plane. He said, "Is this true? They've taken two prisoners of war?" I said, "Yes, sir." So he said, "What is the Tornado?" And I told him it was a very good fighter built in Europe by German, Italian, and British manufacturers. But then I asked him, "Sir, what do you want me to tell Gen. Ali Hussein to do with the pilots?"

He pushed back slightly and crossed his arms, obviously thinking about what to do next. Then he said, "Okay, here's what I want to do. We need a man who speaks English very well, who knows the capabilities and tactics of the aircraft, and who knows how to translate those tactics into air defense. He looked at Gen. Muzahim and said, "No, he shouldn't be the one." One by one, he checked off a list of all the officers in the headquarters, and finally he turned to me and said, "Georges, you will be responsible for the prisoners of war."

The Downed Pilots

By Saddam's command, I was now the officer responsible for coalition pilots shot down over Iraq. So I said, "Okay, sir, I'll do my best." When I returned to the phone, I said to Gen. Ali Hussein, "President Saddam has put me in charge of the POWs. So please send them to me right away." But then I added, "Don't send them by helicopter or they'll never make it to Baghdad. Send them by car with some good officers to the air force headquarters."

The old headquarters building had been bombed and was split down the middle. If it were hit again, it would be a total disaster. So I asked Gen. Ali Hussein to send the POWs to the new headquarters in Baghdad, which was to be located in a large bunker that had been specially built below a civilian bunker. Until now, no one knew that Saddam had built military command bunkers in secure structures below civilian bunkers. It was an act of cowardice contrary to the Geneva Convention to hide military commanders behind women and children. But such things weren't uncommon for Saddam Hussein.

Anyone who followed the events of that war will recall that the international news media had a field day when American bombers struck the Al-Ameriya bunker, which was full of women and children. Scores of civilians were killed, but this was exactly what Saddam had wanted to happen. If he could somehow persuade the Americans to destroy a civilian target, he would then be able to portray the Americans as aggressors and ruthless killers of women and children, when, in fact, he had built our command posts in the same buildings, beneath public structures.

When the main air headquarters was bombed, Saddam gave orders to move everything—radar equipment, radio communications, and personnel—to the civilian bunker at Al-Maamou, which was in the officer city of Yarmook. The upstairs, as before, was reserved for the use of women and children. But downstairs was the operations center for the Iraqi Air Force, and this, as Saddam knew very well, was against the rules of war. There's no question that American and coalition surveillance could detect that military communications were coming from that place, and truthfully they would have been within their rights to attack it. But Saddam also knew that, after Al-Ameriya, the Americans were not likely to risk another media disaster.

So I went to that shelter, and that's where I met with the prisoners of war. It's also where I continued to work until I was discharged from service and summarily retired once again shortly thereafter. The first prisoner I interviewed, Navy Lieutenant Jeffrey Zaun, had been flying an A-6 Intruder from the Aircraft Carrier Saratoga, anchored in the Red Sea. He was followed by Flight Lieutenants John Peters and John Nichol of the UK, whose British Tornado was shot down. Commander Scott Speicher had been shot down previously, but he died in the crash, and that's part of a longer investigation I'll come back to momentarily.

Neither of the British pilots was in very good shape when we got them because they'd ejected at low altitude—less than 150 feet from the ground. Their aircraft took a direct hit from an SAM-3 guided missile. In fact, they didn't actually eject; they were forcefully ejected by the force of the missile. Their parachutes opened but at such a low level that they hit the ground very hard, and both men suffered trauma and abrasion injuries.

When they arrived and I saw the condition they were in, I called the director of the air force hospital. I told him, "Doctor, I need you to do something for me, and please don't refuse. I have two guys here, both of them are prisoners of war shot down in the south, and they're in pretty bad shape." As soon as I said the words "prisoners of war," he became defensive and said, "What do you mean, General? I have dozens of patients in here, and more are coming every minute. You expect me to prepare for surgery on two of your prisoners of war?"

So I said, "Look, Doctor. There's no time for this kind of talk. These are prisoners of war, entitled to all the protections of the Geneva Convention, and I want them alive. So I'm asking you to take care of them just as if they were our own soldiers. Do you understand me?" He knew I meant business, so I immediately had the wounded pilots transferred to a van, and I drove them to the air force hospital myself.

Medical Attention

When we got to the hospital, I went to find Dr. Al-Mukhtar, a military surgeon, an excellent orthopedist, and a general officer in the army. I said, "General, I need for you to give these men the same treatment you'd give an Iraqi pilot. They're POWs, and according to your religion and mine, as well as the Geneva Convention, you have a duty to give them proper medical attention. And that's all I'm asking for."

Dr. Al-Mukhtar is a good man, so he said, "Okay, Georges, I'll do my best." Over the next several days he either supervised or performed at least five operations on the men. When they finally went home to England, on March 4, 1991, they were checked out by British surgeons to see if the treatment they'd received was satisfactory. The British doctors said the care they had been given was excellent and nothing more needed to be done.

After treatment, Flight Lieutenant Peters was sent back to the detention center, but Flight Lieutenant Nichol was kept in the hospital for several more days. Whenever I'd go to the hospital to check on him, I could see that he wanted to stay longer. Obviously, he would rather be in a hospital than a prison. When their book, *Tornado Down*, was published in 1998, telling about that time, the British pilots didn't have many good things to say about their treatment in the POW camps. But, then, they didn't say anything very bad either. Obviously, we were at war, and they were strongly against Saddam and the Iraqi military. The good news was that they came out of it alive. Later, Flight Lieutenant John Nichol credited me with saving his life. He was quoted in the *London Telegraph* as saying, "I'd like to meet Georges and shake his hand."[2]

When it came time to prepare my report on Capt. Zuhair's mission, I learned that Lieutenant Commander Scott Speicher's F-18 had been hit by an R-40 guided missile. He was hit head on and there was no time for the pilot to react, so Speicher went down with his plane. Several days later, however, the story was circulated that Speicher had ejected and might possibly still be alive. But I'm certain that story was not true. The airplane was completely destroyed, and Speicher did not survive.

We found what was left of his F-18 years later in 1995 with the help of American satellites. We even took a group of American investigators to the site to look for evidence. We examined the wreckage and found the remnants of a flight suit, but no sign of Lieutenant Commander Speicher. Because of the uncertainty involved, the U.S. military changed his status from Killed in Action (KIA) to Missing in Action (MIA). But I believe that was more wishful thinking than anything else.

Several years later, a number of American Christians, whom I had met through my work in the reconciliation movement, came and asked for my help in finding out if Commander Speicher could possibly be alive. I was certain of the facts of this case, but they wanted to check every angle, so I agreed to help. We looked again but found nothing to change my mind. Scott Speicher is dead. There's no way he could have survived a direct hit from an R-40 missile. That's a huge weapon, and you don't walk away from a crash like that.

What did happen, however, was that some Iraqis had taken advantage of the situation for money and even for American citizenship in one case. There was never any possibility that Speicher had survived, but his family and others continued to hold out hope. After the liberation of Iraq in 2003, one of the first delegations to come from America was a group of twelve people looking for Scott Speicher. They called me once again, and once again I agreed to help.

They told me they had talked to some Iraqis who had solid evidence that Speicher had ejected from his plane and somehow managed to evade capture. When they told me the names of the men who said that, I realized I knew one of them. He was a distant relative of Saddam's. So I said, "Bring them to me." They had to fly the men to Iraq from America, and when they finally arrived I asked them to tell me the whole story. They said they'd seen the pilot. They fed him, gave him clothing, and then helped him escape across the border into Syria.

I didn't believe it for a minute, but I asked for more proof, and they told me they had given Speicher official documents. I asked if they had copies of those documents and they said they did. They showed me the copies, and they looked official. But I knew they were a forgery the minute I saw them, because of the title at the top of the page.

Uncovering a Fake

At one time, many years ago, Iraq was called "The Iraqi Republic," and in Arabic that's a feminine title, because of the endings of the words. When Saddam first saw it, he said, "How can Iraq be a feminine name? We're a strong, masculine country!" So he ordered the government to change all the official documents and also to change the official name of the country. Instead of the feminine form, "The Iraqi Republic," would now be "The Republic of Iraq," with the masculine construction.

When the men who claimed to have seen Speicher showed me their papers, I realized the documents had the old feminine title for Iraq, so obviously they had forged them. I knew their story was false, but I gave them one more chance to show me the rest of their proof. At that point they claimed they had been to the crash site, so I told the Americans to ask the men to take us to the crash site. I knew by then that the wreckage of Speicher's plane was far away, in the western desert, and it would be very hard to find it again. The men admitted they had no idea which way to go, and at that point everybody knew they'd been lying.

I brought with me another Iraqi general from the intelligence service who might be able to help in the investigation. But as soon as he arrived, the intelligence specialist told the Americans, "You know, you really ought to listen to General Sada." He said, "He's the one who will tell you the truth." He knew that I had already spent a lot of time on this case. They agreed with him, and they asked me to handle the investigation.

They had offered us money, but I said we didn't want any money. We weren't doing this for money, but out of respect for the men and women who had fought to liberate our country from Saddam. I told them we would be honored if they would simply think of us as allies.

Ever since attaining the rank of brigadier general, and even during my retirement, I was the one responsible for aircraft safety, for aircraft inspections, and for investigation of accidents and things of that sort. This was an area I understood very well, so I helped those people the best I could, and we examined maps, evidence, and all the various claims from people who said they had seen the downed pilot. It soon became clear to everyone that Lieutenant Commander Speicher had been killed in the crash, so I urged the Americans to let his family know what we'd found out so they could, at long last, have some resolution of this matter. I believed it was better to know the truth than to cherish a false hope.

CHAPTER 7

DAMAGE ASSESSMENT

addam had put me in charge of interrogating prisoners of war, and I began that assignment with some concern for the situation we were in because of Saddam's refusal to leave Kuwait before the United Nations' deadline. Having created our own crisis, we were in no position to punish or harass prisoners who had been shot down or captured in the pursuit of a just mission. But, through detention and interrogation, we could perhaps discover tactics and plans that would help to lessen the destruction being inflicted upon us by the enemy. And that was now my duty.

I insured that prisoners who had been wounded were properly treated, and I arranged for housing and food, which was never easy because of the constant pummeling we were taking from coalition strikes. Day after day, fire and death were being rained down upon the city of Baghdad, and on some of those days the buildings where POWs were housed were struck as well, and this meant moving the men from place to place at various times.

Each day of that first week we followed specific procedures involving meals and hygiene for the prisoners and the internment and classification of the new arrivals brought in from the field. But on January 24, exactly one week into the war, Saddam's younger son, Qusay, came to my office and demanded that all POWs be executed immediately as "war criminals." He was ranting when he arrived and never relented, yelling that these men were butchers and murderers, and they had to die for their crimes.

"Do you see what they've done to Baghdad?" he said. The city was being bombed around the clock, with as many as a thousand sorties a day, and Qusay was infuriated by our seeming inability to retaliate. So, to his mind, the best way to slap the Americans in the face and send a message to the U.N. and the rest of the world was to execute the pilots being held in our military jails.

Imagine my position. The son of Saddam, immoral, unpredictable, and more brutal than his father, had determined on his own self-proclaimed authority that these men must die. Trying to defend the pilots by the standards of the Geneva Convention against the wrath of such a man was not going to be easy. In fact, for more than ten hours we argued back and forth. I said, no, it could not be done. But Qusay wanted to kill them immediately, all of them: Americans, British, coalition flyers, and especially the Kuwaiti pilot, Staff Colonel Mubarak, who managed to take off after the airfields were destroyed and kill or wound hundreds of Iraqi troops on the border.

Qusay yelled, "I want you to kill that Iraqi. He's a traitor, and that is our business." He claimed this man was a traitor to his country. Like his father, Qusay insisted that Kuwait was the nineteenth province of Iraq and not a separate country. But I challenged him. "Do you mean the Kuwaiti?" At this he yelled even louder, "Don't say Kuwaiti! He's an Iraqi, and he dropped bombs on his own people."

I knew I must not speak harshly to this boy if I valued my life, but I glared at him sternly and said, "Mr. Qusay, excuse me but the Geneva Convention states very clearly that the uniform, the ID card, and the aircraft of a captured pilot may be used to identify the nationality of a prisoner of war. When he was captured, this pilot, Col. Mohammed Mubarak Sultan Mubarak was wearing a Kuwaiti uniform, he was flying an American Skyhawk fighter, which is a Kuwaiti aircraft and not an Iraqi aircraft, and his ID card said that he belongs to the air force of Kuwait. By the rules of war, I have no choice but to say that this man is a Kuwaiti."

Justifiable Defense

By any measure, that Kuwaiti pilot was a skilled aviator and a hero to his people. When the Iraqi Army entered Kuwait on August 2, 1990, one of the first things they did was to drop bombs on the runways so that the Kuwaiti fighters could not take off. So almost immediately, the entire air force of Kuwait was disabled and could not fly. But Col. Mubarak didn't use the runway; he taxied his plane onto the service road that surrounds the airfield and, miraculously, he had just enough room to take off and become airborne.

He climbed quickly, and as soon as he gained altitude, he spotted four massive columns of Iraqi tanks, armored personnel carriers, trucks, and vehicles of every description—stretching for miles, as far as the eye could see—and they were coming across the border into Kuwait. Obviously, those vehicles were easy targets, so he opened up on them, flying up and down, back and forth, column by column, until he ran out of ammunition. Then he flew to the air base in Dharan, Saudi Arabia, where he remained for the next five and a half months, until the air war started on January 17, 1991.

At that time, the Kuwaiti pilot returned, and that's when his plane was hit by anti-aircraft fire and he was shot down. When he ejected, Mubarak was captured and taken as a prisoner of war, and there was no doubt that he was the same pilot who had managed to do such damage to our forces on the morning of August 2. The television news cameras had captured the horror of that grisly scene: miles and miles of burned-out tanks, columns of acrid smoke rising from those burned-out hulks in all directions, and hundreds of bodies scattered along the roadside. No wonder Qusay and the others hated him; but no wonder his own people today consider him to be a hero.

When news of that first attack reached Baghdad, Saddam and his sons were furious, and I'm sure this is why they wanted to take revenge on all the captured pilots. But I also realized that if I could save the life of that one man, I could save all the others. Qusay and his family would likely say that I was only defending the pilots because they were Christians like me. So I thought, *By the rules of war, the religious background of the prisoners doesn't matter at all. But, still, it will be much better if I can make the case by saving the life of this Muslim pilot.* And that's what I did. I defended him vigorously, and doing that gave me the credibility to defend all the others.

I should also mention that during the Gulf War, a total of 606 Kuwaitis were captured and held by our forces as either hostages or prisoners of war. Of those, 605 were killed by Saddam, and only one is alive today. That one man is the pilot, Staff Colonel Mohammed Mubarak Sultan Mubarak, whom I defended on that day.

Unspoken Threats

It was not an easy task. The more I resisted, the more Qusay became enraged at me. He was relentless, and it was obvious that he was becoming exasperated and volatile as the day wore on. Normally, Qusay wouldn't think twice about chopping off my head if I didn't agree to his demands, and no one would have said a word. There must have been twenty or thirty officers, pilots, and other staff members standing there watching all of this taking place, and, believe me, none of them would have said a word if Qusay had shot me on the spot.

But he continued to argue, and when he finally stormed up the stairs toward the exit late in the evening, we passed through the shelter where the women and children were housed, and I breathed a silent prayer, *Jesus, please help me to know what to say to this man.*

As he stood near the door, Qusay looked at me with utter contempt, and he said, "Don't you want to obey the orders of the president?" And I said, "I'm sorry, but I'm the man who was commanded by the president, your father, to obey the orders in this book." For the tenth time I held up my copy of the Geneva Convention, and I said, "As you know very well, the nation of Iraq signed this document too. But if you disagree with this, then go ahead and tell your father exactly what I've said."

He was silent for a moment, but at length he said, "All right, then. Let the Americans execute the Americans. Take the pilots out of the prisons and put them at the targets their own bombers will hit. Then we'll just let the American pilots do the job for us." But I said, "I'm sorry, I can't do that either. That's the same as murder, and, again, the Geneva Convention specifically forbids using prisoners of war as human shields."

"If the American intelligence is as good as you say it is," Qusay shouted, "they will know we've done this. And if they know their pilots are at the targets, maybe they will change their plans and not hit the targets. Surely they don't want to kill their own people." But I said, "It's still the same thing as executing them."

I was exhausted by this time and tired of the whole debate, and I thought, *My God, what can I possibly say to this man to make him change his mind?* At that moment I knew what I had to say to him, so I said, "Mr. Qusay, here's the last thing I can say to you about this matter. At this moment we are at war with America. It's a war between Iraq and America. But I can assure you, if you kill these twenty-four pilots, it will no longer be a war between Iraq and America; it will be a war between America and your family. If they discover that their pilots have been executed, they will come for you, one by one. And, believe me, they will not stop until they have done the job. Is this what you really want?"

When I said that, all the officers and pilots standing with us began looking around at each other, wondering what was going to happen next. Some of them were certain that Qusay was going to kill me on the spot; others were afraid he was going to kill us all. But a few thought that maybe this time Saddam's undisciplined son had actually heard what I was saying. But Qusay said nothing. He simply turned on his heel and walked off into the night.

The moment he left, several of the officers who were standing there all at once began shouting at me very loudly, "Georges, why did you do that?" they said. "You know that man can have you killed! What were you thinking? Why didn't you just agree with him and be done with it? Do you want to die?"

That was a very dark hour, I must say. Imagine the situation I was in. Coalition pilots were still attacking Iraq. And in that command bunker I was fighting for the lives of pilots who, to many of those men as well as to Saddam and his family, were considered nothing more than war criminals. But thank God, by some miracle, I was given the courage, the words to say, and the ability to save the lives of those men.

Even so, I didn't know what my destiny would be, and it turned out to be a costly effort on my part. I couldn't sleep after that because I knew there would be a price to pay. Sure enough, the next day, on January 25, Qusay sent intelligence officers to pick me up. They were surprisingly polite. They said, "Please, sir, will you come with us?" And I asked, "Where are you taking me?" But they didn't tell me. They just said, "Just come along. You'll see."

I was sure I was going to be killed, so I just said to myself, *Thank God that I was able to do my job in a proper way, as a good general. If I must die for that, then I am satisfied I've done my best.*

Counting the Cost

The Mukhabbarat took me to a room in a nearby school. When the air force command center was destroyed on the first night of the war, Saddam gave orders for a new facility to be set up and they decided to use the bunker under the women and children's shelter. So for several days operations were directed from there, but a few days later they moved it again, to the school, and that's where I was taken.

They held me there as a prisoner for the next week, and this was a very difficult time for me. I didn't know what would happen, whether I would be killed or put on trial. I eventually learned that the air force commander and several others in the leadership had deserted me and turned against me, so my fate was uncertain.

The waiting was difficult, especially when I thought about what would happen to my family after my death. At that time I was wearing a beautiful Swiss-made watch, a chronometer especially made for pilots, with sophisticated time and navigation features, and I decided I wanted to leave it to my son. So from my prison cell I managed to signal to my driver who was waiting nearby, and I said to him, "I want you to take this to my son and tell him I want him to have it as a memento from his father."

Sometime later when I spoke to my son, I asked him what he thought when that watch arrived, and he told me he didn't know what to think. Mostly, he said, he was frightened, because he knew I loved that watch, and if I was sending it to him, then something terrible must have happened. But Saddam was the one who made the decision about what to do with me, whether I was to live or die, and he decided that I had done the right thing.

Saddam was capable of diabolical evil, but he was also a very practical man, and he realized that killing the pilots would only have made the situation worse for him. So he decided that they should not kill me. In reality, only God knows what would have happened if I had agreed with Qusay and let them execute those men. I know many Americans were divided over the war; many thought the war was wrong, and the public was divided on this issue. But news that all the coalition pilots had been executed may well have been enough to galvanize public opinion against us, and the pressure to punish Iraq—not just in America, but in Europe and the Middle East—would have been greater than ever.

Eventually, there were forty coalition pilots and five support staff from Saudi Arabia who ended up as prisoners in Iraq in that area. But when the decision was made not to kill the first twenty-four pilots, that meant that I had saved all of them. So I'm glad my actions turned out to be the right ones, and I'm also glad, for my sake, that Saddam recognized it before it was too late.

Col. David Eberly, who was shot down on January 19, 1991, was the senior coalition pilot captured at that time, and became the leader of the POWs. He had evaded detection for three nights but was captured in the early morning hours of January 22, on the Syrian border. After the war, he wrote about his experience in his book *Faith Beyond Belief.* He describes what happened, day by day and hour by hour, how he was shot down and how he came to us. He doesn't talk about the fact that he wasn't badly treated, but in the letter he wrote to me after the war, he thanked me for saving his life. David's story was described previously in Rick Atkinson's book about the war, called *Crusade*, which reveals many of the conflicting images of that war.

Col. Eberly told me that his book was the story of how his Christian faith sustained him through those stressful times. More recently, I have visited with him in America. We have shared our common faith and have become good friends. David has thanked me many times for saving the downed pilots from execution. Of course he couldn't praise the enemy, and we were enemies for the duration of the war. But he has been clear about the service I rendered. After all, if I had obeyed Qusay's command, as most others in my position would have done, there would have been no story to tell.

Casualties of War

Exactly five and a half months after Saddam gave the order to Gen. Hussein al-Tikriti to "Let the boys get in," the first Gulf War began. Coalition forces had been preparing for war since the first day our soldiers crossed the border into Kuwait on August 2, 1990. Then the first missiles hit Baghdad on the morning of January 17, 1991, and after forty-two days of sustained combat on the ground and in the air, and after more than 88,500 tons of bombs had been dropped by coalition aircraft on the nation, a ceasefire was finally declared and the armistice signed. On February 28, 1991, the first Gulf War came to an end. Saddam's outrageous gamble had failed, and the rest of the world had won.

During the five months preceding the commencement of hostilities, the United Nations Security Council put forth twelve separate resolutions condemning Saddam's actions and calling for immediate withdrawal from Kuwait. His refusal to cooperate with those demands led to the formation of one of the most formidable coalitions in military history, representing thirty-one nations from five continents. Joining the Americans, the British, and the Australians were ten nations with predominantly Arab or Muslim populations. This fact was not lost on Saddam.

While America and Britain provided the lion's share of men, money, and materiel, they were joined by Argentina, Australia, Bahrain, Bangladesh, Belgium, Canada, Czechoslovakia, Denmark, Egypt, France, Greece, Hungary, Italy, Kuwait, Morocco, the Netherlands, New Zealand, Niger, Norway, Oman, Pakistan, Poland, Qatar, Saudi Arabia, Senegal, South Korea, Spain, Syria, and the United Arab Emirates. It was to be America's largest military engagement since Vietnam, involving a half million troops, more than two thousand aircraft, and one hundred warships.

The devastation unleashed upon my country at that time was entirely due to the arrogance and avarice of one man. Saddam could not restrain either his ego or his greed, and his total lack of moral boundaries cost the nation dearly. In addition to the tens of thousands of soldiers and airmen killed in the war, as many as 3,500 innocent civilians were killed in collateral damage. These were tragic losses, yet for Saddam the deaths of civilians was a good thing because it served his purposes: exploiting the deaths of civilians as propaganda has always been a favorite weapon of tyrants.

To his own tally of war casualties, Saddam could add the 8,000 who were killed in the brutal massacre of the Kurds in 1983; the attack on Halabja in 1988, carried out by his cousin, Ali Hussein al-Majid (better known as "Chemical Ali"), which killed 5,000; and at least 182,000 Kurds murdered at Anfal the same year. The total is still not complete, but more than 275 mass graves have now been discovered, each containing from fifty to several thousand bodies. This is the true legacy of Saddam. Murder, torture, rape, and wholesale genocide were his trademarks, and it may be years before the world discovers the full extent of his evil deeds.

Certainly there were other casualties, both before and after the war. Some estimates by international agencies place the total number of Saddam's victims at more than a million dead. It may have been more, but even that wasn't enough for him. Saddam wanted desperately to drag Israel into the war. If he had succeeded, it probably would have fragmented the coalition and led to thousands more casualties, which would have pleased Saddam immensely.

Ultimately, the war would cost Iraq more than $200 billion. But this was only a fraction of the price we paid. During Operation Desert Storm, coalition fighters and bombers flew more than 60,000 sorties and made more than 41,000 strikes. Two-thirds of these actions were directed against our ground forces. Approximately 227,000 bombs and missiles were deployed by the coalition, and the damage this caused was staggering.

The toll in human terms was even higher. Of the approximately 360,000 Iraqi soldiers on the field of battle, 28 percent of them (or nearly 100,000 men and boys) were killed in action, and as many as 200,000 sustained serious injuries. In addition, coalition forces captured 60,000 prisoners, and by some estimates there may have been as many as 150,000 deserters. As for casualties on the other side, 390 American soldiers, sailors, and airmen died in combat, while 458 were wounded in action. Among coalition forces, there was a total of 510 casualties. The financial cost to America was approximately

$80 billion, of which coalition nations contributed $54 billion. In the end, it's clear that Saddam had underestimated the resolve of the American forces, and he completely misjudged the unity and determination of the coalition.

An Uncertain Victory

When the war ended, Gen. Sultan Hashim, who had commanded the Iraqi infantry, met with coalition commanders in a tent at Safwan, on the Iraqi side of the border with Kuwait. Gen. Norman Schwarzkopf, commander of coalition forces, and Gen. Khalid bin Sultan, commander of the Arab coalition forces, were there to negotiate the ceasefire. The document before them testified to the fact that the multinational forces led by the Americans had gotten everything they wanted. But even the statement of surrender didn't solve the problem.

For one thing, Schwarzkopf had agreed to let Iraq keep its remaining helicopters, which allowed Saddam to use them to attack and punish those who had carried out the uprising in the fourteen provinces. And, worst of all, nothing was done to change the regime or restrain what Saddam and his deputies could do to us in the future. When news of what happened that day reached the people of Iraq, many felt that America had deserted and abandoned us.

Just weeks later—as soon as they could load their tanks and artillery and personnel—the Americans left, and there was no one to save us from the wrath of Saddam. Within days he had turned defeat into a victory. He admitted that the Americans had managed to take back Kuwait, but he boasted that three of the world's most powerful nations had attacked us in the "Mother of all Battles," and we had won. Iraq was still there, Saddam was still in power, and we would rebuild our forces.

The Americans thought that sanctions would cause Saddam's regime to collapse, but it didn't happen. Anyone who knew Saddam could have told them what was going to happen. Sanctions made the nation weak but they only made Saddam stronger. He hijacked the nation. He even took the bread rations and sold them. Whenever U.N. inspectors would come to see if the people were getting bread, he would open the warehouses and show them bread. But the minute they left, he would shut the doors. And if he ever suspected that someone had been against the regime during the war, he would cut off their bread rations, cut off their electricity, and in this way gradually starve them to death.

Saddam always had ways of maintaining the appearance of victory even in defeat. When the armistice was signed, Gen. Sultan had agreed to all the points of surrender. But what Gen. Schwarzkopf and his aides didn't realize was that on the way to the tent, Gen. Sultan received a call from Saddam on his cell phone. Saddam said, "Look, Sultan. I don't want you to take off your pistol when you go in there to sign the agreement. I want the world to see you with your weapon on your belt. If they tell you to take it off, I want you to refuse."

Once again, Saddam was proving that his authority was still supreme, and thereby he was undermining the coalition's victory. I'm sorry to say that Gen. Schwarzkopf didn't notice what was happening and didn't say anything about it. Consequently, Gen. Sultan managed to sit through the entire proceedings wearing his pistol on his belt. In his book, *Crusade: The Untold Story of the Persian Gulf War*, Rick Atkinson also reports that coalition commanders had agreed before the signing that Gen. Schwarzkopf was not to shake hands with Gen. Sultan, as a sign of disrespect. But at the last minute, when the Iraqi officer extended his hand, Schwarzkopf shook it anyway, which reportedly outraged Gen. Colin Powell and the top brass at the Pentagon.

For years afterward, Saddam often pointed to the pictures of that day, and he would say, "Look, let everybody know that we signed the document in Safwan, but Gen. Sultan Hashim was still wearing his pistol." It was a tiny victory, little more than a way of saving face. But to the people of Iraq this was one more sign that, despite the overwhelming strength and might of the enemy, Saddam had won again. For anyone not familiar with Middle Eastern culture, it must be difficult to understand how a man who was such a tyrant could still be seen as a hero. But Saddam understood, and he mastered the art.

The reality was that the entire Iraqi Army was destroyed. Most of Saddam's tanks had been destroyed. The images of Iraqi tanks and equipment lying smoldering and burning beside the road for more than a hundred miles between Kuwait City and Nasiriyah were broadcast by satellite to the entire world. Yet Saddam was still in control. He had told his general to wear a pistol to the surrender proceedings, and every Iraqi knew that as long as Saddam was still alive, he would always win. And we knew that one day Saddam would rise again.

The Source of Weakness

The Baath Party came back as well, and before long everything was very much as it had been before the war. Furthermore, when the Americans left, they turned everything over to the United Nations, and the U.N. officials were corrupt, taking money to look the other way. They were selling the food and supplies they were supposed to be giving to the people as part of the recovery effort. Today the media and investigators are discovering the tip of the iceberg in the Oil-for-Food scandal, but this sort of thing was happening from the beginning.

Over the next twelve years, things got better and better for Saddam while they just got worse and worse for the people. But what made Iraq weak in the first place, in all fields, was the system that put weak people in charge of all major departments and functions. This was the true nature of all the systems put in place by the Baath Party. If you look at the principles of the party that empowered Saddam and allowed him to rule for all those years, you can't miss the irony.

The motto of the Baath Party was "Socialism, Unity, Freedom." The phrase was meant to be poetic, in the same way that the rallying cry of the French Revolution in 1789—*liberté, fraternité, egalité*—had galvanized the republic. In the aftermath of the revolution in France, there was not much liberty, no fraternity, and there was equality only in the suffering endured by the people. The motto was all symbolism with little meaning. By the same token, there was no freedom or unity in Iraq under Saddam either, and his idea of socialism was a joke.

The slogans of the Baathis were loaded with symbolism, but it was a symbolism that mattered only to members of the party. If the party had really cared about the people, they would have given us a free-enterprise economy, or at least allowed the people to use their native skills as businessmen and entrepreneurs to improve conditions in Iraq. But this never happened, and it was a great loss to the Iraqi economy.

For example, when I was retired from the military, I was given ten thousand acres of arable land. In years past this land would have been managed by the government. We had a nationalized agriculture program at one time, but it was terribly unprofitable. It was like the Soviet system in that way, only worse. But one day Saddam thought, *Why do we have all this land in agriculture and we can't make any money with it? We pour so much money and equipment into it, and still we get nothing back. We should get out of the farming business.* So he said, "Give the land to the people and let them farm it. Maybe they can make a profit."

That's what happened, and it was one of the few economic measures Saddam ever took that actually helped the people. The minute the people began farming the land for themselves, it became profitable. The lucky thing for me was that my property was well prepared. The land had been cleared and leveled during the days of the collective farms. Concrete irrigation canals were installed and there were barns, outbuildings, harvesting and storage facilities, and I was able to buy modern equipment on the open market. These benefits from the socialist era were helpful, but the ingenuity and hard work were all mine, and that was what made the real difference.

With a combination of government funds and some of my own money, I was able to buy the things I needed. It wasn't the biggest farm in Iraq by any means, but it was one of the most productive farms in the Middle East. For four years I lived the life of a prosperous farmer. But my question is, why couldn't the Baath Party have followed that model, empowering people to take command of their own welfare? Instead, they were merely defenders and enablers of the ceaseless quest for power and domination that consumed our corrupt leader's every waking thought.

Decline and Dissent

Part of the problem in Iraq was that Saddam Hussein was a creature of the Baathist political apparatus. It was the Baathist agenda that brought Saddam and Al-Bakr to power in 1968, and that agenda was never benign. The Baathis were fiercely political and unaccountable to anyone. They were brutal to rivals and they couldn't even maintain peace in their own ranks. The only two countries actually ruled by the Baath Party were Syria and Iraq, and they were two of the biggest enemies in the Arab world. Despite the motto of the party calling for unity and freedom, there was no unity among them.

The man who fought hardest against unity and freedom was Saddam. He wasn't the least interested in Arab unity, and he wasn't interested in giving the people freedom unless it was the freedom to bestow honors and riches on him. The slogans of the Baath Party were only that: slogans. Saddam wasn't interested in the well-being of the people, whether it was a socialist system or any other. And the Baathists gave him no reason to behave otherwise.

Now the whole world is able to see the evil that was done under that evil regime. Today investigators are uncovering the mass graves and examining records of atrocities revealing, at last, the corruption in everything that Saddam touched. The truth is, Saddam Hussein killed more Arabs than anyone in history, and he wouldn't hesitate to abuse, torture, and kill his own people if he felt threatened. There was nothing he wouldn't do to maintain his grip on the country, and there were no principles he wouldn't sacrifice for the sake of his own greed.

The Baath Party claimed to be dedicated to a socialist welfare system. But if I tell you how Saddam and his sons dealt with the wealth of the nation, and especially how he dealt with the nation's oil and gas resources, you will see that it had nothing to do with the welfare of the people, and everything to do with their own venality and corruption.

And freedom? Let me give you a graphic example of freedom under Saddam. It was the unspoken rule in Iraq that if Saddam gave a speech on TV—and he gave hundreds of them, ad nauseam

—everyone in the entire country was supposed to watch it. There was no freedom of the press in Iraq; all the news was about Saddam. There was no freedom of speech in Iraq; any word of dissent would be met with swift and often fatal punishment. Every day, in all the news media, the subject was what Saddam had done that day. Not to watch a broadcast when Saddam was giving a speech could be very dangerous to your health.

If anyone disagreed with Saddam over even the slightest thing, he would have his head cut off. If anyone spoke against him, he would have his tongue cut out. If they didn't like the army, he would have their ears or their nose cut off. In some cases he would have brands seared into the flesh of their foreheads to show that they were cowards.

On one occasion that I know about, a man was watching a speech by Saddam on TV. He was sitting there with his family and at one point became fed up with hearing the same old lies, day after day. So he simply reached over and turned off the television. He said, "I don't want to hear that anymore. I've heard it all too many times." And that was all. But the next day at school, his son, who was about seven or eight years old, told his teacher, "My daddy turned off the TV because he didn't want to hear President Saddam last night." An innocent comment? Less than a week later, undercover agents of the Mukhabbarat showed up at his door. They took that father away and he was never seen again.

No one had to ask. We all knew what happened to that man, and this was a well-known and constant threat under Saddam. But what kind of "freedom" is it when a child can turn in his own father and the result is that the man will be killed for turning off the television? And this wasn't even the tip of the iceberg in my country. Iraq was a nation gripped by fear, night and day, and, believe me, there were many things more horrible than this taking place in every village and town.

When Saddam wanted to punish the people of a certain province, he wouldn't say, "I'm going to punish you for rebelling against me." Instead, he would say it was because of the sanctions. We can't build a school in your city because of the sanctions. You can't have a hospital because of the sanctions. You can't have medicine or food or good roads because of the sanctions. But if he wanted a new palace, he would build it wherever he liked and there were no sanctions.

In some cases he would punish the people of a certain region to the degree he believed they had been against him; and by the same token, he rewarded those who had been for him, meaning primarily the four provinces in the Sunni Triangle who were strong Saddam loyalists, with jobs and money and political appointments. Today, it's the other way around. The provinces he rewarded are the ones where the insurgency has remained strongest, and that's where most of our problems have come from since the end of the war.

But this is what Saddam and the Baathis gave us. Their motto was a lie. There was no unity, no freedom, and their idea of socialism was a fraud that corrupted the people. Life in Iraq was precisely the opposite of what we were told to expect, but the fear was so great that nobody dared say a word. The system Saddam created did not make us better, stronger, or more prosperous. It diminished us and weakened us in many ways. Saddam's government shriveled the souls of the people and weakened our standing in the eyes of the world. The only thing that grew bigger and stronger day by day was Saddam Hussein and his insatiable ego.

The Human Toll

After the first Gulf War ended in 1991, and to a much greater extent since April 2003, international agencies have been able to examine areas in Iraq that had previously been off limits. So they went in to determine if rumors of mass graves in Iraq were true. The fact is, mass graves were being used in Iraq for many years before 1991. The Baathis had used mass murder as a tool for decades, and the tragedy of what happened to the Kurds in the north at the hands of Chemical Ali was well known long before the Gulf War began. Kurds were taken from their homes and villages and massacred in the tens of thousands.

It was not until the investigations of 2003, however, that those Kurdish graves were finally uncovered, and what they discovered was horrifying. Thousands of men, women, and children from the northern regions, referred to as Kurdistan, had been seized and taken from their homes in the north, massacred, and buried in the south. The people who opened the graves knew immediately where the victims were from by the bits of clothing that remained on the bodies. Some remnants of their distinctive Kurdish garments were still intact.

We also know that thousands more were taken from Halabja and murdered somewhere near Babylon in the south. So long as Kurdistan was being protected by the American forces based in Turkey, the Kurds had a measure of protection. But when they left in 1991, Saddam ordered his soldiers to take these people as prisoners and execute them. They massacred them in the tens of thousands and buried them in military camps where U.N. peacekeepers and international forces could not go. There were vast areas within the three biggest military bases in the south where mass graves were dug, and Saddam believed no one would ever know the difference.

The graves were well hidden, and access to those sites was strictly prohibited by the military and the government. But even before liberation in 2003, people would sneak into those areas at night and dig, hoping to find evidence of their loved ones and even entire families that had been taken away and killed. Imagine their horror when dogs began digging in the graves and pulling out parts of human bodies. Finally, after 2003, the camps were opened and hundreds of searchers showed up, digging for evidence of the atrocities that had taken place under Saddam.

Human rights organizations, peace activists, private religious groups, and many others were part of this. And in some cases they had access to satellite imagery that showed them the most likely places where mass graves could exist. There's still so much that we don't know. But many official records from the Saddam era are now being brought to light, and the agencies are finding long lists with the names of those killed, how and when they were killed, and even who did the killing. But it will be years, I suspect, before the whole dark secret of Saddam's savagery is known.

There are also mass graves of the Shia people and their clerics. The strict laws followed by the Shia go back more than 1,400 years, and each member of Shia society is obedient to a particular *imam* or religious leader. Each of these leaders is obedient, in turn, to another cleric at a higher level. And this continues to the level of the ayatollah who is obedient to the highest Shia leader of all, a grand ayatollah. In Iraq, the Shia make up about 55 percent of the country. Their first loyalty was not to the government but to Islam, and this made Saddam very angry.

Consequently, Saddam thought nothing of capturing, torturing, and killing these people. Especially in the south, where the majority of Iraqi Shia live, he kept the people of the region in constant fear. Some families lost four, five, or six members in a single day. And because it was impractical to put so many people in prisons—many times the intelligence officers would round up thousands of them— they usually ended up in mass graves.

The persecution of the Marsh Arabs, who live in the wetlands to the east of Nasiriyah and south almost to Basra, was very much the same. Saddam was afraid of these people, who live and make their living in a very different way from most Iraqis. Because of their unique customs and fiercely independent nature, the Marsh Arabs were among the first to challenge Saddam's edicts, and he feared that one day they would rise up against him. Because they lived in the land between the Tigris and Euphrates Rivers, where tanks and heavy vehicles couldn't go, he decided that the best way to control them would be to drain the marshes, fill them in, and then drive the people off the land.

This was an ambitious project because the marshlands cover an enormous area—more than 7,500 square miles, an area equal to the state of Massachusetts. But over a period of years, the military engineers sent in by Saddam were able to divert the rivers and reduce the size of the marshlands to less than 500 square miles. Less than a third of the land was spared, and the way of life of these people, who depended on the rice crops, fishing, water birds of all kinds, and an active river commerce, was shattered. Water was the basis of their entire civilization. But this wasn't even the worst of it, because once the tanks and armored vehicles began penetrating that territory, they rounded up men, women, and children, and marched them off to places where they, too, were killed and buried in mass graves.

Saddam took revenge on anyone he believed had worked against him in the past or who might be a threat to him in the future, and he did it in the most brutal ways imaginable. This is where the mass graves and torture chambers came from, and those things are a dark stain on the history of our country. I haven't seen any official reports documenting the total number of Iraqis who were killed by Saddam in this way, but I'm inclined to believe that the unofficial estimates of 200,000 to 300,000 deaths wouldn't be unrealistic, and it could be substantially higher.

A Sinister Caricature

For Iraqis to move beyond all the disasters that have happened in Iraq over the past forty years, we will need to learn about human compassion and the importance of working together, regardless of our religious and political differences. We will need to appreciate the importance of the miracles that are happening now in Iraq, and we will need to have faith in the capacity of the human spirit to survive in the midst of suffering, humiliation, and defeat. But we also need to remember what we've learned about evil, and that it was our own complacency that allowed this man (who will one day rank in history beside Stalin, Hitler, and Pol Pot) to rise and seize power in our midst.

Some people have asked me in recent years, "Georges, do you really support what the Americans and coalition forces did when they came to Iraq and turned our world upside down?" And I say to them, "Yes, of course I do. And I support it for one simple reason: I have known that man since the early days, when he was first coming up as an ambitious young hoodlum and a tool of the Baathis. He was very clever, that's true. But too late we discovered that all his cleverness was directed toward doing evil."

God only knows what evil he would eventually have done if he had remained in power. His intentions were very bad and he would pay any amount of money to gain greater power and control. He dreamed of resurrecting ancient Babylon as his capital, and he claimed that one day he would be the emperor of all the Arab nations. He would have spent any amount of money or committed any atrocity, no matter how barbaric, to make that arrogant boast come true.

For a man like Saddam to possess nuclear weapons was a threat of such immense proportions that it was inconceivable that he would be allowed to continue to pursue them. The collapse of the former Soviet Union may have ended, or at least postponed, the threat of a nuclear holocaust from that part of the world, but that didn't mean that the world was a safer place. Saddam was willing to pay any price to gain control of a nuclear arsenal, and he wouldn't hesitate to use those nuclear warheads if he had them.

Saddam knew he could get those weapons if he put enough money into the hands of certain people, and he was actively courting displaced nuclear scientists from the former Soviet regime. He paid large sums to bring back many Iraqi nuclear scientists who were working in the West, and he used every trick imaginable to expand his superweapons program. By the late 1980s, he had a functioning light-water reactor as well as dozens of nuclear weapons facilities in operation, from one end of Iraq to the other.

I'm convinced that Saddam came close to having nuclear warheads by the beginning of the second Gulf War, but it was difficult to maintain secrecy about these operations. To the best of my knowledge, he never managed to acquire all the pieces to make that happen. However, I know that he made payments to a group of Asian scientists to manufacture nuclear components abroad, and had even made the first multimillion-dollar down payment. What he was thinking about doing was so dangerous that the only solution was for coalition forces to remove Saddam from power. And that's why I applaud the liberation of my country, despite the losses we suffered in two successive wars. Someone had to stop Saddam from fulfilling his plans, and the Americans were the only ones with the military and moral resolve to do it.

You can't begin to imagine what Saddam would have done if he had been given just a little more time. His personality was so full of ambiguity, and the way he saw the world had nothing to do with the world as it really is. Saddam fooled some people for a time—he made himself out to be a peacemaker, a good Muslim, a teacher, a lawyer, and a statesman. But he was none of those. He was never anything but a common thug.

I knew this man. I saw him as closely as anyone, and what I saw was a sinister caricature of a human being. He was nothing but a gangster in a uniform he was unworthy to wear—the living embodiment of evil and a danger to the world. There are millions of Iraqis today who, like me, can only look forward with anticipation to a time when the world will finally be rid of him once and for all.

CHAPTER 8

BEATING THE SYSTEM

For more than a decade, from the end of the Gulf War in 1991 to the beginning of Operation Iraqi Freedom in 2003, I suspect most Americans were wishing that the Iraq problem would just go away. With a presidential election less than a year away, Americans were ready to return to business as usual. And the United States Department of State, committed to a doctrine of stability at any cost, even if it meant winking at a dictator like Saddam Hussein, was doing its best to look the other way.

They wanted containment in Iraq, and with the cooperation of the United Nations they were hoping that military and economic sanctions would provoke the people to rebel against the dictator. But this wasn't just unrealistic diplomacy; it was bad policy, for many reasons. Nothing but force and the threat of death or imprisonment would ever cause a tyrant like Saddam to give up his base of power. As I've said repeatedly in these pages, he continued to confiscate the wealth of the nation and to use it for his own pleasure and amusement. The subtleties of international diplomacy would have absolutely no effect on such a man.

Sanctions never touched Saddam, but they did hurt the people of Iraq very much. And when people in the provinces did rise up to rebel against Saddam, the diplomats were nowhere to be seen. The rebels were left to fend for themselves, and they were decimated by the Republican Guard. Any who survived the conflict were destined to become victims of Saddam's revenge. They were slaughtered like sheep. The situation couldn't have been worse.

The first President Bush was disinterested and ineffective by the end of the Gulf War. Later President Clinton favored a doctrine of appeasement. He refused to strike back at terrorists when American forces were hit, which was seen by most people in the Middle East as a sign of cowardice. Many in Iraq were laughing at America during those years, and terrorists like Osama bin Laden were emboldened, broadcasting the message that Americans are cowards. America was brave once, he said, but no longer. And it was hard to argue with those messages when the American leadership had seemingly gone soft on so many things.

When President Clinton did authorize an air strike in Sudan, in August of 2000, he was apparently responding to faulty intelligence, and as a result the U.S. military sent cruise missiles to destroy an aspirin factory. I wasn't following the invasion and bombings in Kosovo or Bosnia very closely at the time, but I was fairly certain that those operations would have little impact on the situation in Iraq. And the efforts of the international community to encourage democracy in our part of the world were meaningless. Before long even the State Department had to acknowledge that their policy of containment wasn't working.

Organized Corruption

In 2001 it became apparent that the world had changed since the end of the Gulf War. The terrorist attacks in New York and Washington, D.C., on September 11, 2001, were a wake-up call for the West. In his State of the Union address, given on January 29, 2002, President George W. Bush identified Iraq, Iran, and North Korea as an "axis of evil." The media in Europe and the Middle East made fun of this idea. But for many of us, it was a clear signal that America was finally getting the message.

I thought at the time that it was likely that the Americans were already planning to come back to Iraq and finish the job by removing Saddam once and for all. I'm absolutely certain that Saddam believed they were coming after him. He was very perceptive in that way, and he was also paranoid.

Members of the Iraqi opposition abroad, many of whom had been talking to President Bush and Secretary of State Colin Powell, were urging the U.S. military to take action. The expatriate community had detailed information about what was happening in Baghdad, and I believe the mere existence of Saddam, with more and more news reaching the West about the evil he had done, was becoming an embarrassment for the Bush White House. They had no option but to listen to what the dissidents and expatriates were telling them.[3]

They had once hoped, naively, that Saddam would just fade away or starve to death. But Saddam had only grown stronger and richer over the previous decade. He had more palaces, more soldiers, more oil, more power, and more weapons, and he unleashed more death and destruction against his enemies in Iraq than ever before. News of what he was doing to his own people was beginning to make head-lines in the West, so surely some sort of response had to come.

The survival of Saddam and his regime had to be a concern for President Bush and Prime Minister Blair in England. After ten years of sanctions, they looked around and he was still there, and very much in charge. He had palaces more beautiful than the White House. He had more money than ever—literally billions of dollars that he had stolen from the people—and millions of barrels of oil were still going out of the country illegally. Furthermore, it now appeared that members of the United Nations were involved as well, taking kickbacks and raking in billions of dollars for themselves.

Washington had underestimated the capacity of a man like Saddam for doing evil. And they had overlooked his capacity for drawing others into his conspiracy, including individuals at the highest levels of the United Nations. I could tell you many stories about the people we call the United Nations. Whenever people hear the name United Nations, they may think of some big, powerful organization. But if they would go to the borders of Iraq and see for themselves who these people really are, they might not be so easily impressed.

More often than not the people we call the United Nations are ordinary men from Third World countries who have no great visions of world peace. Chances are you'll see three or four guys from Third World countries, and they're supposed to be monitoring trucks coming and going across the border. They're supposed to make sure there's no smuggling of contraband; but they're all taking bribes—ten, twenty, thirty thousand dollars at a time—to look the other way. And hundreds of trucks are going back and forth, in both directions, and no one is saying a word.

A Master of Deceit

Unfortunately, it doesn't stop there. I believe that one day the Oil-for-Food program will prove to be the biggest bribery scheme in modern times, and Saddam Hussein will be seen as the man who used it to perfection. He was truly a master of deceit. And thanks to the corruption of U.N. officials, Saddam was able to get whatever he wanted.

After a dozen years of sanctions, the Iraqi people became experts at how to work the system. Millions of tons of oil went through the Persian Gulf under the noses of the U.N. and multinational forces. There were days when dozens of barges loaded with contraband would sail out of our ports. And each one was carrying anywhere from 1,500 to 2,000 tons of oil. Because of the restriction on oil, Saddam had to sell it very cheaply. But because of the volume of contraband going out, the profits were enormous.

With the high price of oil today—recently in America it reached nearly seventy dollars a barrel—it would shock you to know that smugglers were selling Iraqi oil at one time for as little as four dollars a barrel. When dealers could buy it for four dollars and sell it for thirty dollars, believe me, people were clamoring to get it, and this included people from many countries that were supposedly America's allies.

Saddam used to tell the smugglers, "Bring your ships to our ports, fill them up with oil, and take them away. After that, I don't know you anymore." After that the ships would sail out into the Gulf, and often they were stopped by American patrol boats that were there to prevent smuggling. Specialists would test the oil to see if it was from Iraq—they knew the properties of all the different types of oil in the region—and they would say, "Nope, this is Iranian oil. Okay, you can go." And the smugglers would pass through with no further problems.

What the specialists and other officials didn't realize was that Iraqi smugglers had made a deal with Iranian smugglers. He would send Iraqi oil to Iran, and they would send back Iranian oil in return. So when our ships left Basra for Europe or the United Arab Emirates, or wherever they found buyers, there was no one to stop them because the oil wasn't Iraqi.

And that wasn't all. Saddam's agents were selling oil to Iran at very low prices, and Iran was shipping the same oil in the same ships from their ports, but under the Iranian flag. No one was checking them because those ships weren't under the embargo. So the Iranians would sell Iraqi oil on the open market for whatever they could get—and I can assure you it was much higher than the four dollars a barrel they had paid Saddam.

I can say without reservation that the sanctions imposed on Iraq by the United Nations were a 100 percent failure. They had a disastrous effect on the people of Iraq and absolutely no effect on Saddam. Even under the eyes of the U.N. inspectors, Saddam was constantly beating the system. He had a million ways to cheat. And even though the inspectors found and destroyed many prohibited weapons, they never found all of them. Believe me, Saddam was laughing the whole time, and his regime was only getting stronger.

Despite U.N. regulations, Saddam also found hundreds of ways to sell oil illegally. There are many people who will cheat or cut corners to make money when the temptation is so great, and this happened constantly during those years. As just one example, some of our neighbors were given permission to receive from seventy thousand to one hundred thousand barrels of oil per day from Iraq. This was permitted under Item 50 of the U.N. agreement because those countries had been helpful to the coalition during the war, and they depended heavily on Iraqi oil.

But who was checking to see whether it was seventy thousand barrels or two hundred thousand barrels going out? At best, there would be two or three men standing there counting the trucks coming across the border. But if the driver were to strike up a conversation and along the way give the men ten thousand dollars or twenty thousand dollars to look the other way, the monitors would quickly forget how many it was supposed to be and let all the trucks pass on through. And the profits from the sale of contraband oil went right back to Saddam. This was common practice throughout the nineties.

I've heard many stories about how oil was sold at the docks in some of these countries. Saddam would sell it to the Europeans, and in turn they would send him electrical appliances, porcelain toilets with solid gold handles, and the finest Italian marble for building more palaces. If you go to any of the new palaces built since 1991—as many as sixty were built during the time of sanctions—you will see all these things. And then ask yourself, how did all this Italian marble and these expensive gold fixtures get here?

Returning to Abnormal

Saddam was slowed but not stopped by sanctions, and the Saddamists came back as strong as ever. Before long everything was just as it had been before the war. When the Americans left, they turned everything over to the United Nations, and the U.N. officials we saw were uniformly corrupt. They were selling the food and medical supplies that were supposed to be given to the people.

His greed was so great that Saddam would take the grain and the emergency supplies purchased under sanctions and sell it to Iraqi merchants, and then he would give them permission to resell it abroad. Large amounts of money were changing hands all the time. And millions of barrels of Iraqi oil were smuggled out of the country in the same way.

The young, the old, and the poor of Iraq suffered enormously during this time, and the combination of high inflation, the lack of medical care, and the economic impact of all these things on the job market led to high unemployment and, as a result, the deaths of many, many people. The Oil-for-Food program may have kept a few people alive, but it was an ineffective and unmanageable system, and the world would soon discover that it was also a system that was contaminated by corruption.

The program was designed by the U.N. to be operated through an escrow account managed by the French-based international banking consortium of BNP Paribas. The bank was authorized to receive all proceeds from the sale of Iraqi oil and gas. These funds were then kept in escrow to be used in making payments for humanitarian supplies and other items specifically licensed by the United States

Department of Treasury's Office of Foreign Assets Control. These payments could only be made from the BNP account to suppliers who presented letters-of-credit or coupons that met the terms and conditions of the U.N. sanctions regulations. But, as the scandal that unfolded in 2002 quickly revealed, the program was being manipulated by corrupt officials on both ends.

There were bribes, kickbacks, or unauthorized commissions in virtually every transaction under the program, and revenues that were designated to aid the people simply never reached them. According to a report from the United Nations Children's Fund (UNICEF), as many as five thousand Iraqi children a month were dying from diarrhea, pneumonia, breathing problems, and malnutrition as a direct result of the economic sanctions imposed on our country.

Even if the actual figures were half that, it was still a tragedy. Under U.N. regulations Iraq was allowed to sell $5.26 billion worth of oil every six months in order to purchase food and medicine, but most of that money never made it to the people, and that was another source of the suffering we endured. Economic sanctions cut commercial revenues in Iraq by as much as 90 percent, and whatever profits were made through normal trade flowed directly into the coffers of Saddam and his family. And all Iraqis suffered as a result.

Overlooking Differences

If the world thought the hostility between Iran and Iraq was a buffer against illegal trading between these old enemies, they were dead wrong. There was nothing separating the two countries, and there was no one to stop Saddam's tankers from going back and forth across the border. From time to time we would hear that American satellites had spotted trucks going across the border into Iran. Alarms would go off in Europe and America, but there was no way of knowing whether those trucks were carrying food or machinery or contraband; in any event, nothing happened to stop the two countries from trading illegally.

For the entire twelve years between 1991 and 2003, Saddam was buying and selling and making huge profits. The black market was thriving in both Iraq and Iran, and despite their long history of hostility, these two countries became active trading partners. When large amounts of money are involved, even the worst enemies can manage to behave as friends. In particular, the sons of wealthy families in Iraq were in regular contact with the sons of wealthy families in Iran, and they did a huge business back and forth. Chief among these, of course, were the two corrupt and wicked sons of Saddam who were making, literally, billions of dollars on the black market.

Millions of barrels of oil were shipped to the United Arab Emirates, and from there they went around the world. Even when the oil was being sold for only a few dollars per barrel, it was still enough to make Saddam Hussein one of the richest men in the world. He had bank accounts in Europe and the Middle East, and his personal wealth—which was in fact the wealth he had stolen from the Iraqi people—was truly staggering.

The sons of Saddam, especially Uday, would play with the value of currency in Iraq in order to make more money for themselves. For example, Uday would buy all the U.S. dollars he could get his hands on. He bought them from banks, businesses, and exchange services, and he would keep them out of circulation so that the value of the dollar would rise to anywhere from five hundred to two thousand dinars per dollar. Before long the people would panic, and they would start bringing all their money to the bank, and they would exchange thousands, even millions, of dollars so that they wouldn't lose the value of their cash. But as soon as this happened, Uday would dump all those dollars back on the market, buying millions of dinars and virtually bankrupting everyone who had any money at risk.

For their own personal profit, these men were willing to throw the entire Iraqi economy into turmoil. Today, thanks to the new administration and systems put in place by the Americans, the dollar is worth 1,450 dinars, and it's not moving at all. This gives our currency great stability. People aren't worried anymore, and they all know just how much money they have. In the new government, no one is playing with our currency for profit. If you want dinars, you can have them. If you want dollars or English pounds, you can have those too. This has been excellent for Iraq. But under Saddam, we were never secure. We never knew if we could survive from one day to the next. Just imagine what kind of life it was, trying to survive under those conditions.

Rewarding Incompetence

And what did the Baath Party do for Iraq? For one thing, the Baath Party made certain that those who were the most capable were never allowed to become leaders. In every area it was those with second- and third-level skills, who happened to be members of the Baath Party, who were always put in charge. The main reason was because these people would do whatever Saddam wanted them to do without question. And the result was that Iraq continued to slide backward while the rest of the world was moving forward.

Not only was the nation going backward, but we had been pushed into fighting three major wars that consumed any gains we might have made if we had simply been able to pursue our own goals peacefully. In the process, Saddam drained the wealth of Iraq. There we were, a country roughly the size of California, with an army of 6,400 tanks. Compare that to Great Britain, which has so much more at stake, and they only have about 950 tanks altogether.

There is a saying that if you want to understand what's most important to a man, look at where he spends his money. If you want to know what was important to Saddam, look at where he spent the wealth of Iraq. Tanks, missiles, bombs, guns, and explosives—not to mention the millions he poured into the technology and technicians he needed for producing weapons of mass destruction. We were starving and he was buying weapons! And thanks to the corruption of the Baath Party, they were putting our resources into the hands of the least qualified people.

As a general in the air force, I worked with highly specialized equipment. When we bought missiles for our fighters, such as the French Exocet, we had to pay $1.2 million for each one. When we bought a new jet fighter, we had to pay $21 million each. But if we put a second-rate pilot in charge of that aircraft, we soon found out that he didn't have the skill or the courage to fly it, and he would eject at the first sign of trouble. So then what happened to that big investment?

On one occasion I received a call from Tammuz Air Base near Habbaniya, in the south, telling me that one of our pilots had ejected and crashed his plane in the desert. When I asked which aircraft he was flying, I realized that the plane he was in had been flown less than eight hours. It was a brand-new Sukhoi, which was a beautiful Russian-made fighter. So when I got to the base, I told the commander, Gen. Saad, "Round up everybody. I want to talk to them."

They all came, and there were about five hundred of them from eight separate squadrons: pilots, crews, mechanics, radar operators, ground personnel, administrators, and many others. When I came into the room, I said, "Which one of you is the pilot who ejected?" A young first lieutenant raised his hand and said, "It was me, sir. I ejected." So I said, "Come here." He walked up to the front of the room and I said, "What was your mission, and what was your position in the formation?"

He said, "Sir, I was number four. Numbers one and two took off, and, according to procedure, they were to pull high so that when number three and I took off at low level under them we wouldn't get hit by the jet wash. But one and two didn't go high enough, so when I took off I hit the jet wash of number two and my aircraft became unstable. I started losing control, so I ejected."

The air base where this happened is very near Habbaniya Lake, where there is a beautiful resort built several years ago by the French. When that pilot ejected, his plane headed straight for the resort, and if it hadn't somehow veered away on its own, by the grace of God, many people would have been killed. And the reason would have been because this stupid boy thought the world was ending. He didn't think twice about destroying a $20 million jet aircraft that had flown less than eight hours.

Why is this important? Because if you put an unqualified person in charge of something that you value highly, you will be putting everything at risk. And if you do this long enough, sooner or later everything of value will be destroyed by incompetent people. An airplane could care less whether the pilot is British or American or Iraqi. All that matters is that the pilot is competent and properly trained to operate the equipment as it was designed to be used. But a fool can destroy the best fighter in the air force in a matter of minutes.

Saddam built a military with more than 1,000 aircraft, 6,400 tanks, and thousands of missiles of every kind, from laser-guided rockets to the new energy bombs; each one of them was worth more than a million dollars. Such weapons in the hands of a man like Saddam Hussein could drain the entire wealth of the country. Why? Because this man wanted to be big. He wanted to be a hero, to conquer, and to be feared. And in the process he robbed the people, terrified them, and made them poor.

He destabilized the entire region and made his country the enemy of the world. Who would do such a thing? A politician must have good common sense. At the very least he should want to improve the prosperity of the people, but Saddam never cared in the least for how the people of Iraq were actually living. He didn't know the people, and he didn't care what happened to us.

An Empire Built on Sand

In one of my assignments as an air force commander, I was put in charge of six squadrons of jet fighters. Each squadron had about thirty pilots, so I was responsible for 180 pilots and their aircraft. I had trained some of them and given them their solo flights, but of course I didn't know them all. So I watched them, and in time I discovered who the good pilots were, who the leaders were, who followed orders, and who did not. I soon knew who to promote and who to hold back, because my goal was to have the best pilots and the best squadrons not just in the air force but in the whole Middle East.

But this was never the policy in Iraq. Because of the low standards of the Baathis, leaders in all fields and all disciplines were selected on the basis of loyalty to the party, and I believe they actually preferred to have less competent people in key positions. Consequently, the incompetent people who were in charge would make sure that no one who was genuinely competent would ever be allowed to rise.

I remember a conversation that took place in San Antonio, Texas, in 1965, when I was in training at Randolph and Lackland Air Force Bases. There was an officer in the class named Wing Commander Wood who was from New Zealand. I didn't know him very well, but apparently he had been watching me for some time, and one day he came up to me and said, "Georges, I like the way you fly. You're a good pilot, and the flight instructors are saying good things about you. But there's something I'd like to know." So I said, "Sure, Wood. Ask me anything. What is it?" So he said, "Is it still like it used to be in Iraq, where anyone who's doing a good job and advancing in his career, you stop him and pull him back?"

I said, "How did you know that?" He knew what he was talking about because that's exactly the way things were done in my country. He said, "I served in the Royal Air Force in Habbaniya, Iraq, for seven years. We used to have some very good people, but as soon as they would start doing a good job, your people would pull them back to keep them from advancing."

I said, "Yes, I'm sorry to say you're right, only now it's worse. They don't just stop him; they slap him around and say, 'Why are you working so hard? You're not going anywhere!'" And this pilot said to me, "I was afraid of that, and I'm sorry to hear it. Because, even though you're a very good pilot, you'll never be advanced."

He was right, but I'm sorry to say that it wasn't just pilots who were being held back. My country was destroyed—politically, militarily, commercially, and especially in the leadership of the government— because of the Baath Party and their bad policies. Saddam Hussein was an artist in his ability to destroy not just the country but even the party that supported him. He was not alone though. His allies were doing a pretty good job of destroying things on their own.

The nation of Iraq, like all those in the Middle East or elsewhere that operate in an atmosphere of corruption, had been weakened by hatred, suspicion, and fear—all the worst emotions. This was a shame because Iraq has so many natural resources and we've had so many opportunities to achieve great things. But for a time, the country fell into the hands of the wrong men and we paid dearly for that. But thank God, the structure erected by Saddam and the Baathis has collapsed, and Saddam is gone—because it was an empire built on shifting sands. And as the Bible tells us, only a house built on solid rock can stand.

Taking a Demotion

The system in Iraq was so corrupt that even acts of benevolence had disastrous effects. Poor and incompetent leadership combined with Saddam's military adventurism and confiscation of our national treasure had been driving the nation into deep financial trouble for years. But when sanctions began in the mid-1990s, the economy suddenly went into freefall. When Saddam saw what was happening, he decided to intervene by giving money to party members so they could survive in those difficult times. Of course, he controlled all the oil revenues and the entire wealth of the nation, and he could use it however he pleased. So he created a bonus program, the *Makrama*, meaning "the gift of the president."

Originally this was mainly a way for Saddam to solidify his power base, but before long it became a necessity for millions of Iraqis. Inflation was eating us alive, and there was no way to increase salaries enough to make up for the difference. But consider what happened to those like me who weren't party members. In the late eighties, my salary as an air force general was 1,000 dinars per month, which was about $3,000 U.S.—because the dinar at that time was worth three American dollars. That was a good salary in Iraq, but in 1995 when inflation went so high, 3,000 Iraqi dinars was only worth about one American dollar. This meant that my salary, which had been worth $3,000, was suddenly worth just 30 cents.

On paper, salaries continued to increase, and by 1998 a general's salary was shown as 80,000 dinars per month—eighty times my salary a decade earlier—but in reality it was the equivalent of only $40 U.S., and no one could live on that. If you were a loyal party member, you would receive "the gift of the president," which could vary from a half million to a million and a half dinars per household. So while you were receiving just $40 in your pay envelope each month, "the gift" could come to $2,000 to $3,000 or more every month.

So what did this mean to the country? It meant that suddenly the people's loyalty was no longer to the government or the military or their employers but to Saddam Hussein, who held their lives, their welfare, and their future in his hands. The "gift of the president" could be ten to twenty times the amount of your salary, and it varied based on your position and rank. If your rank increased, the gift also increased, and it could reach as high as 10 million dinars every month, which was about $5,000.

Ultimately this meant that Saddam had made Iraq, its industry, its oil, and everything else, very small in the hearts of the people; but he had made himself bigger than Iraq because he was the gracious benefactor who was giving the people such wonderful gifts. And this is why people who supported the Baath Party were so loyal to Saddam after the war. In their minds, their loyalty wasn't just to Iraq but to this man. And most of them had never considered that this wasn't how it was supposed to be.

Imagine the devastating impact this had on the nation. Inflation was destroying us and sanctions were just as bad, but Saddam was able to solve the problem by giving his people "the gift." Thus, by his generosity, he restored what had been lost because of inflation. Party members were doing very well, but the rest of us had no alternative but to be quiet and wait.

This also meant that non-party members had to begin selling off personal items—cars, clothes, televisions, furniture, even the good wooden doors inside our homes—just to be able to buy food to eat. We sold everything we could live without and many things we couldn't. Some high-ranking officers who had beautiful chairs, lamps, light fixtures, and fans in their homes had to sell all of it, and in some cases they even had to sell the large ornate doors on the outside of their homes and replace them with plywood or simple sheets of tin.

A Nation in Decline

This all started after Saddam invaded Kuwait in 1990. That's when things really started going downhill for us. The lucky ones were those who had family living abroad, and fortunately I was one of them. My son and his family were living in Europe, where he had his medical practice. He wasn't a wealthy man, but if he was able to send us just one hundred dollars a month, that was an incredible blessing, because it was a great amount of money for us. And that was the only way we managed to have anything like a normal life.

Those who had no family abroad and who had no other means of earning money were in terrible shape at that time, especially the women. For some of those women, the only way to survive was to sell themselves to men who were members of the party and who could pay them for their services. This contributed as much as anything else to a coarsening of morality and decency and the breakdown of Iraqi society.

Little by little, corruption began eating its way into every field and profession. The military was being run by men who were corrupt and, in many cases, incompetent. This meant, in turn, that the army was not able to defend the nation. The good officers were often forced to take lower-level jobs, or they were simply forced to leave the military altogether. The military commanders would keep non-party members if there was no one else to replace them; but as soon as they found a party man who could do the job reasonably well, they would push the non-party man out the door and release him.

The Baath Party modeled itself on the Communist Party in Russia. In the Soviet system, children from eight to ten years old were encouraged to become *Oktyabryata*, or Octobrists. That was the Communist Youth Organization's program for indoctrinating young people into the beliefs and policies of the party.

The youngest ones were called "the children of October," as a reminder of the Bolshevik Revolution of October 1917. Between the ages of ten to sixteen, they could become Pioneers, which was sort of like Scouting, with a lot of outdoor activities. Then, from nineteen to twenty-three, they were expected to join the Komsomol. These children were taught how to be good communists, so that one day they could become full-fledged members of the party and unquestioning servants of Mother Russia.

I was a student pilot in Russia for three years, so I was able to observe that system closely. This was the model Saddam had decided to follow; but as we saw in the late-1980s when the Soviet Union was beginning to collapse, there were many problems with the communist ideology. I think it was inevitable that the system would fail. And I think Saddam's commitment to the same political ideology played a big part in the ultimate collapse of his regime.

The only way I was able to keep my job and rise to the rank of two-star general was by being an excellent pilot and working harder than everyone else. Saddam knew that, as a Christian, I was no threat to him. Besides that, he knew that I was honest and he could count on me to tell the truth, whether he liked it or not. In some ways I think he was proud of me because I was the only officer in Iraq at that time who had been trained as a pilot in Russia and America, and I'd also spent time as an officer in England, France, Italy, and other places. I worked hard and was loyal to my country. These things pleased him, but not enough to make him listen to my objections or take my advice.

Things in Iraq were getting progressively worse. We weren't modernizing like other nations; we were going backward. Why? Because in every area of our lives, we were at the mercy of second-rate party officials and bureaucrats, and these men were incapable of restoring order or of coping with the problems created by the U.N. sanctions and the restrictions placed on us after the Gulf War. So the country continued to deteriorate, and life for all Iraqis became very, very hard.

Risks and Rewards

When we were still going through all of this, I asked myself at one point, *What are the attributes of a Baath Party man? How is he different from me? And what are the benefits of being a party member?* The answer was obvious. Those who were not especially capable—whether it was in the military, the administration, in politics, or simply being an accountant—could advance to the top of their career because of their membership in the party. In fact, the main value of membership in the party was job security.

The important jobs were not given to those who were talented and hard working; they were given to members of the party, regardless of their skill. And the reason was that Saddam and the leaders of the party understood that rewarding party members with jobs and money and other benefits was the best way of preserving their own authority and power.

Consequently, what you would find in Iraq, where the Baath Party was in control, was that the leaders in politics, science, medicine, administration, and every other field were, virtually without exception, the least efficient and least capable men. And these men, in turn, were always jealous and suspicious of those who were more capable, so they would hold them back and make it impossible for them to improve their status.

The men who surrounded Saddam were never the best and most capable people in the government. They were the worst ones, but they were faithful to him because they had been given positions they knew they didn't deserve. They owed everything to Saddam, and because they were loyal and would say or do whatever he wanted, they were also well rewarded for their service. It's true that Saddam managed to build a large and powerful regime, but it was not built on the basis of skill and efficiency. Rather, it was built on the basis of blind loyalty to Saddam. And this is the only way that someone like Izzat al-Douri, who had been a lowly ice seller in the village of Dour, could rise to become Saddam's top deputy, a four-star general, and ambassador of the president.

Foreign Relations

The only authority in Iraq was the authority of Saddam, and this was the only thing he created. His acts of generosity and benevolence were a sham. We were all puppets and he was the puppet master. Our government became one of the weakest government systems in the entire civilized world. While the system may have worked in Iraq for a time, simply because of the scope and brutality of Saddam's repressive regime, it was a categorical disaster to everyone else in the world.

Internationally, Iraq was seen as a loser, and the ones who paid the greatest price for this were the citizens who had to live under Saddam's tyranny. Now that Saddam and the Baathists are gone, the people of Iraq are discovering that this person who had the power of life and death over them was a nobody. He was the biggest liar and the biggest loser of all. And the systems he created were among the weakest in leadership, organization, and administration of any in the entire world.

Once in a while during the first year or so after liberation, I would hear someone say, "Now that Saddam is gone, who will take his place?" Some would even say, "Where will we find another Saddam?" Frankly, I was shocked to hear that kind of talk. It made me angry to think that there were Iraqis who still believed that two plus two is nine, and anything that Saddam had said or done was just fine. But I realized, of course, that most Iraqis have never known any other kind of government, and they can't imagine what will come next.

But I would ask those people, "What are you talking about? Who was Saddam Hussein that you still think of him as some kind of hero? He was nothing but a gangster in the streets, a criminal, a common thug! Why are you worried about who will take his place? Anyone would be better than Saddam." But this is what happened. For more than forty years the people of Iraq have been beaten down, oppressed, robbed, brutalized, and stripped of their resources and power by a tyrant. We were all victimized by a despot who would stop at nothing to enrich and empower himself. Now that we have a new government, a new constitution, and a new opportunity to join the community of nations, we have to look forward to what is next. With God's help, perhaps we can even regain some of what we've lost.

It's sad for me to think about all the Iraqis who moved away during those terrible years. The Iraqi community in America, Australia, England, and many other places is very large now, and some of those people would love to be able to come home to their native land. And when they come, they will bring knowledge and experience and wealth, and they will be able to help us find what we've been missing for so long.

It will not be an easy transition, but we need those people, and I think they need us. So it is my prayer that this sort of transformation will be possible in the months and years ahead. There's so much we need to learn about self-respect and opportunity and freedom, and the Iraqi people are eager to learn.

Iraqis who managed to survive all those years under Saddam may resent the fact that some of the people who have been living abroad will have a chance to come and take important jobs in business, industry, and the government, as if they had never left. But we need to understand why they left in the first place; and we need to understand that, at this moment, we need the knowledge and skill that they can bring to Iraq from abroad.

A System That Works

The Iraqi people also need to understand the importance of what America, Britain, and the other coalition nations have done for us. They have helped us regain our freedom, and they have helped to restore our credibility and give us a voice in the community of nations. They risked a lot to do this for us, and many of their sons and daughters gave their lives for our freedom. We should be grateful for what they've done and show them our appreciation by making the most of this incredible opportunity.

We know, of course, that Europe and America have other interests in our area—they want to secure the peace because it is good for them too. Many of these countries have diplomatic and commercial interests in the Middle East that they want to secure, and this is also what they were fighting for. So we need to be realistic about that. But we Iraqis must now be willing to participate in the restoration of our nation and our honor, and to build a new government that is worthy of our hopes and our great and ancient history.

Unfortunately, there are some Iraqis, and others in the Middle East, who are still pro-Saddam and pro-Osama bin Laden, who are saying, "The Americans are there to take your oil and occupy your country." But this is not true. I know why the Americans are there. They want stability and peace in the region, and they want to make sure that their interests are protected.

America is the longest surviving republican democracy in the entire history of the world, and they believe that a free democratic nation is the best system for guaranteeing the peace and prosperity of the people. The task now is to help the Iraqi people, who have known nothing but tyranny and fear and suspicion for their entire lives, to understand this and believe it.

Americans and Iraqis need to understand that America's interests will be served, naturally and fairly for everyone, if there is peace in the Middle East. One of the hats I wear today is that of Executive Secretary of the Iraqi Institute for Peace (IIP) in Iraq, and peace and reconciliation are very important to me for two reasons. First, I'm a Christian and Jesus Christ is the Prince of Peace. Second, peace is the universal condition of nations that are prosperous and happy. And I believe that's what we ought to be pursuing.

The remarkable thing is that the American military and the U.S. State Department are still working to make sure that the people of Iraq feel that we have ownership of our government and its policies. In the past, armies have come to Iraq to conquer and colonize our land, but this is not what's happening now. America and Britain do not want to own Iraq but to help us stabilize the country and get it going again. Our task now is to make sure that whatever we come up with in the future—at the polls and in the halls of government—will be a system that really works.

PART III

CHAPTER 9

THE WAR OF LIBERATION

When I was discharged from the air force on February 5, 1991, I returned to the job I had been doing before the war, working with the Christian community in Iraq, and I was elected president of the Baghdad Evangelical Church. This was an organization of all the evangelical churches in Iraq, and it's where I spent most of my time. I had served as leader of the evangelical churches from 1986 to 1990, but not on a full-time basis. The farm was my main occupation in those days. But from 1991 to 2003 I was able to go back to this work full-time, and they were some of the most wonderful years of my life.

During this time I met with people from all over the world, and I traveled frequently. Even though I was no longer an active duty officer, and certainly not a member of the Baath Party, the prime minister's office called me on several occasions. They asked me to travel to Europe and North America as a representative of Iraq, and I was glad to do it. One of the most important trips was one I made to Coventry in 2000 to meet with leaders of the Anglican Church who were engaged in developing an alliance for peace and reconciliation. Participants in these meetings represented churches from all over the world—more than eighty men and women from North America, Europe, Asia, and Africa.

On that trip I spoke with evangelical leaders and the directors of several Christian organizations. I also made my first visit to Coventry Cathedral in England—that great church which had been erected upon the ashes of the one destroyed by German bombers in the Second World War. The resurrected cathedral didn't replace the old one, which was only a shell, but incorporated the fractured walls and towering spire in the new atrium, and those ruins still stand today as an even greater tribute to faith and freedom.

After that, I was invited to conferences in Europe and America to talk about peace and reconciliation, and my knowledge and enthusiasm for this new area of interest were constantly being expanded. I continued to develop these relationships throughout 1999 and 2000, and in November 2001 I was invited back to Beirut, Lebanon, for a conference of pastors and laymen who were working for peace in the Middle East. At one of those meetings I was asked to serve as director of the International Centre for Reconciliation (ICR) in Baghdad, sponsored by the Bishop of Coventry and his emissary to the Middle East, Canon Andrew White. I understood the importance of the project, and I gladly agreed to take on the added responsibilities.

A Life-Saving Message

The church leaders in Britain were very encouraging to me, and they were eager to avert another war between Iraq and the West. They introduced me, in turn, to their counterparts in the United States who were pursuing similar goals, trying to improve relations between America and Iraq. Canon Andrew White, who was a young priest at Coventry Cathedral, just thirty-five years of age at the time, was convinced that if we could gather enough support, we could persuade Saddam to cooperate. Andrew was leading the mission in the Middle East, and he soon became a good friend and ally. It was through him that many of my contacts were established around the world.

All the men and women I met in those days were dedicated to reconciliation between the Sunni, the Shia, the Christians, and the other religions in Iraq, and their support and encouragement eventually made it possible for me to take leaders such as Dr. Abdul Latif al-Hemayem, who is the leader of Sunni Muslims in Iraq, and Ayatollah Sayid Hussein al-Sader, the Shia leader, to meet with prominent Christian leaders in England and America. And all of this had been arranged by my friend and colleague, Canon Andrew White.

The first of those trips, widely reported in the media at that time, was to meet the Right Reverend Colin Bennetts, Bishop of Coventry. The group also met with the former Archbishop George Carey and from there they traveled to North Carolina to meet with the Rev. Billy Graham. I felt that these were remarkable accomplishments, that even in those difficult days we were able to take a deputy of Saddam Hussein and the secretary of the Islamic Conference to meet with men of that stature in the West. The meetings were informative, constructive, and eye opening; and I believe they helped create a new level of trust and respect between us.

Everything was done with the aim of expanding the reconciliation and peace movement that I was trying to establish in Baghdad. Leaders of the government in Iraq, on the other hand, were hoping that these meetings would help to lift the sanctions, or at least reduce restrictions on trade. They wanted Iraq to be able to rejoin the community of nations and be accepted once again as part of the civilized world. I often felt that the people of Iraq were living on another planet. We were totally isolated from the rest of the world and in such bad shape, politically, economically, and spiritually. We needed all the help we could get.

All our neighbors—Iran, Syria, Saudi Arabia, Turkey, and especially Kuwait—were enemies of Iraq now, and we were struggling to survive under United Nations sanctions. So my goal was to help regain my country's standing in the world. The sanctions were bad enough, but we also had to live with Saddam, and he was at least as bad as sanctions. These were the real suffering years for us. But I felt that becoming involved in the religious life of the nation would give us renewed hope and new ways of improving our chances for reconciliation and peace.

A Direct Confrontation

My most unforgettable conversation with Canon Andrew White took place in the fall of 2002 when he called from England to arrange an official visit to Baghdad. He told me he wanted to bring several members of the ICR in Coventry to talk about ways to improve the situation in Iraq. When he called on September 21, he said, "Georges, it's very important that a group of us come to Iraq on the twenty-third of September. We already have our tickets and we'll be coming to meet with Tariq Aziz, the deputy prime minister, as well as the foreign minister and President Saddam Hussein."

I thought this was very strange, indeed. No one could simply call and then come to Baghdad two days later and expect to meet with Saddam. So I said, "Excuse me, but why are you coming? And what are you hoping to accomplish here?" Andrew said, "I'll tell you when we get there." *Get there?* I thought. *He wants to come and meet with three of the highest-ranking officials in the government, two days from now!?* So I said, "Andrew, do you know what you're asking for? How do you expect me to put something like that together in two days? Look, I'm willing to help make the arrangements for you, but that's much too soon."

But the canon wasn't dissuaded in the least. In fact, I think my hesitation was more of an incentive to him than anything else. He said, "Listen, Georges, you've got to help me. I know you're an important man in Iraq and you can do this for us. It's imperative that we come." At that point I thought, *I wonder who put him up to this? Surely somebody has told him to do this.* Frankly, I wondered at first if the British prime minister's office wasn't behind it. But then I thought, *Well, why not help him? At least I can try.* So I said, "Okay, Andrew. I'll do my best."

After I hung up the phone I immediately called Tariq Aziz, and he was amused by Andrew's request. But when I explained everything to him, he told me, "Sure, let them come. We'll work on it," by which he meant that he would see if Saddam would be willing to meet with an English delegation. But no promises were made.

Tariq Aziz said he would be willing to meet with the English visitors, and he also said that since the delegation would be in Baghdad for four days, he would see what else he could arrange for them to do. In the meantime, I went to see the ministers of religious affairs and foreign affairs to make arrangements for their visit, and then I also went to the residence office to arrange for our foreign guests to stay in the city. All of them were very helpful. If Andrew and his team were able to get their visas and travel arrangements completed in the U.K. on time, then they wouldn't have any problems once they arrived in Iraq. Plans like that didn't usually go so smoothly, but on this occasion I was able to get the job done with time to spare.

Our "Invited" Guests

When they arrived, everything was ready. No foreign visitors could come to Iraq without being accompanied by a member of the intelligence service, however. So an officer from the Mukhabbarat was assigned to them. These men call themselves tour guides, but everyone knows they're only there to make sure that no secret transactions will be taking place. And they would also have a staff member from the ministry of foreign affairs traveling with them the whole time, to translate and to advise the delegation on protocol when necessary.

When they first came to Iraq, I didn't know most of them. I had never met John Holliman or Michael Smith who work with the ICR in London. Canon Andrew White, who became a friend and colleague during my time at Coventry, was especially gracious. Andrew is a tall and uninhibited young man and visibly passionate about his work. He refuses to be slowed down by obstacles—including even a diagnosis of multiple sclerosis. Andrew was named to serve as emissary of the Archbishop of Canterbury and director of the International Centre for Reconciliation in Coventry. I was named to head the ICR in Iraq.

Our first meeting with Tariq Aziz was not very successful. Andrew and his friends were concerned that Iraq was on a collision course with the U.N., and they were very confrontational and demanding. Tariq Aziz was not pleased with their approach. Andrew made it clear that they were trying to prevent another war, and they said it was essential that Saddam allow the U.N. weapons inspectors to come back in, either on the first of October or the first of November.

Tariq Aziz reprimanded Andrew and told him it wasn't his place to tell President Saddam his business, at which time Andrew said, "Mr. Aziz, I hope you understand what I'm about to say to you, because I can't say it more clearly than this. But if you don't allow the inspectors to come back in, as I've just said, your country will be flattened." That's the word he used, "flattened," and Tariq Aziz was upset that Andrew would speak to him in that way. And, honestly, I was surprised by it as well.

Tariq Aziz said, "Reverend Andrew, you really shouldn't be speaking to me like this." But Andrew said, "Mr. Aziz, believe me when I say that I'm your friend. But I would be no friend if I didn't speak honestly to you. I'm only saying this to make sure that you understand that the situation now is very, very intense, and President Saddam cannot continue to ignore and insult the whole world."

Andrew didn't say that war was coming immediately or at some date certain. He wouldn't have been permitted to go that far, I'm sure, but Andrew left little doubt that this was really the heart of what he had come to say. If Saddam continued to resist the United Nations weapons inspectors and thumb his nose at the world, as he had done consistently for the past five years, it was only a matter of time until the second Gulf War would begin.

Tariq Aziz wasn't the only one who was shocked by the confrontational approach our "invited" guests had taken. But Andrew's message must have gotten through to Saddam because the inspectors were allowed back in before the November first deadline that Andrew had mentioned. When they arrived, the inspectors already had a list of sites to be examined, and they made quick work of it. But at one key site, they were stopped at the gate by security guards and weren't allowed to go in.

Saddam's agents blocked the doors and claimed the site wasn't on the list that had been approved by the president. The inspectors showed them the document and, sure enough, that building was on it. Nevertheless, the agents said, "No, you're not coming in here, so you may as well leave now." And that's just what they did. They tried briefly to negotiate with officials from the ministry of defense to gain access to the site, but it didn't work out, and that's when the inspectors took their equipment and left Iraq for good.

Taking the Other Side

Tariq Aziz told me that he would speak to the president about the delegation and try to set up an appointment for them to meet with Saddam, but after a long series of frustrating delays, they still hadn't been permitted to go to the palace. With only a few days until Andrew and his friends would have to fly back to England, I said, "Let's see if we can get an appointment with Abdul Latif al-Hemayem, who is the secretary of the Islamic Conference and leader of Sunni Muslims in

Iraq. He's one of the most important sheiks of the Sunni tribes in the Sunni triangle. Maybe he can help."

Dr. Al-Hemayem was very close to Saddam. He had made the pilgrimage to Mecca (the Hadj) on Saddam's behalf. Islam allows those who cannot go on Hadj to send a substitute in their place, and Hemayem was the one who went for Saddam. He had also made a copy of the entire Koran by his own hand with Saddam's blood. He also happened to be the owner of the Islamic Bank of Iraq and a close personal friend of Saddam, so meeting with him would be an important step. When we arrived at Dr. Al-Hemayem's office, Andrew gave him a letter that explained what he wanted to say to Saddam.

At two o'clock in the afternoon, the Sunni leader agreed to call the palace and set up a meeting, and he said we would be able to see Saddam at eight o'clock that evening. Then he gave Andrew a beautiful *abaya*, which in this case was a long gentleman's robe worn by Arab sheiks, and he gave him two more to take back to England—one for Rowan Williams, the Archbishop of Canterbury, and one for George Carey, the former Archbishop. They were very elegant gifts, and Andrew was obviously pleased to receive them.

We went back to the Al Rashid Hotel at that point and waited expectantly for a call. But eight o'clock came and went and nothing happened. At one thirty in the morning we were still waiting, but the call never came. The delegation also included two English vicars. Both of them were military officers in the chaplaincy, one a colonel and the other a lieutenant colonel. We all waited there together for two more days, but eventually Andrew and the others decided they would have to give up and return to England. Before they left, however, Andrew requested one more meeting with Tariq Aziz, and when that last meeting took place he disclosed there was going to be a meeting of parliament very soon in which the issue of Iraq would be discussed.

"There will be a vote," he said, "on whether or not Britain should go to war against your country as a member of the multinational coalition led by the United States." But then Andrew said, "Mr. Aziz, don't you think you ought to have someone you trust at that meeting?" He looked across the room at me and said, "We would like to recommend that you send General Sada, who speaks very good English, and he can report back to you on what happens in London."

I could see that Andrew was concerned about the likelihood of another war, and he was worried about my safety. But it wasn't just the war that concerned him. After the hard way he had spoken to these highly placed government officials, Andrew was afraid that someone might want to hurt me. I had put myself in harm's way by arranging the meetings, and Andrew had not attempted to spare the deputy prime minister's feelings when he spoke to him so bluntly.

As the deputy prime minister and confidant of Saddam, Tariq Aziz had immediate access to the president. Saddam was both president and prime minister, as well as the head of the revolutionary council, which was the most powerful group in the country. And he was the commander-in-chief of the military, so as Saddam's chief deputy Tariq Aziz had a great deal of authority. He would certainly want to know if the British Parliament voted in favor of another war with Iraq, and sending me as an insider would be a prudent step for him to take.

A Timely Exit

I was convinced that another war was the last thing we needed. Sanctions and corruption were already destroying the country. But my strong convictions about the need for a more conciliatory relationship between America and Iraq made Saddam and his deputies, including Tariq Aziz, more suspicious of me. I didn't know whether they would give me permission to go with Andrew or not, but I was ready to go and hopeful the answer would be yes.

After he considered Andrew's suggestion, Tariq Aziz said, "Yes, I think it's a good idea. Why don't you take Georges with you to England?" And then to me he said, "Georges, I agree that you should go to London, and I want you to attend that meeting of Parliament. I would like to know what happens there, and I will be very happy if you call me any time, day or night, and tell me exactly what they decided at that meeting."

Then after telling me to go with Andrew, he took a notepad from his desk and wrote some numbers on it. He handed me the slip of paper and said, "Georges, I'm giving you two telephone numbers. These are private numbers, and no one else answers these telephones but me. As soon as you go to the meeting and find out what they're thinking, I want you to call me on one of these numbers and tell me in detail what took place. Do you understand?" And I said, "Yes, sir. I understand, and I will be glad to do that."

What Andrew had not told him was that the parliamentary meeting that would be taking place was not the political body that sits at Westminster but the clerical body composed of members of the clergy. Most people know that the primary political bodies of the English Parliament are the House of Lords and the House of Commons. But there is a third body, the Synod, which represents the Church of England, which is the state church. The Synod has a voice in legislation whenever social, cultural, or religious matters are involved. That was the meeting that Andrew and I were going to attend.

I was so happy to be given permission to go with Andrew to England. I breathed a silent prayer: *Thank you, God. You've saved me from the mouth of the lion!* Even though I was well known in Iraq, and generally well respected by Saddam and his deputies, they knew that on this issue I was with the other side. Saddam was adamant about resisting the West and continuing to build his own power, but I knew that was a suicide mission, and I was becoming more and more aggressive in my own involvement with the movement for reconciliation. I dreaded the prospect of another war, and this made Saddam and Tariq Aziz wary of me.

No one in the government had forgotten that I'd been imprisoned for a short time after my debate with Qusay Hussein, and I had been sent back into retirement for the second time. But there was never any effort on my part to undermine the government. I was concerned for my people, and that's why I was eager to join the reconciliation movement and encourage Saddam to allow the inspectors to come back and finish their job.

But going to London at that time proved to be a real blessing. This was especially true since my family were all out of the country as well. The only problem was that, under Iraqi law, at least one member of the family had to remain in Iraq at all times. It was like the Soviet system in that way: if a son or daughter went abroad, at least one parent had to remain behind. If both parents went abroad, at least one child had to remain behind. In this case, I was going to England while my family members were all outside the country; but I was going with the blessings of the deputy prime minister and, indirectly, of the president himself. So once the clearances had been given and my travel documents were ready, we left Baghdad and I traveled with Andrew's delegation back to the U.K. on September 27, 2002.

An Unavoidable War

When I got to England, it didn't take long to realize that the game was up. It was obvious from everything I saw and heard—newspapers, television, conversations in the street. And when I observed the political mood of the country, I realized that Prime Minister Blair and the members of parliament, for the most part at least, were convinced that another war with Iraq was unavoidable. The only question was when.

When I visited the British Foreign Office at Whitehall, in London, they told me they were very concerned about conditions in Iraq. Saddam's obstinate denial to allow full access to our weapons facilities, and his attempts to mislead the U.N. and confuse the issue, were having the opposite effect of what Saddam intended. Before I left, I offered the military planners some counsel that I felt was very important. I said, "If it turns out that Britain and America conclude that you must attack again, please do not attack the whole country as you did in the first Gulf War. Attack only the targets that will weaken the regime, but please don't destroy the infrastructure, the bridges, the homes, and the property that belongs to the people."[4]

Then, on November 11, 2002, I was in the gallery when the members of the Synod met to deliberate our fate. Even before we entered the chambers at Westminster, everyone knew I was there. I had been introduced as an air vice marshal and a delegate of the Iraqi government, and they proceeded to discuss the situation in Iraq and the Middle East at length. I listened intently, and I was amazed as the deliberations went back and forth, often with great intensity. When they concluded the discussion, however, a vote was taken to determine whether or not that body would be willing to support a resolution of war.

As it turned out, there were 121 votes by members of the Synod in favor of going to war with Iraq with the authorization of the United Nations, and 142 votes in favor of joining the coalition led by the United States without going through the U.N. This was an overwhelming decision. Either way, whether with or without the U.N., they had agreed that war with Iraq was the only option.

I immediately called Tariq Aziz using one of the phone numbers he had given me, and I said, "Sir, the war has been declared against us, so please do something. You must speak to the president and tell him what's happening." We spoke for nearly twenty minutes, and I gave him as much detail about the meeting as I could, offering my own suggestions. But I had no idea what he would actually do. Tariq Aziz was really shaken by this news. He said, "Georges, how could they make such a decision? What made them decide to go to war against us?" He asked me, "Did you see the Archbishop of Canterbury?" I said, "Yes, sir, I saw him. He's here, and all the clergy are here. They are all agreed that war is unavoidable."

I told him that as of that date, November 11, 2002, war was already declared against us. But neither Tariq Aziz nor any of the members of the Iraqi government seemed to understand what that would mean. Instead, Tariq Aziz said, "Georges, I want you to stay there and wait for me. I'm coming to Europe on the fourteenth of February. I will have an audience with the pope in Rome on that day. I'm sure he will be able to do something about this and tell them to stop the war."

"February?" I asked, incredulously. "Sir, do you understand what's happening? The fourteenth of February is three months away and a lot can happen before that." It was obvious that he had no idea how serious our situation had become. With the Synod, the British Parliament, the United States Congress, and the United Nations now demanding that Iraq come to terms with the rest of the world, it should have been obvious that an invasion could come at any time, and Tariq Aziz was talking about waiting three months for an audience with the pope that, more than likely, would have no effect at all.

So, again, I said, "Sir, that's too long, and, believe me, the pope will do nothing." At that point, I was convinced that war was inevitable. But Tariq Aziz didn't believe me.

An Unusual Visitor

As conditions in Iraq continued to worsen, I decided it would be good for me to take the deputy prime minister's advice and stay in England for a while longer. I had a place to stay, and there was a lot that I could do there to try and help the cause back in Baghdad. I was already recognized as someone working for peace and reconciliation in Iraq, and I was becoming known as a spokesman for religious reconciliation. People in England, America, and Iraq knew my name, and this helped to increase my involvement in public policy matters.

I had planned to continue as president of the evangelical churches, but since I was staying in England there wasn't much I could do. I was also a board member of the Holy Land Trust, a foundation based in California and headed by Dr. Robin Wainwright. And I was also asked to join the board of World Compassion, headed by Dr. Terry Law, and I now serve as the director of the programs in Iraq for that organization.

While I was still in England, during the first week of December, Canon Andrew White called to tell me that a man was coming from his alma mater, Cambridge University, to speak with me about the war. This was to be, he said, the last and final effort to avoid another major conflict in Iraq, and someone had told this man that he ought to go to London to meet with Gen. Georges Sada. Andrew told me the gentleman was well known in the peace and reconciliation movement. He had worked with former Russian Premier Mikhail Gorbachev to end the violence in that country after the fall of the Berlin wall in 1989. Subsequently he was in Eastern Europe, working with the governments of Bosnia and Herzegovina to restore peace in that troubled region.

But the man who arrived at my door a few hours later looked nothing like the Cambridge scholar I was expecting. He was wearing a very odd costume—a long saffron robe with a white tunic underneath, and a heavy topcoat over that. When I opened the door I wasn't sure if this was the person I was supposed to meet or not. But he introduced himself as Junsei Terasawa, a representative of the International Peace Bureau in Geneva, Switzerland.

Suddenly I understood why he was dressed the way he was. He was a Buddhist monk. He told me he was originally from Japan and had been traveling all over the world as a messenger of peace for many years. So I invited him to come in and we talked at length about many things, especially about the problems in Iraq. Dr. Terasawa told me he was heading a committee of international religious leaders who wanted very much to go to Iraq. They wanted to speak directly with President Saddam, or at least to speak with his deputy, Tariq Aziz, who could relay a message of peace. Terasawa said he had learned about my work with the International Centre for Reconciliation from the clergy in Coventry. He knew about my background as an air vice marshal and the fact that I'm an Assyrian Christian. He was convinced, he told me, that I was the right man to help him fulfill his mission.

A Desperate Mission

Honestly, I thought the chances of changing Saddam's mind were negligible. As much as I was hoping and praying that some alternative to war could be found, altering the path we were on seemed impossible, and I was convinced the war was going to happen, one way or the other. Nevertheless, I agreed to help Dr. Terasawa make one last attempt to alter the course of destiny. I told him I would arrange the visas for himself and his colleagues, and I would also make sure they received some kind of hearing from the government of my country. I thought Tariq Aziz, who had been so depressed the last time I spoke to him, might see Terasawa's mission as a sign of hope. So I called him.

When I spoke with him in Baghdad, I told Tariq Aziz about Terasawa's plan, but he said, "Georges, you've got to stop them." By "them," he was referring to the English and Americans who were putting together a military coalition. He said, "You know I have an appointment to meet with the pope, at the Vatican, on the fourteenth of February. So you must make them wait until I go there." I didn't say anything, but I couldn't help thinking that the whole situation was absurd. I was sad for Tariq Aziz because he really believed I could convince the multinational forces to wait for two more months so that he could make a desperate trip to Rome.

I told him that I would speak to someone, but then I asked him to prepare visas for Dr. Terasawa and his committee, and he agreed to do that. When I informed Terasawa what Tariq Aziz had told me, he said, "Okay, that leaves a month and a half. First, I must go to Washington. Then I'll go back to Geneva, and from there I'll go to Italy. Then I will go and meet with Mr. Aziz in Baghdad." Actually, I thought the plan sounded crazy, but that's exactly what he did.

When Terasawa and his group met with Tariq Aziz in Rome, on February 14, 2003, they gave him a document to present to Saddam that offered him a way out of what was now a looming catastrophe. It said that the committee had already prepared places for Saddam to go to in three separate countries—in India, China, and Russia. Saddam would have to leave Iraq, but he would be welcomed in those places with as many of his family members and former government officials as he wanted to bring with him. He could take his personal possessions, and he would be able to live comfortably there for as long as he liked.

It would be weeks yet before they knew Saddam's answer, but I had arranged to have visas for Terasawa and his group waiting for them in Amman, Jordan, on February 24, 2003. At my request, arrangements were made for visas with the embassy for Dr. Terasawa's group, and my associates also made the travel and hotel arrangements in Baghdad. No sooner had the group arrived in Amman, however, than it began snowing very heavily, and within hours all the airfields were closed. They were stuck there for two days, waiting for the runways to clear. But they finally got a flight to Baghdad on the twenty-sixth, and they were able to meet with Tariq Aziz the same day. I had made those arrangements for him in London.

When they arrived at the palace the next day, however, Terasawa was informed that they would have to wait to meet with Saddam until his staff could clear a space in his busy schedule. So every day for nearly two weeks, from February 26 to March 8, they waited for word that they would be allowed to meet with Saddam. But word never came.

They couldn't stay in Iraq forever; they knew very well what was about to happen. So on March 8, they went back one last time and spoke to Tariq Aziz, and Terasawa said, "Sir, we can't keep waiting like this. It's been two long weeks already and we haven't heard a single word of encouragement from you or the president. You know what we want is just one phone call away, so will you please make that call?" And then he said, "This is the last time I will ask you. We will give you one hour to give us some type of news; but if nothing happens by eight o'clock tonight, then we'll have to leave."

Still, word never came. So at eight o'clock on the evening of March 8, they returned to their hotel, and the next morning they went back to Jordan. Before flying, Terasawa sent me an e-mail. It said, "Dear Georges, The mission has failed and we are coming back. Tell the friends." This was the last message I ever received from him. But I passed that message along to Andrew White and his friends in Coventry, and it was relayed by them to Cambridge, to America, and to Europe, and then to many other friends around the world.

Shock and Awe

The war began on March 19, 2003, with an attack that was described by military analysts and the international news media as "shock and awe." On March 18, just hours before the orchestrated assault was supposed to begin, President Bush received word from intelligence sources in Iraq saying that Saddam was in a bunker in the middle of Baghdad. So without taking time to alert his commander in the field, Gen. Tommy Franks, about what he'd learned, the U.S. commander-in-chief gave the order to strike, hard and fast, to try to end the war before it began.

Immediately, dozens of cruise missiles were launched from the aircraft carriers in the Persian Gulf. Cable viewers around the world watched the unfolding drama in real time as those weapons rained down on the city. The fireworks that descended on the capital that night were unbelievable. I was glued to the television for hours, and I watched those scenes with a combination of sadness, fear, and hope.

And I couldn't help but recall my own night of horror when I was nearly a victim of the first night's bombing twelve years earlier in January 1991.

I'm sure Saddam must have been shocked by the fury of that night and the incredible precision of the weapons that fell on the city. But he wasn't in the bunker when the first missiles struck. Television cameras showed the devastation from the explosions, but coalition operatives on the ground in Baghdad reported that Saddam had been somewhere else and was still on the loose. The next day, Gen. Tommy Franks gave the order to launch Operation Iraqi Freedom, and the second war in the Gulf was quickly under way.

From that moment, the war was a rapid succession of air and missiles assaults followed by a rapid mechanized infantry and armor advance to the capital by American Army and Marine units. The tactics of coalition forces surprised everyone. They didn't stop to engage the Iraqi resistance on the way but raced straight up the main highway toward Baghdad. Within days they were able to secure Saddam International Airport and post guards at all the major bridges along the way.

Some of the British and American units that followed the main assault took up positions in major cities and outposts, and they began clearing out the pockets of resistance in the southern cities of Basra, An Nasiriyah, Al Kut, and others. But the rapid dash to Baghdad by the U.S. Marines completely outsmarted Saddam's forces, and just twenty-two days later, when the forty-foot-tall statue of Saddam was pulled down in Fardus Square, on April 9, 2003, it was apparent that the war was over and, finally, Saddam was no longer in charge.

Bringing down that statue, and the scene of young boys pounding on it with their shoes, was a scene the world would never forget. Seeing the image of their dictator torn down, broken, destroyed, and disgraced in that way sent a clear message to the people of Iraq that things were going to be very different for them in the future.

It struck me that this was the first time in forty-five years that I hadn't participated in military operations as an Iraqi officer, and it was an odd sensation. But I was glad not to be there, and my friends in Coventry were even more so. Several of them called me and said,

"Georges, don't even think about going back to Iraq for a while. It won't be safe for you there, and you're too important to the future of your country to risk your life now. We'll let you know when we feel it's a good time to go back." So I said okay, and I remained in London for three more weeks, until it was safe enough to return to Baghdad.

In the Aftermath

I went back to Baghdad on May 8, 2003, and when I arrived I spoke with the American and British generals who were in charge of the occupation. I was able to offer some ideas on the best way to stop the looting and restore order. I spoke to Gen. Jay Garner at that time, as well as his deputy, British Major General Tim Cross, and they were very receptive to my suggestions. I had met Gen. Cross three months earlier when I'd been invited to attend a series of meetings in England dealing with the prospects for a settlement in Iraq.

When I spoke to Gen. Cross in February 2003, he had said, "Georges, I'll be in Baghdad before long, and I hope you'll come to see me when you get back. By that time hopefully Iraq will be free. Come to my headquarters and tell them your name, and I'll make sure you get right in." When he said that, I knew they were already planning the attack and it would just be a matter of time until the invasion began.

I did go to meet with Gen. Cross as he had suggested when I got back to the capital. He told me he had been talking to officials at the Pentagon about how religious affairs would be set up under the new government, and that was something I wanted to know about. He said the decision was made that there would not be a ministry of religious affairs in the new government, as there had been before, but that each of the major groups—Shia, Sunni, and Christian—would have their own councils. They thought that this would be the best structure, and I told Gen. Cross I thought it was a good plan.

A few days later, I was called to another meeting of military officers, and this time I spoke very candidly. Things were becoming increasingly unstable in the city, and I was of the opinion that strong action needed to be taken. I believe they understood my words in an equally forceful manner. I told them, "I know that the coalition forces know many things, and in your joint operations command you have all the firepower and skill you need to win a military victory. But winning the battle isn't everything. To accomplish your objectives, you must also win the peace, and at this moment the peace has not been won."

Because of the speed and efficiency of the coalition assault, Saddam's forces were quickly routed and the American infantry and tank battalions took over in Baghdad. But there was still a vacuum in the city—there were no police, no local authority, no effective security measures, and a foreign army was in charge. Unfortunately, this foreign army was too small at the time to control the country and provide a police presence in the cities. So I told them that providing a strong police presence ought to be their top priority.

Once it was safe enough to move in Baghdad, I returned to my office and began preparing for the work ahead. Many organizations had asked for my help and suddenly I was wearing many hats. It took some time to get everything organized. Then in early November 2003 I received a call from Andrew White in London telling me that I'd been chosen to receive the Coventry International Prize for Peace and Reconciliation. This was an unexpected honor and a wonderful surprise. In addition to the recognition our cause would receive, I was to be named a Companion of the Church of England and I would have my own pew at Coventry Cathedral. Along with the peace prize I would receive a very special award called the Cross of Nails.

That ceremony took place on November 14, 2003, in a commemorative service at the cathedral. I still wear the Cross of Nails on special occasions as a symbol of my commitment to the cause of peace and reconciliation. The large silver and gold cross is an artistic representation of one formed by the nails that fell from a large crucifix in St. Michael's Church when it was destroyed by the Nazis. When fire fighters and rescuers examined the wreckage of the church after the bombings in November 1940, they found that spikes from the hands and feet of Christ had fallen in the exact shape of the cross and had been fused together by the heat of the blast.

Very much like the cross of girders that remained standing in the ruins of the World Trade Center in New York City after the terrorist attacks of September 11, 2001, the cross of nails was seen as a dramatic testament to the survival of faith amidst chaos. I was told that only ordained clergy and recognized Companions of the Church of England may wear this unique cross, and that's another reason why receiving it was such a great honor. I enjoyed the celebration very much, and I was delighted that my wife, my son and daughter-in-law, and my daughter and her husband were able to be there with me. But the visit to England had to be brief because I had so much work ahead of me in Iraq.

Mobilizing for Peace

Today we need peace more than anything. As of this writing, the peace between Shia, Sunni, and Christians in Iraq is very fragile, and if there's ever a major clash, it could be bad for the Christians. Iraqi Christians are industrious and prosperous people, but we're few in number and politically weak. When the terrorists came in the early days of the insurgency and bombed eighteen of our churches, many Assyrians left the country. Within three months, between thirty-five and fifty thousand Christians left Iraq. If this happens again, I'm afraid many more will go. So we pray each day for peace.

So far we've recruited and trained more than 150,000 police officers in the cities. The numbers are good but the training isn't as good, and the police presence is still poor. The quality of the army is much better. Gen. David Petraeus, the former commander of the 101st Airborne, is training our military now, and he's an excellent commander. Some of our brigades are beginning to look like the American brigades. They're well trained, tough, determined, and they're learning to be disciplined under fire. In time, they will be a first-rate fighting force, and they'll be able to maintain peace and deal with some of the other problems. That's our hope.

As I've said elsewhere, I believe in preemptive action, not only in the military but in politics and everywhere else. If you're a farmer, as I was for a time, you must be preemptive against rats, grasshoppers, and other insects; otherwise they'll destroy everything you've worked for. And the process is the same whether you're defeating rats in your cornfield or insurgents on the battlefield. When I talked about these ideas in the Staff College, I used the terms *prehap* and *mishap*, and I think this is a good way of thinking about the importance of planning and preparation.

Here's what I mean. Anytime there was an accident or a crash involving one of our aircraft, it was my job to find out what happened. The first thing I would do in most cases was to get the black box and read the data. Once I put it into the computer, I could ask as many as ninety-three thousand questions; I could follow the flight from taxi and takeoff until the moment the defect happened, right up to the moment of impact. I may have had the skill to review all that information and find out what happened, but what did I really have? Nothing, because the accident had already happened and the pilot and plane were lost.

Think how much better it would have been if we had been able to detect the structural or mechanical flaws before takeoff so that we could have saved both the pilot and the plane. Many times when I've examined the black box after an accident, I ended up saying, "This squadron made a big mistake. This aircraft had a serious defect that should have been caught by the crew in the preflight review."

That's what prehap does: it prevents accidents before they happen. Spotting a problem before it's too late is prehap; afterward, it's a mishap that should have been avoided. And this isn't just for airplanes; it's also true in politics and many other areas. If we're paying attention, there are many problems that can be avoided in the prehap stage. In the negotiations process that follows a war, politicians may be able to resolve certain issues and stop the conflict; but how much better if they had resolved them on the front end instead of waiting until it was too late? Prehap beats mishap every time.

Ironically, more than a year after Junsei Terasawa's visit to Baghdad, I made an interesting discovery. In another meeting with the Sunni leader, Sheik Abdul Latif al-Hemayem, I happened to mention that Saddam had been given a chance to leave Iraq without penalty. When I told him about the offer of asylum from three Asian countries, he said, "Ah, now I understand!" Then he told me that he had once asked Saddam, "Sir, can we avoid this war?" and Saddam replied, "No. The price is too high." Sheik Al-Hemayem told me, "I didn't know then what he meant by that, and I didn't ask. But now I know what he meant." The price of giving up control of Iraq, even for a comfortable sanctuary abroad, he said, was more than Saddam was willing to pay.

In October 2005, there was another report that Saddam had agreed to accept an eleventh-hour offer of asylum from the United Arab Emirates, or one of several other Middle Eastern countries. But once again he waited too long and the invasion began before the plans could be finalized. In the end, though, justice was served. Saddam fled Baghdad and his humiliating capture, recorded and broadcast by satellite on December 13, 2003, was an object lesson for the whole world.

The hope I have for Iraq today is that democracy and freedom will come quickly, and that as we mobilize our energies toward greater prosperity and autonomy for all the people, we will be able to avoid tragedies like the ones we experienced under Saddam. It's my daily prayer that we will have the courage and the foresight to stop tyrants and their bad ideas before they become a problem. Democracy is the best form of "prehap" I know of for doing that, and this is something my people need to understand. We've learned some hard lessons in recent years, and somehow we've survived. Now we need to be prepared and make sure that no tyrant will ever conquer or mislead us again.

CHAPTER 10

INSURGENCY AND SURVIVAL

Anyone with eyes to see could have seen what was going to happen after liberation. When I realized what was happening, not just the looting, but the pockets of resistance and signs of a growing insurgency, I went to one high-ranking American official, a general officer who was in Iraq on the fourteenth of May 2003, and I said, "General, someone who knows what they're looking at needs to get involved and help stop the disturbance and disorder that's going on here."

He asked me very seriously, "General Sada, can you do this?" I said, "Yes, sir, I can do it. Let me take forty thousand men from the Iraqi Air Force and we will take care of the security of Baghdad, I assure you. Furthermore," I said, "I don't need you to give me one rifle, one pistol, one truck, or anything else. The people know us and we know our people. We know our city, and we know where the troublemakers are located. All I need from you is the go-ahead and I will take my forty thousand men from the air force and we will take the city."

When I told him that, I also said, "When we do this, you can go back to your mission as soldiers. You've done a great job here. You've won the main battles. The statue has fallen in Fardus Square and Saddam is on the run. So let us finish the job." He seemed to think my idea made a lot of sense, but when he gave me his answer a few days later, he just said, "Two armies cannot operate in the same war zone." I asked him, "Why not? If there's good coordination and cooperation between these two armies to achieve one common aim, why can't they work together?" But he refused, and that was that.

As a consequence of that decision, the instrument that was used to restore order in the city was totally inappropriate for the task. Tanks, self-propelled cannons, APCs, and mechanized vehicles are great for combat, but they're not the right tools for restoring security in a large urban center like Baghdad. Anywhere else, I'd want them too; but not in a place like Baghdad.

In the city, those vehicles become perfect targets for those who want to destroy them. And the coalition knew very well that the insurgents and the remaining Baath loyalists had rocket propelled grenades (RPGs), land mines, and rifles, because it was the coalition forces who let them take those things. So when the Americans and the British took over security, it meant that the terrorists would be able to choose the time and place of engagement. They could choose the targets, and they could choose the weapons with which to attack the targets, whether they were tanks, APCs, or platoons of soldiers on foot.

America made the right decision to come in and liberate Iraq, and despite some mistakes, I have to say they've done a great job. They broke Saddam's regime and eventually captured the dictator in his spider hole—that was a tremendous victory, and no one in Iraq or America should miss the symbolism of the way it was done. But the peace is still not won, and the future is uncertain. At the end of a war, there ought to be peace. If there isn't peace, you've done something wrong. Today there's still fighting in the streets and villages of Iraq, and only time will tell how this war will end.

Supplying the Insurgents

The decision to disband the army was not a bad one, but the way it was done was not very good. What the coalition should have done was to remove the commanders and senior Iraqi officers who had been loyal to Saddam. The first thing they should have done was to activate the law of retirement and, instead of simply disbanding the military, retire high-ranking officers who had been close to the old regime in a more respectful manner. That way these men would have gone away quietly rather than joining the insurgency. There were at that time about five hundred thousand soldiers and officers in the army, and many of them would have been glad to serve under the new command. But rather than keeping those men and getting rid of the Baathis and the Saddam loyalists, the Americans simply disbanded all of them, and as a result, thousands took their weapons and joined the insurgency to fight against America.

It seemed so obvious: the last thing you want to do is to take five hundred thousand trained warriors and turn them loose on the streets with no salary, no pension, no jobs, and nothing to do. Not all members of the Baath Party were bad people. There were four to five million members of the party, and it would be wrong to punish them all indiscriminately. Those who were punished unfairly would be easily persuaded to join the insurgency, and this is a big part of the problem in Iraq today. Besides that, there was no supervision of the ammunition and weapons depots of the army, and they allowed civilians (including many dissidents) to go in and take whatever they wanted—rifles, rockets, anti-tank weapons, and just about everything else. They may as well have said, "Help yourself!" You want RPGs? "Help yourself!" Land mines, C4 explosives, detonating caps, and even surface-to-air missiles were taken by the people.

More than eight million AK-47s had been distributed to the popular army by Saddam, and another four million were stolen from the military arsenals. Just imagine what twelve million Russian-made rifles can do in the hands of people who are angry and disappointed with the way they've been treated. Something was very wrong, and this all happened because the victors who liberated Iraq didn't solve the problem of popular unrest in the first place when they had the chance.

In addition to small arms and conventional weapons, the United Nations inspectors also found a lot of weapons and ammunition that were forbidden during the period between the wars. They destroyed thousands of tons of artillery shells, rockets, and components for building chemical and biological weapons. But I can assure you, they didn't find everything. Because of his rapid rebuilding capabilities, Saddam managed to hide many of these weapons, along with the raw materials for building weapons of mass destruction (WMDs).

During the times when these weapons were not actually in production—mainly because of the threat posed by the United Nations inspectors—Saddam gave orders that the scientists who had been working on these programs were to keep their plans, diagrams, formulas, raw materials, and everything else in highly secure underground vaults so that they could continue their work the minute they were no longer being observed.

Saddam was committed to using WMDs and he wouldn't hesitate to use them on his enemies. The level of expertise among scientists who were developing our nuclear weapons systems was very high, but it was difficult to acquire the specialized equipment that was needed for weapons development. So while he had plans—Saddam had set very ambitious goals for the nuclear engineers—we weren't as far along in the nuclear program as we were with biological and chemical weapons. But we were very sophisticated with those, and we had plenty of them.

If Saddam ever suspected that there was any chance the inspectors would find something, he would have everything destroyed. But even then, nothing was really destroyed: the scientists had the knowledge and the budget, and when the time was right they would simply begin again. This was even true in the nuclear weapons program. Even though we had not yet developed actual nuclear warheads, we were working on them. We had some components, and Saddam had developed sources in Europe, Asia, and America who were willing to supply whatever we needed.

I learned in 2005 that Saddam had even made arrangements with a group of nuclear scientists in China to produce nuclear arms for him overseas. At least $5 million changed hands at that time, and as late as 1992 these plans were apparently still ongoing. But to my knowledge our own scientists had not yet produced—or acquired by other means—any nuclear warheads that could actually be deployed against an enemy.

An Eyewitness Report

Iraqi engineers were very good at manufacturing chemical weapons systems for artillery shells, rockets, missiles, and other ordnance. By August 2002, Saddam was convinced the Americans were coming; but even then the chemical and mechanical engineers continued building and developing all these systems, on into 2003 and after the American invasion began. Eventually he decided that he would have to gather everything—whether it was complete, partially complete, or only raw material—and take it out of the country, and that's what he did.

Prior to Operation Iraqi Freedom, no one in Europe or America ever doubted that Saddam possessed weapons of mass destruction. No one could possibly deny that he had used them on many occasions. It's well known that Saddam ordered chemical weapons to be used against the Kurds at Halabja and Anfal. And there were occasions when the artillery shells and bombs that were used during the Iran-Iraq War were armed with chemical agents.

Before any military operation would begin, the orders given to commanders in the field would tell us when, where, and how to conduct our operations. Within the operations orders there were certain code words that would only be used when air or ground units were supposed to deploy chemical weapons. We never used these code words when conventional weapons were to be deployed. But that's not the end of the story.

For years now people have been asking what happened to the WMDs. It's not something that has been widely discussed either in Iraq or America, mainly because of what might happen if these matters were made public. Part of the concern, I believe, is because of where these weapons and materials were taken. Until now, I've never spoken about this subject and it hasn't been made public to the best of my knowledge. I have discussed the subject with officials at the Pentagon, but until now the way these weapons were transported has been a military secret.

Whenever Secretary of State Colin Powell would visit one of our neighboring countries—such as Syria, Jordan, or Saudi Arabia—it's probable he talked about these things. I don't know whether he did or not, but there is a tremendous volume of intelligence on these matters, and mountains of anecdotal evidence. These are issues the Americans would likely have pursued diplomatically. But if they did, they have not wanted to make any of that information known to the media or the public.

I am in quite a different situation, however, as a former general officer who not only saw these weapons but witnessed them being used on orders from the air force commanders and the president of the country. Furthermore, I know the names of some of those who were involved in smuggling WMDs out of Iraq in 2002 and 2003. I know the names of officers of the front company, SES, who received the weapons from Saddam. I know how and when they were transported and shipped out of Iraq. And I know how many aircraft were actually used and what types of planes they were, as well as a number of other facts of this nature.

Weapons of Mass Denial

Since none of this information has been made public, there's been a feeding frenzy in the media for years now, coming particularly from opponents of the Bush administration, claiming that there never were or could have been WMDs in Iraq. This is not true, but I've often wondered why this information hasn't appeared in the media. Why has it been withheld? The Israelis have not hesitated to talk about it. Israel's intelligence service, the Mossad, is notoriously well informed about military and paramilitary operations in the Middle East, and they've said repeatedly that Saddam had weapons of mass destruction. They have also said that some of those weapons were transferred to countries in the region.

The Israeli Army and Air Force have taken military action against arms traffickers and terrorists, and they've intervened to stop arms smugglers and drug runners who are implicated in terrorist operations in some of these countries. But the Americans who know what actually happened in Iraq and how Saddam managed to hide these weapons, have not as yet been willing to speak publicly, about the WMDs and what became of them. As a result, those who oppose the war in Iraq have dominated media accounts, claiming they never existed.

When I speak here about weapons of mass destruction, I am referring to the biological, chemical, and nuclear weapons that Saddam had built or was trying to build. Everyone in the international arms community knew that Saddam had them and that he was spending like a sailor to buy more. In a July 2003 interview on CNN, former President Bill Clinton said, "People can quarrel with whether we should have more troops in Afghanistan or internationalize Iraq or whatever, but it is incontestable that on the day I left office, there were unaccounted-for stocks of biological and chemical weapons."

The White House knew Saddam was armed and dangerous, and the international community knew from past experience that if Saddam had WMDs he would not hesitate to use them—at a time and place of his choosing. Madeline Albright, who was secretary of state during the Clinton administration, said in February 1998, "Iraq is a long way from [here], but what happens there matters a great deal here. For the risks that the leaders of a rogue state will use nuclear, chemical, or biological weapons against us or our allies is the greatest security threat we face."

Later that same year, Representative Nancy Pelosi, who is now Minority Leader in the United States House of Representatives, said, "Saddam Hussein has been engaged in the development of weapons of mass destruction technology, which is a threat to countries in the region and he has made a mockery of the weapons inspection process." There are members of the Democratic Party in America who oppose the war today who understood the risks involved in Saddam's possession of WMDs and said as much at the time. President Clinton's National Security Adviser, Sandy Berger, warned, "He will use those weapons of mass destruction again, as he has ten times since 1983." So the fact that WMDs were present was never a secret.

Saddam's Special Weapons

Everybody understood that reality at the start of the war; I'm convinced it was only politics that made some people change their minds after the fact. But the world has been thinking about WMDs since at least 1990. This was one of the reasons that America and coalition forces decided to invade Iraq in the first place. And that's why it's important for me to address some of these things now, to set the record straight.

The point is that when Saddam finally grasped the fact that it was just a matter of time until Iraq would be invaded by American and coalition forces, he knew he would have to take special measures to destroy, hide, or at least disguise his stashes of biological and chemical weapons, along with the laboratories, equipment, and plans associated with nuclear weapons development. But then, much to his good fortune, a natural disaster in neighboring Syria provided the perfect cover story for moving a large number of those things out of the country.

It's important to understand, particularly in light of all the controversy of recent months, that Iraq did have weapons of mass destruction both before and after 1991, and I can assure you they were used. They were used on our own people. They were used in artillery shells, cannons, and by aerial dispersion of toxins by both helicopters and fixed-wing aircraft against Saddam's enemies. And this was always done in a particular way. Whenever we received ops orders to attack using WMDs, the orders never said, "Okay, use WMDs on this one." Instead they said, "Special mission with special weapons," and the commanders all knew what that meant.

I'm certain that many of those ops orders were recovered later by coalition forces after liberation in 2003, although intelligence officers may not have known what those words, written in Arabic, actually meant. But let me be very clear: in every case, "Special mission with special weapons" meant that the field commanders were to use chemical weapons to attack the enemy.

Large stockpiles of weapons were destroyed by the United Nations weapons inspectors between 1991 and 2003, but I can assure you they never got them all. There were tons of raw material, shells and shell casings, rockets and grenades, both half-completed and fully completed devices hidden in large caches. In 2001 and then again in 2002, Saddam called a meeting of all the top scientists, researchers, and technicians involved in developing weapons systems, and he told them to memorize their plans. Before the paper trail was destroyed linking Saddam to these plans he made certain, on the threat of death and dismemberment, that every single plan and every schematic was committed to memory.

Eventually he ordered most of the papers, plans, schematic drawings, formulation details, and other data relating to WMDs production to be destroyed, but he wasn't worried in the least. In fact, he authorized our engineers and scientists to show the inspectors everything that had been destroyed, and to make it clear that all these plans had been shredded and burned. He could do this without any fear of detection because he also knew that every scrap of information was in the minds of his scientists and researchers, letter by letter, line by line, because they had memorized every word. And he knew that, sooner or later, they could reproduce those plans and begin all over again.

The Nuclear Industry

The evidence of Saddam's nuclear and chemical weapons programs from the 1970s onward, from reliable sources inside and outside of Iraq, is overwhelming—so much so that it's difficult to understand why so many people in the West have been unwilling to acknowledge the fact that WMDs were not only a fact of life in Iraq for more than thirty years but they were Saddam's obsession. Dr. Khidir Hamza reveals in his book, *Saddam's Bomb Maker*, that German scientists created the chemicals that Saddam used on the Kurds at Anfal. Later it was German, French, and Russian scientists who helped the Iraqi engineers begin the process of enriching uranium for nuclear weapons.

Dr. Hamza was one of the scientists trained in the West who was brought back by Saddam to head up the Iraqi nuclear weapons program. Between 1970 and 1987, he served as a top research scientist and adviser to the prime minister. At that point he took over as head of our entire nuclear weapons program. With his help, Saddam was able to buy enriched uranium from both France and Russia, and German companies supplied parts and tools for the weapons programs. He had also negotiated with France and Russia for nuclear reactors, including the French-built Osiraq plant.

The Osiraq reactor was the best-known nuclear installation in Iraq. It was a forty megawatt light-water nuclear reactor housed at the Al Tuwaitha Nuclear Center, located about eleven miles southeast of Baghdad. This facility was designed and built by French engineers, who supplied at least 27.5 pounds of 93-percent Uranium-235 to fuel the reactor. The French called this type of reactor the "Osiris," for the Egyptian god of the dead. But the Al Tuwaitha plant was renamed "Osiraq" to incorporate the name of the country. Saddam, however, preferred to call it the *Tammuz 1* reactor, using the Arabic word for *July*, which was the month the Baath Party seized power in 1968, and again in 1979, when he became president. When that reactor was destroyed by Israeli F-16s in 1981, it made headlines around the world.

The Al Tuwaitha Center also included several research reactors, plutonium-separation and waste-processing operations, a uranium metallurgy shop, a laboratory for neutron initiator development, and several labs for a variety of different methods of uranium enrichment. Records of the United Nations Special Commission (UNSCOM) state that all the nuclear fuel stored at this site was removed and destroyed under supervision of the International Atomic Energy Agency (IAEA). One would have to be incredibly naïve, however, to believe that Saddam would have allowed all of this material to be destroyed.

In addition to the Osiraq reactor, UNSCOM also reports that there were dozens of known active WMD production facilities in operation during the 1990s. Al Tarmiya was the main site for electromagnetic isotope separation, which was part of the overall program for uranium enrichment. Much of the equipment there was disassembled and hidden from inspectors. The Al Atheer Centre was the primary facility for nuclear weapons development and testing. Activities at this site included uranium casting and metallurgy, core assembly, explosive lens assembly, and detonics testing.

A high-explosives test bunker near the Al Atheer site was used for hydrodynamic experiments. The buildings and bunkers were destroyed under IAEA and UNSCOM supervision in 1992, but plans, schematics, and other materials from these facilities were removed long before the inspectors ever arrived. And the list of nuclear labs goes on from there. The Al Furat lab was used for design, assembly, and testing of gas centrifuges for uranium enrichment. Al Jesira was a factory for production of uranium dioxide, uranium tetrachloride, and uranium hexaflouride.

The Akashat mine produced uranium ore. A similar facility at Al Qaim produced refined yellow cake uranium ore. Rashidiya was a facility for centrifuge design and testing; the Al Sharqat reactor site, which was still under construction when coalition forces attacked in 1991, was going to be the second of Saddam's Tammuz reactors. In addition, scientists had completed the Petrochemical-3 Centre, which housed the Iraqi nuclear weapons design team. When inspectors examined this facility in September 1991, they recovered thousands of files and documents that described in detail the scope and nature of Saddam's nuclear weapons programs.

The Chinese Connection

More recently, I learned from a close family member of a high-ranking Iraqi official that Saddam made arrangements in August 1990 to acquire nuclear weapons directly from a group of nuclear scientists in China. After the invasion of Kuwait, Saddam realized that scrutiny of his weapons programs was going to be much too intense for Iraq to continue nuclear development, and it would have been next to impossible to maintain secrecy. So he made a deal to pay the Chinese scientists $100 million to manufacture weapons for him.

However, when the chief accountant of the Ministry of Military Industrialization tried to transfer the first payment of $5 million from an account at the Rafidan Bank, Al Riyadh Branch, on August 4, 1990, he discovered that the transaction was being blocked on orders from America—this was apparently being done in anticipation of the beginning of the first Gulf War. After several failed attempts to transfer the funds by wire, it was decided that a courier would come to collect the money.

According to a report that I have seen, the courier arrived in Baghdad on October 15, 1990. He took the $5 million in cash and returned to China the same way he had come. I don't know what happened to the money or the relationship after the Gulf War, but I certainly believe that Saddam would have continued to pursue those arrangements throughout the 1990s, using a portion of the more than $11 billion he received through the Oil-for-Food program. To insure the secrecy of those plans, however, Saddam simply eliminated anyone with detailed knowledge of them, including the accountant who had managed the transfer. That man died of cancer in 1994, but suspecting that his disease was no accident, he revealed the details of those transactions to a family member before his death, and that individual subsequently related his story to me.

Underlying all of Saddam's secret operations was a foundation of fraud and corruption. According to the report of the Independent Inquiry Committee of the United Nations, headed by former Federal Reserve Chairman Paul Volcker, released in October 2005, more than 2,200 companies participating in the United Nations' Oil-for-Food program paid at least $1.8 billion in kickbacks to Saddam. More than sixty-six countries were involved, and manipulation of oil profits in violation of the sanctions agreements helped to increase Saddam's personal wealth by as much as $11 billion.

In another highly acclaimed book called *The Bomb in My Garden*, published in 2004, Dr. Mahdi Obeidi describes his work on the centrifuge programs in Iraq. Obeidi served as director of the Ministry of Industry and Military Industrialization, which was the weapons development arm of the Iraqi government. At one point he had in his own possession all the records of the nuclear enrichment programs in Iraq as well as extensive documentation on the entire history of Saddam's WMDs programs—hidden in an oil drum buried in his back yard.

Many of those documents were eventually turned over to the U.S. State Department and were reportedly the largest collection of evidence of Iraqi WMDs in the West. So there's no lack of evidence that all of this had been going on in Iraq for more than three decades. But the question of how Saddam hid these weapons and equipment prior to and during the second Gulf War involves another brilliant bit of deception.

A Natural Disaster

Saddam had ordered our weapons teams to hide the WMDs in places no military commander or United Nations weapons inspector would expect to find them. So they hid them in schools, private homes, banks, business offices, and even on trucks that were kept constantly moving back and forth from one end of the country to the other. And then fate stepped in.

On June 4, 2002, a three-mile-long irrigation dam, which had been drawing water from the Orontes River in the northwestern district of Zeyzoun, Syria, collapsed, inundating three small villages and destroying scores of homes. Many people and livestock were killed, and the flood waters covered an area of nearly forty square miles. As soon as word of the disaster was broadcast on television, help began arriving from all over the Middle East. The Red Crescent, which is the equivalent of the Red Cross in our area, brought in aid workers to set up shelters and render medical care.

But when Syrian president Bashar al-Assad asked for help from Jordan and Iraq, Saddam knew what he would do. For him, the disaster in Syria was a gift, and there, posing as shipments of supplies and equipment sent from Iraq to aid the relief effort, were Iraq's WMDs. Weapons and equipment were transferred both by land and by air. The only aircraft available at the time were one Boeing 747 jumbo jet and a group of Boeing 727s. But this turned out to be the perfect solution to Saddam's problem. Who would suspect commercial airliners of carrying deadly toxins and contraband technology out of the country? So the planes were quickly reconfigured.

All the passenger seats, galleys and toilets, storage compartments, and other related equipment that would be needed for civilian passengers were removed, and new flooring was installed, thus transforming the passenger planes into cargo planes. The airliners were then used for transporting hundreds of tons of chemicals, armaments, and other paraphernalia into Syria under the cover of a mission of mercy to help a stricken nation.

Eventually there were fifty-six sorties. Commercial 747s and 727s moved these things out of the country. This was another of Saddam's tricks. Instead of using military vehicles or aircraft which would have been apprehended and searched by coalition forces, Saddam's agents had used the civilian airlines. He arranged for most of these shipments to be taken to Syria and handed over to ordnance specialists there who promised to hold everything for as long as necessary.

Subsequently, I spoke at length to a former civilian airline captain who had detailed information about those flights. At the time he held an important position at Iraqi Airways, which is the commercial airline in Baghdad.

Fraud and Corruption

The plans for transferring these weapons were concocted by Ali and Ali. Our Ali was Ali Hussein al-Majid (Chemical Ali), and their Ali was General Abu Ali, who was a cousin of Syrian president Bashar al-Assad. For once in the long history of belligerence between Iraq and Syria, there was complete agreement between them. They arranged for the operation to be conducted like a regular business deal, and everything was paid for, up-front and in cash. The tab for moving fifty-six sorties of highly dangerous contraband was enormous, but for Saddam it was worth every penny.

In addition to the shipments that went by air, there were also truckloads of weapons, chemicals, and other supplies that were taken into Syria at that time. These weren't government vehicles or military equipment but large cargo trucks and eighteen-wheelers made to look like ordinary commercial operators. Saddam was convinced that commercial trucks could pass right through security checkpoints on the borders without raising alarms, and they did, without drawing the attention of American and international satellite observers. Another source has reported that even ambulances were used to carry weapons and equipment across the border.

To keep all these illegal transfers under wraps, the two Ali's worked through a false company called SES. This company played a key role in transporting equipment back and forth between Syria and Iraq, as well as in smuggling many former government officials out of Iraq prior to and immediately after the U.S. invasion in March 2003. These are the same people who had previously organized the illegal sale of oil, natural gas, gasoline, sulfate, and other resources produced in Iraq to countries in the region, defying United Nations sanctions.

And also it's the same company that brokered the sale of weapons and equipment to Saddam while Iraq was under sanctions. This part, at least, is not news. A major story broke in the *Los Angeles Times* on December 30, 2003, confirming Syria's role in undermining sanctions—names, dates, and places were given. The CIA and the State Department were aware of all this and more, but the Syrian role in ferrying WMDs out of Iraq has not previously been confirmed. My own knowledge of these transfers doesn't come from any of the published reports but from a man who was actually involved in the transfers—a civilian pilot who witnessed the commercial 747 going back and forth between Syria and Iraq at that time. And he has confirmed for me that it happened just this way.

On July 28, 2005, members of a congressional committee and the Bush administration were informed about some aspects of these dealings. Daniel Glaser, assistant secretary monitoring terrorism funding at the U.S. Treasury Department, reported that the American government was conducting further investigations into the dealings of SES. "On June 9, 2005," Glaser stated in his testimony before a House of Representatives subcommittee, "we also designated two associated Syrian individuals, General Zuhayr Shalish and Asif Shalish, and a related asset, the Syria-based SES International Corporation, for their support to senior officials of the former Iraqi regime."

SES, Glaser reported, had acted falsely as the "end-user for the former Iraqi regime" and had managed and directed Saddam's acquisition of arms and munitions, which was a violation of the sanctions agreement. What Glaser did not say, however, was that this same organization also managed the transfer of WMDs out of Iraq in 2002 and 2003, and that they had transported high-ranking members of Saddam's cabinet out of the country into Syria, before they could be apprehended by coalition forces. But these are the facts.

Aid and Comfort

Between the end of the first Gulf War and the beginning of the Oil-for-Food program in 1996, Saddam was robbing the people of Iraq and building a vast network of international collaborators to help him circumvent the military and economic sanctions that had been placed on him by America and the United Nations. He had many covert partners in these operations, but it wasn't until the first large transfers of capital under the Oil-for-Food program came through that the Iraqi president was able to put all these plans into action.

During the twelve years between the first and second Gulf Wars, Saddam accumulated billions in unauthorized currency and credits, and most of that money came through or because of the Oil-for-Food program. As a socialist country, we didn't have an income tax or corporation tax in Iraq. As I've indicated in previous chapters, bribery had become an art form, and even the police and medical professions had been corrupted. But it wasn't until the United Nations began paying Saddam for oil and monitoring trade agreements that he was able to return to business as usual with certain client nations. After that Saddam was able to accumulate the funds to expand his wealth and pursue his favorite hobby of deceiving the world about WMDs.

Saddam was brilliant at this, and his ability to lie, cheat, and deceive carried over into all his business tactics. Contracts for food, clothing, furniture, paper products, and every other essential purchased abroad provided him with the perfect opportunity to exploit the system, by demanding bribes and kickbacks, or by disguising his purchases of armaments and banned technologies as something other than what they were. Shiploads of goods from Russia and France labeled in shipping manifests as "replacement parts" or "factory equipment" were, in fact, missile-guidance systems, rocket engines, and even the barrels of antiaircraft guns.

Government officials, under orders from Saddam, would use oil certificates as cash to purchase goods and services to rebuild and restore the regime, but seldom to benefit the people for whom the Oil-for-Food relief effort had supposedly been designed. The United Nations gave Saddam a mechanism that allowed him to bribe, steal, coerce, and smuggle whatever he wanted, and in the process he was able to amass billions of dollars worth of weapons, weapons components, and the raw materials to manufacture whatever he wanted.

Saddam instinctively understood how to take advantage of the $64-billion Oil-for-Food program. His personal wealth in 2003 was estimated to exceed $10 billion. Most of that had been stolen from the people over the past thirty years. But he also pocketed at least

$1.8 billion through kickbacks, bribes, and illegal commissions in his dealings with suppliers under the U.N. program. In addition, he was able to collect another $8.4 billion through the direct smuggling operations he set up and supervised between 1996 and 2003.

Whenever his operations were threatened, Saddam took advantage of his old propaganda tricks to create a diversion. When he expelled U.N. weapons inspectors in December 1998, for example, he claimed that there was political bias against him and that the inspectors were breaking their own rules in the selection of sites. On many occasions he would orchestrate vocal confrontations with the inspection teams, entirely for the sake of the media. It wasn't until November 2002, with the threat of war hanging over our heads, that Saddam finally allowed the United Nations Monitoring, Verification, and Inspection Commission (UNMOVIC) back in.

As part of the armistice signed by Gen. Sultan Hashim at Safwan in 1991, Saddam was required to sign both the international Biological Weapons Convention (BWC) and the Chemical Weapons Convention (CWC). Unfortunately, both conventions were weak, and neither agreement provided strong incentives or a monitoring apparatus to guarantee compliance with the terms of the documents. And for someone like Saddam, that meant no compliance at all. It was a loophole he was only too glad to exploit.

Toward Reconciliation

In June 2004, Demetrius Perricos, who serves as president of UNMOVIC, confirmed these and many other facts in a report to the United Nations Security Council. He made it clear that Saddam had smuggled WMDs out of Iraq before, during, and after the war. In his report, Perricos provided evidence that documents recovered in Jordan, Turkey, and as far away as the Netherlands revealed that thousands of tons of biological warheads had been shipped out of Iraq to other countries in the Middle East. And along with chemical and biological components there were nuclear reactor vessels and fermenters for preparing chemical and biological warheads.

Perricos didn't mention the Syrian connection, but field reports from Iraqi informants and information supplied by the Israeli intelligence service, the Mossad, confirmed that members of Syria's Baath Party were very much involved. And two months prior to the UNMOVIC report, U.S. officials received word from the Jordanian intelligence service that they had broken up a plot by Al Qaeda to explode a large chemical weapon in the center of Amman, Jordan.

The plot masterminded by the Jordanian terrorist Abu Musab al-Zarqawi was designed to create a "toxic cloud" in the city that would permeate not only the U.S. Embassy but also the office of the prime minister of Jordan and the intelligence service headquarters. The collateral effect would lead to the death or serious impairment of at least twenty-thousand Jordanian civilians.

During the operation to foil this diabolical plot, the Jordanian agents captured several of the terrorists involved, as well as some twenty tons of nerve gas and Sarin gas that were to be used in the attack. No one could say where the biological and chemical agents had come from, but there was only one logical source. They were, more than likely, merely a small portion of the contraband that had been shipped out of my country by Saddam, and that had now fallen into the hands of a notorious terrorist whose base of operations since the early days of the Gulf War has been in Iraq.

Life After Saddam

I assure you that most Iraqis were shocked and surprised by the way Saddam was captured—dirty, frightened, and hiding in a spider hole. For thirty years that man tried to make everyone believe he was invincible. He smoked his big cigars and fired his weapons in the air, always strutting before the TV cameras. The first report on every news broadcast and the main headline of the daily newspaper had to be about Saddam every single day. But on that day, December 13, 2003, there he was for the whole world to see, and there was nothing brave or inspiring about it. He was just another coward running from justice.

If Saddam had decided to fight and die like a man, I suspect he would still be admired by some people in my country. Those who loved him would say he was a hero who fought for what he believed in. But he lost all respect after being captured with a pistol he didn't even try to use. It would have been better for him to have been killed, or even to have killed himself, rather than surrender. But, instead, he was dragged from a hole like an animal.

Now the world will see him standing trial before a special tribunal. The charges against him are very serious, and I have no doubt he will be convicted. Even his own lawyers know that Saddam is guilty. In one interview, Abdul Haq al-Ani, who was hired by Saddam's daughter to head the defense team, told reporters that he thinks Saddam is "despicable" for the illegal imprisonment and torture of innocent Iraqis. The only reason he accepted the case, he said, was because he is anti-American and defending Saddam was his way of showing it. But he will, in any event, have a hard case to prove, and the charges against his client are enormous.

Among the many serious charges, Saddam will be accused of the massacre of Kurds at Anfal in 1987–88, in which nearly two hundred thousand were killed or expelled from the country. He will be charged with ordering the bombardment of Kirkuk, and the slaughter of thousands of Shia Muslims who were buried in mass graves in the south. He will be charged with the chemical attacks on Kurds at Halabja in 1988, and execution of eight thousand members of the Barzani tribe—which happens to be the family of the president of the Kurdistan region. And these are just a few of the most notable accusations Saddam and his lawyers will have to deal with.

Eighty percent of the people of Iraq are eager for this trial to begin and for justice to be served. Another 15 percent don't really care one way or the other; they're just glad to know that Saddam is gone and they're alive. There is, however, a small group of "Saddamists" who still feel loyalty for him because they had prospered under his corrupt regime. But I can also tell you that there is another large group, made up mainly of journalists and broadcasters and officials of foreign governments, who were paid very large sums by Saddam to say and print nice things about him. Hundreds of people in newsrooms and network boardrooms all over Europe and the Middle East are learning how to live on less these days, since the bribes and the extortion money that was being paid to them by Saddam has suddenly dried up.

A Personal Appeal

As a former fighter pilot and an air force general who has been engaged in wars and revolutions throughout my entire career, I know what war means, and I understand what these weapons can do. And this is why, in 1998, I began working with organizations dedicated to peace and reconciliation in the Middle East. Since that time I've led the International Center for Peace and Reconciliation and I've been awarded the "Cross of Nails" at Coventry Cathedral in England, which was a very great honor. Seven months after the liberation of Iraq, on November 14, 2003, I was awarded the International Peace Prize at Coventry.

All of this happened because I believe sincerely that our part of the world needs peace—not just in Iraq, but peace throughout the Middle East. And we have to learn how to live in peace with others if we are to survive. It's in this spirit that I have decided to issue an appeal to my brother in the Middle East, Syrian president Bashar al-Assad, who is a young and gifted leader, not to withhold the truth about these matters any longer.

I'm asking President Bashar now to tell the world the truth about the WMDs and then to hand them over to a neutral organization that will make sure they're transported out of Syria and disposed of in an appropriate manner. Whether it's the United Nations, the Red Cross, or some other international body, these weapons and everything else sent there by Saddam Hussein need to be handed over in order to bring this troublesome matter to a close. To possess them is a threat to world peace, and using them would be a crime that can only end in even greater tragedy. Now is the time to dispose of them.

If President Bashar will take this important step, it will earn him and his nation the goodwill of the entire world, and it will help to solve many problems that have been created by Syria's poor relations with its neighbors in the past. As an Iraqi general and now a director of peace initiatives in the Middle East, I can think of no more important action than this for restoring hope and prosperity to our region.

Fifty years of fighting between our two countries is enough. Fifty years of bloodshed, the loss of millions of our sons, the devastation of hundreds of towns in Syria, Iran, Jordan, Saudi Arabia, and Iraq, and the waste of billions of dollars of our national treasure that could have fed and clothed the people of our countries, is a terrible price to pay for our pride and resentment.

So this is my plea, and I say it with all my heart: Mr. President Bashar al-Assad, please turn over these weapons. Let the United Nations take them away, and the whole world will thank you for it.

CHAPTER 11

THE WAY FORWARD

The International Centre for Reconciliation (ICR) was established in Iraq in 1998 when Canon Andrew White made his first trip to meet with me in Iraq. On that occasion Andrew and I laid out the general guidelines for the work ahead based on our commitment to creating an environment in which people of all faiths and backgrounds could speak freely and resolve their differences without fear or the threat of intimidation. After Andrew returned to Coventry, I took steps to organize the operations in Iraq, and since that time the activities of the group have grown tremendously. The outreach of this movement has expanded, and my own responsibilities have expanded even more.

As director of ICR in Iraq, my mission was to help encourage the various groups in the region to talk through their problems rather than immediately resorting to verbal or physical attacks. The work was slow and sometimes dangerous, but we could see signs of progress as we persevered. One of the most important events took place on February 24, 2004, when Canon White and I moderated a large convocation of tribal and religious leaders who had come together to talk about our common concerns. We met at the Babylon Hotel where, at the conclusion of that meeting, we drafted a document called the "Baghdad Religious Accord," which called for religious and ethnic tolerance in Iraq.

Following the signing of that document by leaders of all faiths, we established a new entity to serve as a center for dialogue and reconciliation. This effort was originally funded by the Religion and Peacemaking Initiative at Coventry Cathedral. The United States Institute of Peace (USIP) in Washington, D.C., was also instrumental in organizing and helping to plan our activities. We decided to choose a name for the new organization as close to USIP as possible, and that's how the Iraqi Institute for Peace (IIP) came into being.

I had served as director of the International Centre for Reconciliation since 1998 and served the new organizations in a similar capacity until February 2004 when I left to assist with the creation of the new Iraqi ministry of defense. They found other people to manage the IIP, though I returned to help resolve some of the problems that emerged after my departure.

I took no salary or stipend when I served in those positions for seven years. As a Christian, I was giving a tenth of my income to the church, so I often used my own money to host visitors or do other things for the IIP and its affiliates. Eventually an order came from the USIP saying they would only send funds for operation of the institute to me personally. So even though my duties had expanded many times over, I am still working with them, and I serve today as executive secretary of the IIP in Iraq.

Reconciliation and Rebuilding

Since 2004, the work of the IIP has grown to include hostage negotiation, mercy missions, intervention in cases of religious persecution, and many other things. We have met with Sunni leaders from all the different areas, and we worked closely with them in selecting the fifteen individuals from that region to serve on the committee drafting the new national constitution. We have hosted conferences for as many as a thousand people at a time, and I also began working with Sunni leaders to improve relations between the tribes and religious groups in the northern part of the country. In the beginning, the British Foreign Office funded those meetings, but today American organizations are doing it.

But then on March 21, 2004, I was called to a meeting with American Ambassador Paul Bremer and Mr. Brusqa Nuri Shawez, who is a prominent leader of the Kurdish people in Iraq, to sign the new law creating the ministry of defense. On that day we began building our military forces, and Mr. Shawez was named to the post of General Secretary of the Iraqi Defense Ministry. Six weeks later, on May 10, 2004, I was sent to Washington, D.C., for a special course designed for new members of the senior executive service, which is the highest level of civil service in the government of the new Iraq.

I had been nominated to become the spokesman for the ministry of defense and director of public affairs in that office. But while I was awaiting further word on the nomination, I received a call from the director of the Office of National Security Affairs (ONSA) in Baghdad, Fred Smith, who said, "General Sada, I want to be the first to congratulate you on being appointed spokesman for the new prime minister of Iraq." That was very good news, so I said, "Thank you, sir, but who is the new prime minister?" And he said, "Nobody knows. But you're already appointed, and the new government will be in place on June 1."

That conversation took place on May 24, 2004, and I was excited to see what would happen next. Later that day I was contacted by the Department of State and they told me, "Georges, on May 26 you're scheduled to meet with Secretary of State Colin Powell, and he's going to introduce you to a very important person who will be going to Iraq." So two days later I went to that meeting and I was introduced to Secretary Powell. We talked for some time about the situation in Iraq and how my work was going, and he was very warm and encouraging. Then after a few minutes, he said, "General Sada, I want to introduce you to this man, John Negroponte. He's going to be the American ambassador to Iraq."

I was delighted to meet Ambassador Negroponte. As the principal representative of the United States to our country, he was going to be an important person for us. We shook hands and he said, "Georges, it's a pleasure to meet you. I've heard so much about you." And then he told me, "When I come to take my post in Iraq, even before presenting my papers to the government, I want to see you and say hello." So I said, "Yes, I hope you will do that. And call me at the prime minister's office when you arrive." I gave him my business card, and sure enough he did call when he arrived in Baghdad one month later, and we spoke briefly before he went in to be presented to the prime minister.

On May 28, 2004, I was organizing my office, awaiting the arrival of the new prime minister. At one point I said to Ambassador Bremer,

"Come on, sir. Tell me who's going to be the new prime minister." And he said, "Believe me, Georges, I don't know." I said, "Sir, that's just three days from now. Surely somebody must know who it's going to be." Well, along the way I got the slightest hint that it might be Dr. Ayad Alawi, but it wasn't until June 1 that I actually knew for sure. It was Dan Senor, the spokesman for Ambassador Bremer, who introduced me to Dr. Alawi.

Actually, we had met two months earlier when I was in the ministry of defense and we both attended graduation ceremonies in Jordan for our new brigade commanders. Dr. Alawi was a member of the governing council at that time and head of the Iraqi National Accord, which was his political party. Previously, he had been living in London for more than twenty years.

Dr. Alawi took his duties seriously from the start, and Ambassador Bremer began handing the affairs of government over to him almost immediately. We were very busy for the next twenty-eight days, preparing for a formal exchange from an American administration to an all Iraqi administration. We were originally scheduled to finish everything on June 30, but we finished two days early.

Ambassador Bremer, who was supposed to leave Iraq on the thirtieth, came around to the prime minister's office on June 28 and said, "Good job, gentlemen. You've got everything now, and I'm leaving today." This surprised everybody, especially the media. But there was no reason for him to stay. We finally had a new government in Iraq, and it was being run by Iraqis. Ambassador Negroponte arrived that afternoon, and from that moment we began rebuilding the government of Iraq.

Fighting for Nothing

On March 21, 2004, I met with Fred Smith at ONSA in Iraq, and with David Gompert, who was the senior advisor for security policy under Ambassador Bremer. I was briefed on plans for the new ministry of defense. They told me that there was to be a meeting of Iraqi leaders, and *The New York Times* would be there. The pictures and proceedings of the meeting couldn't be made public at that time, but photographers would be there to record the occasion, and details would be published at some time in the future.

I went to the meeting and many pictures were taken. When we signed the document creating the new ministry of defense, I felt that my years of military service were finally being rewarded. At last my country would have a military we could be proud of. We found a building for it, and today that ministry and the new government are in business. I was proud to be there as spokesman for the minister of defense, whomever that turned out to be. Later they announced that the nominee for the position would be Dr. Ali Alawi, who was a member of the governing council and had also been named as minister of commerce and trade. For several months, while the government was being organized, Dr. Ali Alawi actually served in three separate posts.

From March 21 to May 10, 2004, we made plans for the structure of the ministry of defense, deciding on key posts to be filled in the administration. During that time I was asked for my suggestions about the shape of the new army in Iraq. Among other things, I told them that the three divisions they originally planned wouldn't be enough. I said we needed at least nine divisions and 150,000 uniformed personnel, but ten divisions would be even better. Fortunately, they agreed with me, and since that time the number has increased from nine to eleven divisions.

When the 101st Airborne Division was withdrawn from Iraq to return to America, Major General David Petraeus was promoted to Lieutenant General and given the assignment of training the new Iraqi Army. I can tell you that he is doing a great job, and he works from early in the morning until late at night. I've seen him there at the defense ministry until late in the evening. He's a faithful officer, and he knows how important it is to train the Iraqi soldiers to take over the job of defending the country; I'm very proud of the work he has done.

The hard job for the military now is mainly in the five provinces where the insurgency has been such a problem—Diahla, Ramadi, Baghdad, Saladin, and Mosul Provinces. These are mainly the Sunni

Provinces. Saddam was from that area, and even though the Sunni Arabs make up only about 25 percent of the population of Iraq, they were very much in control under the old regime. Now that they no longer have the advantage, the Sunni leaders are struggling with how to best achieve their objectives. And sometimes they're doing it the wrong way. For example, many Sunnis decided to boycott the elections in January 2005. That was a huge mistake, and they paid a heavy price for it by not getting their people elected to important positions.

There were many officers and soldiers from this area serving in the Republican Guard and the special security forces under Saddam. Many of those men are in the insurgency now because they feel they've been neglected. Also, they realize that they will never regain the same level of power that they had before liberation. They believe the insurgency will help them regain their power, but I can assure you this will never happen. Ultimately, they're not fighting with America; they're fighting their own people and their own government, and this needs to stop.

Whatever weapons they may have—a few AK-47s, grenades, and explosives—will not last very long. And they're nothing compared to the massive supplies of weapons in the hands of the new military. So the smart ones are beginning to realize that it's time to get involved in the political process, because resistance will not work in the long run. And even if the insurgents are having some success today—thanks primarily to the large numbers of foreign fighters who are coming from abroad—this will not last either. It's only a matter of time until these forces will be destroyed.

Learning to Cooperate

We all need to understand that the solution to the problems in Iraq today are not military but political. And when the Sunnis abandon the insurgency, it will be much easier to track down and destroy the black sheep fighters from abroad. And once the Sunnis begin to take part in the political process, foreign insurgents will have no place to hide. They must either surrender, leave the country, or be killed. There's no other choice.

I have personally spoken with many Sunni leaders, and I have brought some of them to meet with the American officials—including Ambassador Paul Bremer, Ambassador David Newman, Ambassador Richard Jones, and British Ambassador Sir Jeremy Greenstock—and these people are now saying they want to take part in the elections and to present candidates for office. They told us that they're ready to lay down their weapons, but they want the new government to take steps to involve them and look after their interests.

At one point a group of Sunnis told me, "We expect the new government to put our leaders in the parliament." Of course I told them that's not how a democracy works. If they want their people to be in parliament, then they will have to run for office and convince the voters that their candidates are the best qualified. They were still under the impression that leaders could be appointed based on the percentage of Sunnis in the country. But now they know this will not happen.

Though they're only a quarter of the population, the Sunni Arabs had nearly 100 percent control of the government under Saddam, so life now is a little harder for them. But the old system is gone forever. More and more of the Sunni leaders are coming around now, and the men who had thought they could be appointed proportionally decided to go back home to find candidates that the voters would support. And I'm pleased to say that Sunnis in Iraq are now taking part in the election process.

In the fall of 2004 I had a conversation with a prominent Sunni who was the head of the physicians union in Iraq. He said he was worried that after liberation the Americans would try to punish the Sunni Arabs because they were involved in the insurgency and had been strong supporters of Saddam. But I assured him the Americans are not against the Sunnis. I told him that I had been in many meetings in America and Iraq in which high-ranking politicians and military officers had said they wanted the Sunnis to be involved in the political process.

Remarkably, the very next day Dr. Condoleeza Rice, the new American secretary of state, gave a speech in Baghdad in which she said almost exactly the same words. She said, "We want the

Sunnis to participate in the political process." A short time later that doctor called me and said, "Georges, I have to thank you for your comments. You know, I believed you, but for Dr. Rice to say exactly what you told me was very gratifying." So I said I was glad my message could be confirmed in that way. But I also told him that all the people of Iraq—Sunni, Shia, Kurds, Yazidis, Sabbists, Christians, and others—have a right to participate in the new government, and until we all come together to work together, nothing good will be accomplished.

Learning to Forgive

I feel certain that the Sunni Arabs in Iraq, who are well-educated and prosperous people, will not want to miss this opportunity. They have too much to lose and too little to gain by their resistance. I also feel certain they will come around very quickly because these are very smart people. They've been in power for centuries, under virtually every government and every ruler we've ever known in this part of the world.

The Sunnis are doctors, engineers, scientists, government officials, economists, and everything else. They are hard working, and many of them are very rich. But if nothing else, they have learned from the defeats their forces suffered in the battles of Falluja, Ramadi, and Al Qaim that resistance won't work. Those battles were object lessons for them which made it perfectly clear that they cannot hope to win power by military means. The way to affect policy is to run for office and be a part of the system.

There is still a problem with foreign insurgents in Iraq, but we have introduced a plan to stop this invasion. We have put the word out that any region of the country that allows foreign insurgents to live among them will be considered rebel territory, against the government, and there will be more and more attacks on those areas by the military to weed out troublemakers. In the process of cleaning them out, those who shelter, feed, and clothe the terrorists will be in harm's way, and many of them will likely be killed or wounded. So it's in their own best interest not to let the insurgents hide out in their towns and villages. And if we can show them how dangerous it is, I believe that, in time, the problem of foreign insurgents will go away.

In many parts of Iraq today, the people are sick of seeing their families and neighbors being killed and wounded or blown up by car bombs and rocket attacks. So they've started turning in the insurgents. They're showing the military where they're hiding and helping to restore the peace in their area. We've explained to them that security is everybody's business. It's not only the job of the police and the military. In a free country, every citizen has a role. So we tell them that if they know of someone who's doing bad things, they should get on the phone and call the police.

Consequently, the level of cooperation between the people and the government is much higher than before. But there's one thing we still need to remember. The only thing that is not available in sufficient supply is love for other people. The Sunnis love their people; the Shia love their people; the Kurds love their people, but there is no love between them. In many cases, there is animosity that goes back centuries, so it's not easy for them to forget about the past. But somehow we've got to show them how to cooperate and how to share in the freedom and prosperity of the country. And most of all we need to teach them the importance of forgiveness.

You know, at the end of World War II, only about forty-eight people, most of them high-ranking officials of the Nazi Party, were actually put on trial for war crimes. In fact, the majority of the German people had participated in some way with the Nazis. But only their leaders were charged with crimes against humanity, and those men were punished for the crimes of the Nazi regime. But after that, America established the Marshall Plan and the people of Germany were able to move forward, to put the war out of their minds, and to rebuild their nation.

This was good for Germany. They needed to forget about the past and begin again, but even so, they should never forget what the Americans had done for them. By the same token, France should never forget that it was the American Third Army under Gen. Patton that defeated the Germans and gave them back their freedom. Sadly, both Germany and France seem to have forgotten that gift today, but it was important for them to put the past behind them and move on.

So far in Iraq, more than two thousand Americans have given their lives in the struggle to restore freedom in my country, and we must never forget that. And the people of France and Germany and Great Britain should never forget that tens of thousands of American soldiers, who came to help them defeat the Nazis, are buried on their shores. This is the greatest gift of all. Jesus said, "Greater love hath no man than this, that a man lay down his life for his friends" (John 15:13 KJV). This is especially true in war, and we must not forget the sacrifices our friends have made for us.

For Love of Country

The biggest problem in the country now is hatred and revenge, and people who try to live that way will never be able to solve their problems. Countries like Iraq that have made a living from hatred and revenge for so many years must relearn the lost art of forgiveness. They must practice love instead of hatred; and they need to make use of the resources that have been provided to us by America, Great Britain, and the many others who are making substantial contributions to our well-being. These nations have been very generous with us, and we still have enormous reserves of oil. If all these things can be used with wisdom, I'm sure Iraq will flourish once again.

Unemployment is still a problem, but when the level of violence subsides and employment begins to rise—so that most people have jobs and are working productively once again—I believe you're going to see an all new Iraq. This is what we need. Another ingredient for building a secure nation, very much as the first settlers of America discovered in the early days of your Republic, is love of country and a willingness to sacrifice for the common good.

There's a wonderful phrase at the end of the American Declaration of Independence that says, "With a firm reliance on the Protection of Divine Providence, we mutually pledge to each other our Lives, our Fortunes, and our sacred Honor." I love that statement because that's what it's all about. The founders of your country were will-ing to sacrifice for each other because they believed that, with God's help, it was the right thing to do.

So long as the Iraqi people continue to say, "my people, my coun-try, my money, my position, and my power," they can't win. But when we come to the point where we can all say, "My religion and my beliefs may be different from yours, but I will defend you with my life because you are my brother," then they will truly be a nation and more than just a collection of warring tribes.

Until now, this spirit has been in short supply in Iraq. Saddam had a lot to do with that, of course, and the willingness of many in the Middle East to live with a certain amount of violence hasn't helped. We are making tremendous advances, but right now everybody is an individual. Even in the political parties, many leaders are only looking out for themselves, and this is true even at the highest levels. Some of our leaders aren't working to show that they're the leaders of all Iraqis. Each man is primarily interested in providing oppor-tunities for his group. And those who are interested in rebuilding a united Iraq with opportunities for all Iraqis, regardless of race or religion, have a tough time getting into positions of authority.

I would have to say that even among those who have come back to Iraq from abroad, many of them are pursuing their own personal interests instead of the interests of our country. A man who has lived in America or Britain for the last forty years really understands very little about how the Iraqi people have lived during all that time. When they come back, some of them want to make a contribution to growth and change; but some are only thinking about how to make a fortune, how to accumulate millions of dollars, and how to take it back to their families in those other countries.

In the meantime, those who have suffered the last thirty years under Saddam Hussein—and much of that under international sanctions—have next to nothing to show for it. The result is that this situation breeds suspicion and distrust on both sides, and when you combine that with the animosity between the various tribes and reli-gious sects in the country, the situation is potentially very volatile.

At the moment, we have military forces from thirty different nations in our country. Iran is on our eastern border trying to meddle in our affairs, even as they're doing their best to antagonize America and the West by renewing their nuclear weapons program. Iran and our other neighbors, Syria, Saudi Arabia, and Turkey, are all jockeying for more influence in the Middle East. And the tensions between the Israelis and Palestinians are only getting worse, hour by hour. Just look at the mess we have to deal with!

The multinational forces in Iraq today are aware of all these things, because these are the tensions that make their mission more difficult. The young soldiers are struggling to deal with the problems, but no one should expect a nineteen-year-old Marine to be able to deal with all of this and make sense of it. His job is to be a soldier, to find the insurgents and get rid of them. He's trained to wage war, not to build a nation. But these are good young men, good soldiers, and they're trying to do all they can. We ought to understand that there's only so much the soldiers and their commanders can do for us.

Things That Don't Work

Part of what your young soldiers are up against is forty years of bad habits. I'm old enough to remember a time when Iraq was a fair and open country, but the vast majority of our people are under the age of thirty, so they have been born and raised in this atmosphere of hate, violence, distrust, and suspicion. And if you want to understand just how evil Saddam Hussein really was, you should know that he opened all the prisons at the beginning of Operation Iraqi Freedom in 2003 and released 150,000 criminals onto the streets. So into the social and political vacuum we have today in Iraq, just imagine what great harm 150,000 thieves, robbers, murderers, and rapists can do when they're released into the general population.

One of those prisoners, who is back in jail now and awaiting trial, has been charged with murdering 150 people. What kind of justice is there for such a man? Americans come to our country and they want to establish freedom and democracy, but for whom? For murderers like this? You can't give freedom and democracy to men of this sort. And there are already so many limitations on what can be done.

When American soldiers capture a terrorist, their own laws forbid them from interrogating them to get the information they need to save lives.

This kind of thinking can never work in Iraq. If a criminal or a terrorist is taken into custody in Iraq, our police and intelligence will know everything in his head in fifteen minutes. And the criminal will know that the best thing to do is to give them the information, fully and very quickly. Americans, on the other hand, may have to keep these men in custody for years, and still they never get a word out of them. They're told, "Don't slap him. That's a violation of human rights!" and as a result this man who has killed and murdered in the name of his fanatical beliefs may never have to pay a price for his crimes.

Imagine how this sort of behavior looks to the terrorists who are determined to attack your country. You take prisoners who have killed people and destroyed property, with absolutely no regard for human life, and keep them in air-conditioned cells with color television, libraries, telephones, hot showers, clean clothes, and three hot meals a day, and you think this will get you the information you want? Believe me, these killers have never lived so well in their entire lives. That's not prison. For such men, that's a holiday resort with all the trimmings. There are plenty of people on the outside who would give anything to be inside a prison like that.

I told Major General Geoffrey Miller, who had been the commander of the Guantanamo Bay prison, that this was no way to deal with terrorists and criminals in my country. And I said, for that matter, there are many things that cannot be photocopied and given to Iraq by the Americans. By that I mean, what may be good and appropriate for you in America may be totally inappropriate in my country. And this is something that Great Britain has also had to discover the hard way.

Many in that country have been against President Bush and the war on terrorism. They want to think that all problems can be solved by diplomacy, but that's wrong. There are bad people in the world who want to kill you, and the only way to deal with such men is with force. Judging by his speech to a national conference of the Labour

Party on July 16, 2005, Prime Minister Tony Blair may have finally gotten the message: England has decided to tighten down on terrorists and the "evil ideology" that motivates them. But one can only wonder if the English people will ever wake up to what's really going on around them.

The Specter of Jihad

As with Christianity, where there are many denominations with different interpretations of the Bible, there are also many groups of Muslims who have different readings of the Koran, particularly when it comes to the doctrines of Fatah and Jihad. Certain politicians and clerics take certain verses and stretch them, not for religious reasons but to achieve their own political objectives. But by doing this they have politicized their religion and created huge problems for Muslims around the world. At the same time, they have made it virtually impossible for followers of Islam to live in peace with their neighbors.

These divisions aren't only between Islam and other religions; there are also major disagreements between the various sects and denominations within Islam. We see this when terrorists like Abu Musab al-Zarqawi claim that even the Shia people of Iraq are not Muslims. Zarqawi has said that the Shia have nothing to do with Islam, so killing them in the name of religion is the right thing to do.

At the same time, he says that the seven hundred thousand Christians living in Iraq are *Mushriqin*, or polytheists, because we worship three Gods—Father, Son, and Holy Ghost—which is, of course, a total misunderstanding of the doctrine of the Trinity. Nevertheless, Zarqawi makes these kinds of pronouncements in order to give his followers license to persecute Christians. But what Zarqawi and others like him don't seem to understand is that in the long run this type of violence is going to hurt him and his followers more than anyone else.

It was this type of dissension and conflict that led us to launch the International Centre for Reconciliation in 1998, hoping to bring people of many faiths together to build bridges of understanding in the Middle East. I wanted especially to improve communications between the Shia and Sunni people because clashes between the denominations of Islam were making life in Iraq impossible for everyone. There's still a lot of hostility between them, but I've seen signs of hope here and there over the last few years.

The mission of the Iraqi Institute for Peace is vital and in time the world will recognize the importance of these efforts. However, whenever I meet with religious and community leaders in Europe or America, I often find a great deal of anxiety about the rapid growth of militant Islam outside the Middle East. I get many questions about what many now perceive as the growing threat of cultural invasion. The number of immigrants from the Middle East is growing so rapidly that many in Europe and Great Britain are worried that what happened to America on September 11, 2001, could happen in their countries as well.

The Paris riots of November 2005 were certainly a wake-up call for many in Western Europe who had been in denial about the dangers of an unassimilated immigrant population. Prior to that, the world witnessed the terrorist attacks in Spain that impacted the national elections in that country. We're still seeing clashes between Muslims and the police, not just in France, but in Indonesia, India, and other Third World countries. And all these incidents only heighten tensions in the West. The atmosphere is already so volatile, and relationships between Islam and the West have gotten measurably worse since the capture of Saddam in 2003.

A reflection of the growing concern is the number of books warning of the dangers of Islamic extremism that have been published in the West. Many well-known columnists, commentators, and public figures in Europe, Britain, and America are speaking out more forcefully than ever about what they perceive as the dark side of the Muslim religion. This ought to be a concern for every follower of Islam, even as it has become a growing concern to non-Muslims around the world.

A Message of Hope

In March and April of 2005 I attended a twenty-one-day conference in the United States for leaders of all the various religious groups in Iraq—Sunni, Shia, Kurds, Sabbists, Christians, and others—to discuss the proper relationship of religion and politics in a democratic society, and to observe how church-state relations are handled in the United States. In addition to our meetings in Washington, we visited six states to see how religious matters are handled and what the doctrine of "freedom of religion" really means for a constitutional democracy. I must say, it was a very good experience for all of us.

One of the most informative trips was to Denver, Colorado, where we visited both the Jewish Center and the Islamic Center in that city. For me, the most eye-opening meeting was with Dr. Ahmad Nabhan, the senior imam of the Denver mosque, who told us, "Terrorism is absolutely forbidden in Islam." During that meeting, Dr. Nabhan said, as he often repeats in his sermons and speeches, "Terrorism is not our way. It is completely out of Islam."

This was such an encouraging message, and at the conclusion of his talk, I told Dr. Nabhan that I felt like Christopher Columbus who had just discovered a new world. In this case, I had discovered new hope for peace and reconciliation in Iraq. Of course, this view is not yet the mainstream view in Islam, but I would like to believe that it is a message that will resonate with followers of Islam around the world and soon become the dominant view.

For Muslims, it's important to realize that Dr. Nabhan is a graduate of Al-Azhar University in Cairo, which is the world's oldest university and widely recognized as Sunni Islam's foremost seat of learning. To have such distinguished credentials, and to have such a strong message of peace and reconciliation, Dr. Nabhan now has a wonderful platform for helping to transform the militant mindset of contemporary Islam. I certainly want to encourage him in his important mission.

Dr. Nabhan's definition of Fatah and Jihad were equally surprising, because they were different from the interpretation we often hear. He offered us a marvelous understanding of the importance of peace and coexistence between peoples of all faiths. And best of all, the view of Islam that he described was a model for how all the different ethnic and religious groups in the Middle East can live together without hatred and violence.

We simply cannot give permission to those who have a different understanding of Fatah and Jihad to exercise their will on society. That view is nothing but a time bomb that can explode at any time and at any place, doing great damage to society. If the followers of radical Islam try to wage war on the rest of the world in this way, it will ultimately destroy our hopes for peace and will push the nations of both the West and the Middle East toward an inevitable clash.

A Timely Warning

Whenever I speak to people in Europe and America about these things, I find they are worried not just about Islamic terrorism but also about cultural invasion by followers of Islam. It has been shown recently that the native populations of England, France, Germany, Italy, and the Scandinavian countries are shrinking, while the immigrant population in these countries is expanding. That is not necessarily a problem if the new arrivals are committed to living in peace with their neighbors. But if they refuse to live by the laws and standards of the countries to which they have immigrated, and if they insist on waging war in the name of religion, then the situation will only grow worse.

Whenever I speak about the peace and reconciliation movement and the changes that are taking place in Iraq today, I'm often asked about militant Islam and the threat of global terrorism. More than once I've been asked about the meaning of the Arabic words *Fatah* and *Jihad*. What I normally tell them is that to followers of the militant brand of Islam, these doctrines express the belief that Allah has commanded them to conquer the nations of the world both by cultural invasion and by the sword. In some cases this means moving thousands of Muslim families into a foreign land—by building mosques and changing the culture from the inside out, and by refusing to assimilate or adopt the beliefs or values of that nation—to conquer the land for Islam. This is an invidious doctrine, but it's true that it's being carried out in some places today by followers of this type of Islam.

On one occasion I was confronted by a young woman who was very angry because Muslims in her community were spreading these radical teachings in the schools while, at the same time, calling their militant view of Islam a "religion of peace." She told me, "Islam is a religion of peace if we're willing to surrender our nation, our customs, our religious beliefs, and our identity to these people. It's peaceful if we submit to living under Sharia law. But if we're not willing submit to them, then it's war, military conquest, or terrorism, and I'm fed up with it."

I listened politely, because I knew that this is happening in some places. But I told her, "Please understand that there are many Muslims who don't accept this view of Fatah and Jihad any longer." And I went on to tell her about the work of Dr. Nabhan in Denver, who teaches that, "Terrorism is absolutely forbidden in Islam." That message is gaining acceptance among educated Muslims in many places, and that's why we can't afford to give up on the prospects for peace and reconciliation.

In my work, I deal with Muslims of many persuasions almost every day. Many of them are close friends and I have great respect for them and their beliefs. I don't have a problem with the fact that they're Muslims, but I do have a problem with the beliefs of those who believe that Fatah and Jihad are commanded by Allah, and that they have a right and a duty to conquer the world in this way. I am committed to working for peace and reconciliation in the Middle East, but these ideas are absolutely contrary to any hope of peace. So that's where I part company with some of them. But to understand this problem, a little perspective may be in order.

Fatah by Demographics

In the eighth century AD, the Moors of North Africa invaded and conquered Spain. They did it under the banner of Islam, and they remained in control of much of the Iberian Peninsula until they were eventually defeated and evicted by force in the fifteenth and sixteenth centuries. Muslims have never forgotten this and it's a source of resentment for the West. It's unlikely such a thing could ever happen again. A military invasion will not succeed, but in countries such as England today, we can witness a modern nation in the process of being conquered by the militant form of Fatah, in a slow, systematic, and unrelenting overpowering of British culture.

The way of life in Great Britain has been transformed by followers of Islam. This is also true in countries such as France, Germany, and the Netherlands, as well as the Scandinavian countries, which have been undergoing changes for decades, and they don't know how to react. Some of them are trying to pass laws or change policies now, but millions of Muslims have immigrated to those countries from Africa and the Middle East. Millions more have now been born there, as the British have recently discovered, and some of the new residents are not interested in the customs, history, or languages of those countries.

Many of these people have not assimilated with the culture, but have created a culture within a culture. This is what we witnessed in Britain in July and in France in November 2005. The young men who carried out the bombings and the riots in more than 300 French cities were born and raised in Europe. They were citizens by birth, but they were attracted to the militant strain of Islam. They belonged not to Europe but to the Islamic Motherland, and they were following an older and more dangerous view of Fatah and Jihad.

What we're seeing in many places is a "demographic revolution." Some experts have projected that by the year 2040, fully 80 percent of the population of France will be Muslim. At that point, the Muslim majority will control commerce, industry, education, and religion in that country. They will also, of course, control the government, as well, and occupy all of the key positions in the French Parliament. And a Muslim will be president. This is what we're seeing happening in many countries, including the United States. It only seems to be slower in the United States because America is such a large and ethnically diverse country already.

This is a big public relations problem for Islam, and it must be addressed very soon. Violence and conquest are doctrines handed down by militant mullahs and imams, and what many in the West have said to me is that they're worried that those who subscribe to this brand of Islam are trying to take over the world by force. To deal with their fears and concerns, I believe there ought to be more teachers like Dr. Nabhan, a highly regarded imam and scholar, who is dedicated to teaching the followers of his faith to live in peace with their neighbors.

Recently there has been a backlash in America against the immigration explosion of the last several years. It's mainly due to the large numbers of illegal aliens pouring into the country from Latin America, but there's a growing awareness of the numbers of immigrants from other parts of the world. This shows up strikingly in town councils and government offices where the foreign-born population is now electing their own people as mayors, council members, and even congressmen and senators.

In Michigan, as just one conspicuous example, the demographic shift toward a Muslim population is changing the cultural balance so much that in some places it's difficult to find a native English speaker. Very soon Muslims will be the majority and European-Americans will be displaced, and they will have to move away from the places where they were born, leaving everything they've known behind. In such places, second and third-generation American-born Muslims are now in the majority, and some of these people are as committed to the older view of Fatah and Jihad as the new arrivals. So this is another area where the moderate voices need to be heard.

I was deeply saddened by the bombings that happened in London in July 2005, and I'm especially sad for the loss of life. After the bombings, many English people, including many liberals who had been in denial, reacted strongly to what they perceived as the militant form of Fatah and Jihad. Over the following weeks, there were verbal attacks on these teachings in British and other European publications, calling for dramatic reforms at all levels of government. Maybe this will be enough to convince Muslim leaders both in Europe and the Middle East that changes need to be made in the way that these doctrines are taught and understood. But it is certain that we will need a new dialogue and a new commitment to reconciliation in order to restore stability in these places.

Knowing Who to Trust

Denying reality is not just an English problem or a French problem. It's a problem everywhere, and it's very troubling to me that President George Bush is under attack in your country for his decision to wage a preemptive war against terrorism around the world. Your president and his commanders, including Secretary of Defense Rumsfeld, understand that the terrorists are determined, ruthless, and relentless. The men who want to destroy your culture were not satisfied with 9/11, and they're going to attack again if they possibly can. The only way to prevent that from happening is to go now and find these people, wherever they are, and stop them.

I can assure you that the people who are intent on destroying America won't be stopped by appeasement. They are not interested in political solutions. They don't want welfare—their animosity is not caused by hunger or poverty or anything of the sort. They understand only one thing: total and complete conquest of the West and the destruction of anyone who does not bow to them and their dangerous and out-of-date ideology of hate and revenge.

You need to remember that Hitler was not satisfied with Yugoslavia or Poland when the English prime minister Neville Chamberlain stupidly gave those countries to him. He wanted to conquer the world, and it required overwhelming military superiority and a long and brutal war to finally stop him. Millions died because too many people in the West believed that diplomacy and appeasement would do the job. The enemy you face today is not so easy to find as Hitler, and he may not be as easy to defeat. But believe me, you will not stop this enemy until you take the war to him and stop him in his own territory, by any means necessary, including direct action and overwhelming military force.

What I want to say next is not easy for me to say but I think I must say it anyway. One of the nicest things about the American people is that you are generous and friendly people, and because of this you are sometimes naïve and overly trusting. You want to be friendly, so you open up to people and then you're surprised when they stab you in the back. Many brave young soldiers have died in Iraq for this reason, but I think this is also a big part of the problem with the State Department and others in government who fail to understand the true nature of this enemy.

To be more specific, for the Americans to survive in a place like Iraq, where violence and corruption are a way of life, you must do two things: you must be cautious and discerning about the people you deal with, and you must listen to the people you know you can trust—who will not lie to you—but will help you to navigate in an environment that is strange and unfamiliar to you.

Without the input of people from the area who understand these ancient cultures, you will constantly be making mistakes, and many times those mistakes will come at the cost of innocent human lives. It would take a lifetime to understand the culture of a country like Iraq, and honestly, it may take much more than that. By that I mean it takes generations to accumulate the knowledge, the history, the traditions, and the mental disposition of our people as it has been passed down to us from father to son and mother to daughter for thousands of years.

This is not something Americans naturally understand. Or perhaps I should say, it's not something many Americans have experienced. Your nation is very young; your culture is barely three hundred years old. In some ways you exhibit the innocence of children, which can be a wonderful quality. It's one of the things we like best about Americans. But young people can also be rash and hasty, assuming they know more than they do, and this can be dangerous for you now. So please take the time to develop friendships with people from these cultures who can help you avoid some of the pitfalls you will encounter.

My advice, in light of all of this, is simply that your diplomats, military officers, and others who do business in any part of the world where there are long-established and ancient cultures, need to be well informed about those nations and their history; and then they should spend as much time and money as necessary to find people whom they can trust. And when they do, they need to listen to those people and heed their advice. In a world where finding the way forward can often seem like a jigsaw puzzle, it's essential to have friends you can trust.

CHAPTER 12

A TIME FOR PEACE

There is a time for everything, and a season for every activity under heaven:
a time to be born and a time to die, a time to plant and a time to uproot, . . .
a time to be silent and a time to speak, a time to love and a time to hate,
a time for war and a time for peace.
— Ecclesiastes 3:1–2, 7–8 NIV

Because of the work I do, I have to have bodyguards at all times. One day when I was working at home, one of them came to me and said there was a car with four young Muslims going back and forth in front of my house, and they were taking video pictures of my property. We knew what that meant: it's a common tactic of terrorists who are planning to blow something up. So my bodyguards, who are all big, strong Assyrians from the north, jumped in their cars and chased them down. They raced all through the streets of Baghdad at high speeds, three cars of them, and they finally caught them and brought them back to the house so I could question them and find out what they were doing.

When I saw the four young men, I knew these were not ordinary terrorists. They had long beards and Muslim clothing, but they were different. When I asked what they were doing, they admitted that they were planning to blow up my house. I knew I had to decide what to do with them and the options were clear. I called the prime minister and told him what had happened and he told me, "By all means, Georges, take them to be interrogated by intelligence officers at the ministry of the interior. God only knows what they may be able to tell us."

I listened and I thanked him politely, but when I put down the receiver I looked at the boys and just shook my head. They looked like good boys, and they were frightened because they knew what was going to happen next. But after a few minutes I asked them, "Do you know me?" They said, "No, we don't know you." So I said, "Then why do you want to kill me?" and they said, "We were told to kill you." I said, "You don't know me but still you wanted to kill me?" And they answered, "Yes, that's true."

So I asked them, "What do you do when you're not blowing people up?" Two of them told me they were engineering students at the University of Baghdad, and the other two were in their second year of medical school. Again, I just shook my head. Here were four bright young men, obviously from good families, and they had been turned into murderers by foreign-born terrorists and the fanatical clerics of their own religion.

I felt sad for them, and I knew very well what the intelligence officers would do to them when I turned them over to the police. As I was considering my options, I asked them, "Why did you listen to these men who told you to kill me?" They said, "They're foreigners, and they told us that it was the will of Allah for us to kill you. If we didn't do it, we would be cursing Islam." I looked at them and I just said a silent prayer: *Jesus, tell me what to do with these young men.*

After I thought about it for a moment, I knew what I was supposed to do. They were trembling with fear, and they had no doubts about what was going to happen to them. The prime minister was angry, especially since they had targeted my house and wanted to blow me up. There would be no mercy for terrorists—these or any others. But I knew I had to settle it another way.

Finding Another Way

I went back to my office and called the prime minister once again, and I told him that I had decided to let them go. He yelled, "What? Georges, no! What are you talking about? You can't do that. It's against the law!" So I said, "Sir, these people were trying to kill me. You know that I'm a Christian, and we're taught to practice forgiveness. Even Jesus Christ, when they hung him on the cross, said, 'Father, forgive them, because they don't know what they're doing.' So let me deal with this in my own way."

When I came back into the room and told the young men they were free to go, they didn't believe me at first. They were sure it was a trick; they were going to be killed as soon as they stepped outside. But I assured them it wasn't a trick and nothing would happen to them. I told them to go, and they went. But four hours later, I looked out the window and I saw all four of them coming back to my house, this time with their fathers and mothers. I invited them to come inside and immediately the parents fell all over me, thanking me for sparing the lives of their sons. They said I had saved their lives and they offered the boys to me as bodyguards.

They were kissing me and thanking me over and over, but I said, "Okay, thank you very much, but listen to me. I have bodyguards and I don't need any more. The only thing I want from you is that you send these boys back to the university. These two are going to be good doctors, and the other two are going to be good engineers one day. They're our hope for the future, and Iraq needs them. So why are you allowing these bright young men to be in the hands of foreigners and terrorists who are telling them to kill people like me whom they've never even met?"

Most of them had tears in their eyes by this time, but they were listening carefully to what I was saying. So I told the boys, "Please listen to me. Those foreign terrorists are nobody. They're losers, they're killers, and they're cowards. They won't do the dirty work themselves, but they want you to kill your fellow citizens. They're nobody, but you're somebody, because you are the future leaders of Iraq. Please don't throw your lives away for losers like that." And they heard me loud and clear.

To this day, those four boys still come to my house from time to time to say hello and wish me well. They say, "Sir, is there anything we can do for you?" And I say, "No, but how are you doing in school?" And they say, "We're doing very well." So I tell them, "I want you to work hard and make sure you pass your exams. And when you graduate as doctors and engineers, come back to see me and we'll try to put you in good positions in the government."

When I spoke to the prime minister about this, he said, "Georges, sometimes I don't understand you. You Christians always do things like this, but God only knows what they're going to do." And I said, "Sir, the only thing they're going to do is graduate from the university as doctors and engineers, and one day I'll put them in good positions. And I think this is the best way of making our young people whose eyes have been blinded by hate and lies to see the truth. One day you'll see what happens."

It's been nearly two years now since that incident happened, and some people still tell me that one day those young men will come back and finish the job. But I don't believe it. I didn't decide to release them on my own: I prayed about my decision and Jesus told me to release them. So I'm not sorry that I let them go, and I mean that even if something bad does happen to me one day. But I can tell you this. All of their people know this story now, and some of them say, "We know very well what would have happened if General Sada was a Muslim. The boys would have been hanged that same day. But that man had mercy on them because he's a Christian."

When I see these young men now, they're so different than they were. They've shaved their beards, they're wearing very nice clothes, they're doing very well in their studies at the university. I have some friends who tell me I did the wrong thing, because these young men are Sunnis and they wanted to see them hanged. Fortunately, many people in Iraq know this story now, and many of them believe I did the right thing. But I know it was the right thing.

Incidentally, one of my bodyguards took the video camera they were using and he copied the file onto my laptop computer. So we know exactly what they were doing and saying in the car before they were caught. If I had simply made the easy decision and done the usual thing, they would be dead now. It's easy to hate, and I could have hated them and allowed them to be hanged; but I knew that Jesus wanted me to find another way, and that's what I did.

An Unexpected Confession

Throughout this book I have tried to put a human face on the tragedy of Iraq under Saddam and to show how the corruption of the government in my country affected not only the Middle East but the whole world. But the story of what has happened in Iraq is not just my story. It's the story of all of us, because we've all paid a terrible price. The Middle East has suffered, the West has suffered, the United Nations has suffered, and the world has suffered. The world Saddam created, in which he held all the power and received all the glory, was a pitiful excuse for a nation. At the heart of it was only terror and evil. But thank God, Saddam is gone now and it's time for the people of Iraq to find our way back to reality.

The biggest problem we had in my country was not poverty or hunger or homelessness. It was that Saddam Hussein, supported by some people in the Baath Party and his corrupt bureaucracy, was able to create a regime based on lies, deception, and their own wicked ambition. When Saddam said that two plus two is nine, there was no one who would dare to tell him otherwise. If Saddam said black was white, they would have agreed immediately. And everything worked this way for forty years.

If Saddam wanted the air force to attack the people of Tehran with mustard gas, the people surrounding him would trip over each other trying to be the first to tell him what a great idea he had. When he decided to attack Israel with chemical weapons, the same people were there, applauding and telling him he was a hero and a military genius. Some of them would say that Allah must have spoken those very words into his ear. To kill and destroy for Saddam was, in their eyes, to do the work of Allah.

It was a sick and dangerous system, and I'm grateful now to know that when Saddam called me for advice it was never because I agreed with him or gave him the answers he wanted to hear; it was because he knew I would speak the truth, even at the risk of my own life. He knew I would not lie to him, even when he disagreed with me. Somewhere deep inside of him, I think he knew that truth does matter. And he also knew I would always speak truth, to the best of my ability. When I refused to execute the pilots, I could easily have been killed. Refusing to do what Saddam or his evil sons ordered had already cost many of my countrymen their heads. Yet, when I refused to obey, I wasn't killed. Instead, I was simply discharged, retired, and sent away.

In some cases, my promotions were delayed because I wasn't a very good yes man, and I had refused to join the Baath Party. But when Saddam called for me and brought me back as an adviser, he did it because he realized I had been right about the captured pilots. He realized it was the right thing to do, and I had been right about many other things as well. On one occasion I will never forget, I was called to the palace and when I arrived was told that Saddam wanted me to have dinner with him. Suddenly, I was terrified, because this often happened when Saddam wanted to poison an enemy. Eating with Saddam wasn't something I wanted to do.

Nevertheless, I went in and met the president. We exchanged pleasantries and spoke for a short time, and then he called for the meal to be served. During the whole time, I kept wondering if the next bite would be the one that killed me. Then, at one point, Saddam said words that sent chills down my spine. He said, "Georges, you know you have not always been very agreeable with me. Seventeen times you have disagreed with me—I've counted them . . ." On hearing that, I could hardly breathe. Disagreeing with Saddam was almost always a death sentence, and his words seemed to confirm my worst fears. But then he added, "and seventeen times you've been right." Imagine my surprise and joy at hearing that remarkable confession. Despite all the evil he had done, Saddam still recognized that honesty could be a good thing, and that it wasn't always necessary to shoot the messenger.

The problem, however, was that the corruption within Saddam's regime reached from the top to the bottom of the system. It was in the government, the military, the hospitals, the universities, the private companies, and even the families of many of our most prominent people. We were not free to think for ourselves, and no one dared to do whatever they wished, because they knew that only Saddam's wishes would be followed. That's why I was forced out of the military in 1986, even though I was a young forty-six-year-old major general who had earned his commission the hard way. At that time I was rated as the best fighter pilot in the air force, but I had a bad habit of saying that two plus two is four. So I had to go.

Saddam, the Destroyer

Saddam must have had other moments of sobriety, but except for that one occasion I never really saw any of them. To understand what he was really like, you need to know that Saddam was the man who killed more Baath Party members than any other person, from the foundation of the party in 1947 to the present. Saddam killed more officers of the Iraqi Army than any other person or nation, from the foundation of the army in 1921 to the present. Saddam killed more Tikritis, his own cousins in the north of Iraq, from the foundation of the nation of Iraq in 1921 to the present. Saddam killed more clerics of all the major Muslim denominations and tribes than any other man. At first it was the Sunnis, beginning with the Badries in the north, and then it was the Shia and the Sadries in the south.

Saddam is also the man who has killed more military personnel and civilians of his own country than any other person, eventually totaling more than a million men, women, and children. All this he did for the sake of expanding his own power and control over the nation. In his time, the nation of Iraq and its vital infrastructure was destroyed more than at any other time in history. At his command, hundreds of thousands of Arabs were killed in the south, especially in Kuwait. And at his command, hundreds of thousands of Kurds were killed and maimed in the north.

At Saddam's command, more than four thousand villages in the north were completely destroyed, and more than 132 of our ancient churches were wiped from the face of the earth. Because of his own fear and hatred, Saddam attempted to destroy the entire way of life of the Arabs in the marshlands of the south. The rivers were diverted, the wildlife was decimated, the people were driven out and killed, and villages and important waterways were ruined forever. At Saddam's command, our wealthy Arab neighbor, Kuwait, was attacked and pillaged, and all for his own glory and greed.

Under Saddam, the great wealth of my country was squandered on wars, weapons, and wasteful spending. On top of that, he paid millions of dollars to bribe and blackmail journalists and broadcasters, to buy off the authors of books and journals, and to publish lies and propaganda in the Arab world and far beyond. He bribed ambassadors, foreign dignitaries, and heads of state. The amount of money Saddam spent on his wars and other corrupt schemes was greater than all the wealth we accumulated in that nation through the sale of oil from the day the first wells were drilled in 1927 to the present. I've done the calculations and I know this is true.

When I consider all the terrible things that Saddam did to my country during his thirty-year reign of terror, I have to ask myself, How could anyone weep because this man is gone? Saddam Hussein destroyed our country. He destroyed our people, their pride, their hope, and for some, even their futures. The best name for such a man is not Saddam, "The Crasher," but rather the Arabic word Haddam, which means "The Destroyer."

Saddam was the only leader in the world to use weapons of mass destruction against his own people. Even as he was building sixty-eight luxurious palaces and increasing his personal wealth to more than $30 billion, he was destroying everything he touched. The educational system, health care system, and financial infrastructure of the nation were ruined by Saddam. The middle class, which is the foundation of every stable society, was attacked, and anyone who dared to speak freely was destroyed by Saddam. The army, air force, and coastal forces were utterly destroyed, first in 1991 and again in 2003, and yet this villain still believes that he should be free to return as the president and national hero of Iraq.

Restoring Our Dignity

As a military officer, I was taught that the success of every operation depends on the strategy that is used. When a leader has the right strategy, even if he makes mistakes in tactics, most of the time the operation will succeed. But if he has a bad strategy, even good tactics cannot save him. I say this because I believe that all of Saddam's strategies were wrong, from the very beginning in the late 1960s to the present. He frequently had clever tactics. He was manipulative and deceitful, and he managed to fool most of the people most of the time. But ultimately he was bound to lose because all of his strategies were bad ones.

It makes me sad to realize that there are still countries in our region who are taking the same path Saddam had taken. They're using the same strategies and many of the same tactics, and if nothing changes, they're headed for the same dead end. If there's one lesson worth learning in the tragic saga of Saddam Hussein, it's that there must be a major change in the policies and strategies of our neighbors in the Middle East if there's to be any hope of bringing peace and reconciliation to our people. This, I believe, is our last, best hope, and I pray that the leaders of the Arab world will be willing to embrace the needed changes.

But even as I say this, I realize that this will not be an easy concept for many people in my part of the world to accept or understand. It will require wisdom, knowledge, and courage to change directions in this way, but I believe it can and must be done. For one thing, I believe in the resourcefulness of our people. We have many well educated leaders in government, business, science, and the law, and we're not lacking for good ideas. So I'm sure these kinds of changes are possible—if we have enough faith and courage to take the first steps. If the nations of the Middle East will come together in a spirit of cooperation to rebuild the region, they won't just be helping themselves: they will be restoring the promise of peace for the whole world.

This is beginning to happen now, and there are many people who are very important to our future who understand this. In particular, I want to express my thanks and gratitude to President Jalal Talabani, who has given our people new hope and begun the process of restoring our dignity. He is a gifted leader and he has also been an encouragement to the Christians in Iraq. He told us that if any of our people are persecuted in the central and southern regions of the country, they can come to the north, to the villages around Kurdistan where they will find land and jobs, and where they will be protected. I wish I could say that all Iraqis are as sympathetic as Dr. Talabani toward the ethnic and religious minorities in the country, but so far that is not the case.

Dr. Ayad Alawi served as the first prime minister of the new Iraq. He has been a great friend to the people of my country and an inspiration to me. I should also say that his deputy, Dr. Barham Saleh, has also been enormously helpful to those who suffered the most in the north, including the Kurds and the Christian minority. When our churches were bombed on August 1, 2004, the prime minister ordered the government to pay for rebuilding them, and he handed me the entire sum in cash, amounting to $496,460. On top of that, Dr. Alawi contributed $100,000 from his own pocket for the reconstruction effort. All of this money is now being used to restore the hope of the Christians in the north.

Dr. Barham Saleh, who heads up the reconstruction committee in the prime minister's office, arranged for the builders to erect a new cathedral for the Ancient Church of the East in the city of Kirkuk. In addition, he offered to rebuild the Assyrian school in Kirkuk, which is part of the Ancient Church of the East, at a cost of approximately $500,000. During this difficult time, I met with Grand Ayatollah Ali Sistani and leaders of all the Christian churches in Iraq, including the patriarch of the Chaldean churches, bishops of the Assyrian churches, and the bishop of the Armenian Orthodox churches. We were also accompanied by the national security adviser, Dr. Mowaffaq al-Rabaie, who respects the Christians and always tries to help them.

The ayatollah told me he was sorry that our churches had been bombed, and he said that a group of the highest church leaders of all the denominations in Iraq had met together and agreed to make a substantial contribution to help us rebuild our churches. This was such a gracious and magnanimous offer, and I want them to know how much it means to our people. And I thank all of them from the bottom of my heart.

But in that regard, I would also say to those who destroyed our places of worship, who killed, kidnapped, blackmailed, and robbed our people, and who used violence and hatred against the Christian community, that we pray to our Father in heaven that he will forgive them and lead them to a better way of thinking. If we want to build a new and better Iraq, then we must learn to live together in peace and work together for the common good. We cannot continue the habits of hatred and revenge that Saddam employed, and that were accepted under his corrupt regime. To go in that direction will only lead to more bloodshed, war, and disaster. I pray we can work together to find a better way.

A New Strategy

I also want to say a word about the Kurdish people of Iraq who suffered so greatly under Saddam. Today the people of Kurdistan, in the north of Iraq, are led by Massoud Barzani, the president of that region, and Prime Minister Nechirvan Barzani. No people in Iraq have lost more than the Kurds, yet they have been the most forgiving and tolerant. Literally, hundreds of thousands of their people were killed, and they were constantly under attack for decades. They now have a strong militia to protect them from future attacks, but they never resorted to revenge or random violence because of what had happened to them under Saddam.

I want to thank these people and their leaders for the wisdom and courage they've shown, particularly in their relationship with my people, the indigenous Christians of northern Iraq. Mr. Sarkis Agha Jan, who serves as deputy prime minister and finance minister of the Kurdistan region, has also been extraordinarily helpful to my people. The majority of Assyrian Christians live today in the Kurdish regions, and we have been respected by the Kurds and treated fairly. So on behalf of my people, I want to say thank you to President Barzani and all those in Kurdistan for their acts of tolerance and good faith. They are a credit to our nation.

Saddam's policies corrupted Iraq but they also condemned it to destruction. Even a man like Tariq Aziz, who was smart and very efficient, was corrupted by Saddam, and he used his skills to prop up a regime that was built on lies. I'm sad to say that, even now from his prison cell, he continues to support Saddam. I have to believe that his behavior is motivated by fear and the belief that, so long as Saddam is still alive, no one is safe to speak against him.

But look what that sort of loyalty has accomplished. Iraq is a big country, as large as the state of California, right in the middle of the Middle East. Yet we had no friends in the region. Iraq was a pariah nation, the enemy of everyone, and not one of the countries around us trusted Saddam or the regime—and for good reason. At one time or another, Saddam had attacked every one of them. He declared himself to be the new Nebuchadnezzar, and he dreamed of one day becoming the emperor of all the Arabs. How could anyone ever trust such a man?

What America did on March 19, 2003, was the first big step in restoring the dignity and reputation of Iraq. Operation Iraqi Freedom began the process of removing an evil regime and helping the people of Iraq to come back and live in the world instead of living out of the world. Yes, there are still dangerous insurgents around, and the streets and alleys of Iraq are not safe for everyone. There are wicked men who want to stop the march of freedom and democracy in the world, and they have had a measure of success. But thank God, at last we're on the right track, and we will win this war one way or the other. We need time to put the pieces together, but I believe that in time we will learn how to use our freedom and democracy in the right way.

The truth is, Iraq is a wealthy country. We have water, land, oil, and many other mineral resources. In addition, we are industrious people who love life and we know how to work. If we can move beyond the terrors of the past and commit ourselves to a more optimistic future, I'm convinced we can transform Iraq once again into a beautiful country in the middle of the Middle East that will be a light shining in darkness. One day many people will look at Iraq and say that we are an example to the world of what democracy can do. I truly believe that day is coming.

The Greening of Iraq

You know, there was a time not very long ago when the central region of my country was a beautiful green forest. There were acres and acres of trees. The countryside was laced with rivers and streams that abounded with wildlife. There were fish in the rivers, beautiful birds in the trees, deer in the forests, and other creatures living among the rocks and hidden places. It was like the Garden of Eden, but then war came and many of those trees were burned. The homes of those who lived and worked in the forests were destroyed. And because of so many wars over so many years, that paradise disappeared. Military roads were built so tanks and armored cars could pass through. And fires were often deliberately set to clear away timber and everything else that interfered with the soldiers' line of fire. There was no beauty in that world; instead, the land within the forests became just another killing field.

The area remained that way for many years; but do you know what's happening now? Since the liberation of Iraq in 2003, the forests have started growing again. Debris is being cleared away, and the streams are beginning to flow. Bushes and wildflowers are beginning to flourish; they're still small in some places, but the trees are growing, and the forest creatures are returning. For me this is an image of what's happening to my country. For too many years we were trampled down by tyrants and dictators. Our souls were like deserts. We lost our capacity for beauty. But at last, freedom is coming to Iraq and there is beauty once again.

What's happening to the forests can also happen with human beings. We will need time to grow strong again. Beautiful things cannot survive forever in a desert, and for too long our spirits were turned into a wasteland. But if you saw the excitement on the faces of the men and women of Iraq during the recent elections—despite the threats of terrorists, and even as people were being killed while going to the polls—then you have seen the face of hope. And this spirit is awakening once again.

War, terrorism, death, and hatred will never bring us peace and prosperity. The people know this now, and they're beginning to resist the lies they've been told by the insurgents and propagandists who are nothing but merchants of death. If the forests can return to life and become green again, then I believe our nation can come back to life as well. And one day, very soon I hope, our ancient land—which was the cradle of civilization—will be green and beautiful once more.

The hope I have now is that democracy and freedom will help lead us back to reality. Because the culture of the Middle East is essentially tribal, the natural tendency is for people to be intensely loyal to their own tribe. They'll get along with members of their tribe as long as it's convenient, but it doesn't take a lot of provocation to make them want to fight. So we see Shia against Sunni, Shia against Shia, Sunni against Sunni, and even Sunni and Shia against everyone else. Somehow in the process of rebuilding the nation, our people must learn how to love each other, or at the very least, to live with each other in peace.

Love and Forgiveness

The number one problem in Iraq today is that there's too much hatred and too little love in the hearts of the people. Somehow our people, in all parts of the country and in every tribe and faction, must learn to love their neighbors and to forgive and forget what has happened in the past. Saddam taught us to hate, but hatred is a sickness and we don't want to be a sick nation anymore. Our hearts and minds ought to be full of love, especially now as we're trying to turn the country around.

Hatred, jealousy, and envy will eat us up from the inside. They do nothing to the other person. Those bitter emotions are like a crippling disease that eats our nerves, our minds, and our bodies, and leaves us empty inside. If we really want to improve our lives in Iraq, then we need to plant love in the hearts of our people, and that's why I've chosen to work for peace and reconciliation in the Middle East. I know now that there's only one way to solve our problems, and that's through creative dialogue, a commitment to peace, and openness to reconciliation.

Here's something I learned when I was a farmer. When you plant a garden, you have to have a plan. It begins with the idea that you want a crop to grow. When you learn how to make the crop grow, you soon discover that it's not just a matter of putting seeds in the ground. You have to choose the right time and place, and then you have to prepare the soil. When you plant the seeds, you nourish them, water them, and protect them. And when the young plants begin to sprout, you nourish them and take steps to prevent weeds and insects from taking over and destroying them.

In due course, when the crop is ripe and it's time for harvest, all your hard work will pay off and you can enjoy the fruits of your labor. Even so, not every plant in that field is going to survive. You will lose some plants, especially those around the edges where they were exposed to drought or insufficient attention. The heat will weaken or kill some of your plants, and predators may take a few more. But if you've done your job well and tended the field with love and patience, you will not only have an abundant harvest but you will have seeds for the next season. Then, with the blessings of God and the spring rains, you can continue to expand your fields and your harvest, year after year.

In some ways this simple metaphor describes my hope for nurturing and expanding peace in the Middle East. No one farmer can do all of this, of course. But if enough people agree to take up the challenge, and if we can harness our native wisdom and vast natural resources, and then turn our energies toward making peace instead of making war, I believe there's no limit to what we can accomplish. Will it be hard work? Yes, of course. Ask any farmer who has ever harvested a crop if the work was hard. Ask him to show you his hands: they're rough and calloused because the work is unrelenting—from dawn to dusk most days. But he knows that there will be a reward at the end if he is faithful, and that's why he does it.

Our problem is not that we don't have the resources. We have plenty to work with, and we have the talents of many tribes and nations. Our problem is that too many Iraqis prefer to live by the old rules of hate, fear, and distrust, and nothing can grow in that garden. One time I asked a well-respected Iraqi physician who was living and working in the West if he would consider coming back to Iraq someday. He said no. So I asked him, "Would you consider coming back if they gave you a high position in the ministry of health?" Again he said no, and then he added, "I wouldn't go back if they gave me all of Iraq!"

The problem was that he remembered what it was like in Iraq under Saddam, and he sees the headlines each day. He hears about bombings, killings, and people fighting because of their religious or political differences. And on top of that the streets are unsafe and the traffic is terrible. But then he said something that hurt very much. He said, "It wasn't until I came to the West that I knew what it means to be a human being." What a sad statement for my country; but what an opportunity for us if we recognize the problems and begin working together to transform Iraq into the kind of country it ought to be. With God's help, I believe it can be done.

A Light in Darkness

After the terrorist attacks in London in 2005, there were people celebrating in the streets of Baghdad, Amman, and Riyadh. I'm ashamed of the way those people behaved. They were proud that Muslims had done this evil deed, and they were celebrating when they should have been hiding their faces in shame. This was also how they reacted on September 11, 2001, when the planes struck New York and Washington.

If you had seen Iraqi television on that day, you would have been embarrassed for us. The people were boasting so loudly without realizing that millions of people around the world were watching them, and without ever thinking that one day they would have to answer for their behavior. That day eventually came, in March 2003, and we all paid a heavy price for it. But, instead of punishment and torture, we were given something else. They gave us democracy and freedom.

Some may ask why I've never spoken about all these things before, and why I decided that now is the time to write about it. The answer is that I could never have written about any of these things while I was serving in the military of Iraq. As I said at the beginning, I was a loyal soldier and fighter pilot during my military career. There were many things that I didn't like about that job: I was given orders many times that I would have preferred to disobey; but I did not disobey because I was an officer who had raised his hand and sworn to serve my country.

I love my country, and I only want good things to happen in Iraq from now on. Even though I am a member of a minority in Iraq, as an Assyrian and a Christian, I have always tried to be faithful and do my duty at all times. I wanted to fulfill my commitment as an officer and a gentleman to the best of my ability. If I had tried to write or speak about the situation in Iraq during those years, it would have been propaganda. It would have been just one more boast for a regime the whole world knew was corrupt and destined to fail. And I would never have written such a book.

The work of peacemaking has just begun, and there's so much that needs to happen before my country can stand shoulder to shoulder with other nations. But I believe that will happen, and I'm doing all I can to make sure that the nation that rises from the ashes of Saddam's secrets and treachery will be worthy of the price we have paid. For that I put my trust in the God who has blessed us and who has shown us a way out of darkness. With his help, and with a renewed commitment by the Iraqi people to find a better way, I believe we will see changes that will dazzle the eyes of the world.

May it be so.

Notes

[1] In Iraq General Sada is best known as General Georges. The most common form of address in Middle Eastern countries is with a person's first name. It is for the benefit of our Western audience that the editors have chosen to use the name Gen. Sada. All other names presented within the book are in their typical Middle Eastern form.

[2] Philip Sherwell, "Saddam's son 'tried to have pilots executed,'" *The Telegraph*, Feb. 5, 2004. [http://www.telegraph.co.uk/core/Content/displayPrintable.jhtml?xml=/news/2004/05/02/wsadd02.xml&site=5]. (Accessed November 11, 2005).

[3] Between 1991 and 2003, there were dozens of published reports in Europe and America confirming the tyranny of Saddam and the Baathist regime, and offering a wealth of detail about the development of WMDs. For a sampling of the large number of reports in major U.S. newspapers regarding Saddam's overt and covert weapons programs, see especially Robert Kagan, "It Wasn't Just Miller's Story," *The Washington Post*, Oct. 25, 2005. A21.

[4] Thank God, this is what did, in fact, happen. The bombers came, but they didn't destroy a single bridge, and the missiles and stealth attacks which struck Iraq in the second Gulf War pinpointed primarily military and government targets, and they did it with stunning accuracy in most cases. For the most part, civilians and their homes were spared. Water and electricity were only minimally damaged and were quickly back in working order.

Acknowledgments

I would like to publicly thank my good friend, Terry Law, for his encouragement and prayers during this book writing process. Without him, I am unsure if I would have completed the book or found people interested in spreading the knowledge of what really happened to Saddam's weapons of mass destruction.

In December 2002, just prior to the war, I was in London when I received a phone call from Amman, Jordan to tell me about two people who desired to go to Baghdad—one of those men was Terry Law. I was told they were very good, Christian people, humanitarians, and that they needed help with their visas. I fortunately knew the Iraqi Minister of Religion, so I phoned him and we soon had visas for the men.

Terry Law and his associate, Joel Vesanen, visited Iraq just before America declared war on Saddam Hussein's regime. They were some of the first Americans to see with their own eyes the effects of Saddam's dictatorship. They saw the great need in Iraq specifically among the hospitalized children who were dying for lack of adequate medicine. I, along with my Iraqi brothers and sisters, have a deep sense of gratitude for the large quantities of medicine Terry and his organization have given to Iraqi hospitals over the past three years. I have personally seen the love of Jesus Christ demonstrated through them.

On May 1, 2003, President Bush announced the war was essentially over. One week later, Terry, Joel and Terry's two sons, Scot and Jason, and I traveled together to Baghdad against the advice of the American Embassy due to the danger. We traveled 100 miles per hour in a convoy of fifteen SUVs from the border of Jordan into Baghdad.

On that trip, something profound happened to me. We were staying at the Palestine Hotel, bordering Fardous Square where Saddam's statue had been pulled down just days before. Terry spoke a prophetic word from God that has since come to pass in my life. He told me that the Lord had a position of influence for me in the coming government of Iraq and that He was going to use me to help the cause of Christianity in my country. Given the discouragement and uncertainty I felt, this message brought me great comfort and encouragement.

In December 2003 Terry and I were once again together in Baghdad when Saddam Hussein was captured. The entire city erupted in gunfire. Terry and his American friends wondered if a revolution was taking place. Paul Bremer, the head of the interim provisional government, announced on international television: "Ladies and gentlemen, we've got him!" There were pictures of Saddam in a spider hole captured just north of us in the town of Tikrit. It was quite a day for us to be in Baghdad together.

It has been my pleasure to introduce Terry to the various leaders of Iraq, including former Prime Minister Iyad Allawi, current Prime Minister Ibrahim al-Jaafari, President Jalal Talabani, President Masoud Barzani, Prime Minister Nachervan Barzani, the former Prime Minister of Kurdistan and the current Minister of Planning Dr. Barham Salih, the National Security Advisor, Mowafak al-Rubaie, and many Sunni leaders in the Parliament and in the country. Terry and I were very concerned about the new Iraqi constitution. We knew that in Islam, both in the Quran and Shari'a Law, if a Muslim converts to another religion, he is called an infidel and given three opportunities to repent. If he doesn't respond, he is to be killed by any means possible.

Terry boldly petitioned these leaders to include religious freedom in the new constitution, according to the Universal Declaration of Human Rights. He also sponsored a petition drive in the United States, Canada, and the United Kingdom asking Westerners like himself to sign documents urging the leaders of my country to guarantee the Universal Declaration of Human Rights in our new constitution.

In August 2005 when the initial draft of the constitution was issued, there was no mention of the Universal Declaration of Human Rights. Apparently our visit had great impact because two months later when the final document was ratified by the people, the verbiage declared that the constitution of Iraq would honor all human rights agreements signed by previous Iraqi governments. Iraq was an original signatory to the Universal Declaration of Human Rights in 1948.

Iraq's constitution now guarantees religious freedom. The 27 million people of my country now have this right and God used my friend, Terry Law, to help make it possible. Thank you, Terry.